How Doctors Think

Books by Jerome Groopman, M.D.

The Measure of Our Days

Second Opinions

The Anatomy of Hope

How Doctors Think

How Doctors Think

Jerome Groopman, M.D.

HOUGHTON MIFFLIN COMPANY

BOSTON • NEW YORK

2007

ISBN-13: 978-0-7394-9167-6

Printed in the United States of America

Book design by Robert Overholtzer

The illustration on page 139 is by Michael Prendergast

AUTHOR'S NOTE

In order to protect their privacy, the names and certain identifying
characteristics of all of the patients whose medical histories are
described in this book have been changed. In addition, Dr. Karen
Delgado, Dr. Bert Foyer, Dr. Wheeler, Rick Duggan, and
Drs. A, B, C, D, and E are fictitious names.

FOR MY MOTHER

Ayshet chayil

(*a woman of valor*)

We carve out order by leaving the disorderly parts out.

—William James

CONTENTS

Introduction 1

1. Flesh-and-Blood Decision-Making 27

2. Lessons from the Heart 41

3. Spinning Plates 59

4. Gatekeepers 77

5. A New Mother's Challenge 101

6. The Uncertainty of the Expert 132

7. Surgery and Satisfaction 156

8. The Eye of the Beholder 177

9. Marketing, Money, and Medical Decisions 203

10. In Service of the Soul 234

Epilogue: A Patient's Questions 260

ACKNOWLEDGMENTS 271

NOTES 274

INDEX 292

How Doctors Think

Introduction

ANNE DODGE HAD LOST COUNT of all the doctors she had seen over the past fifteen years. She guessed it was close to thirty. Now, two days after Christmas 2004, on a surprisingly mild morning, she was driving again into Boston to see yet another physician. Her primary care doctor had opposed the trip, arguing that Anne's problems were so long-standing and so well defined that this consultation would be useless. But her boyfriend had stubbornly insisted. Anne told herself the visit would mollify her boyfriend and she would be back home by midday.

Anne is in her thirties, with sandy brown hair and soft blue eyes. She grew up in a small town in Massachusetts, one of four sisters. No one had had an illness like hers. Around age twenty, she found that food did not agree with her. After a meal, she would feel as if a hand were gripping her stomach and twisting it. The nausea and pain were so intense that occasionally she vomited. Her family doctor examined her and found nothing wrong. He gave her antacids. But the symptoms continued. Anne lost her appetite and had to force herself to eat; then she'd feel sick and quietly retreat to the bathroom to regurgitate. Her general practitioner suspected what was wrong, but to be sure he referred her to a psychiatrist, and the diagnosis was made: anorexia nervosa with bulimia, a disorder marked by vomiting and an aversion to food. If the condition was not corrected, she could starve to death.

Over the years, Anne had seen many internists for her primary care before settling on her current one, a woman whose practice was devoted to patients with eating disorders. Anne was also evaluated by numerous specialists: endocrinologists, orthopedists, hematologists, infectious disease doctors, and, of course, psychologists and psychiatrists. She had been treated with four different antidepressants and had undergone weekly talk therapy. Nutritionists closely monitored her daily caloric intake.

But Anne's health continued to deteriorate, and the past twelve months had been the most miserable of her life. Her red blood cell count and platelets had dropped to perilous levels. A bone marrow biopsy showed very few developing cells. The two hematologists Anne had consulted attributed the low blood counts to her nutritional deficiency. Anne also had severe osteoporosis. One endocrinologist said her bones were like those of a woman in her eighties, from a lack of vitamin D and calcium. An orthopedist diagnosed a hairline fracture of the metatarsal bone of her foot. There were also signs that her immune system was failing; she suffered a series of infections, including meningitis. She was hospitalized four times in 2004 in a mental health facility so she could try to gain weight under supervision.

To restore her system, her internist had told Anne to consume three thousand calories a day, mostly in easily digested carbohydrates like cereals and pasta. But the more Anne ate, the worse she felt. Not only was she seized by intense nausea and the urge to vomit, but recently she had severe intestinal cramps and diarrhea. Her doctor said she had developed irritable bowel syndrome, a disorder associated with psychological stress. By December, Anne's weight dropped to eighty-two pounds. Although she said she was forcing down close to three thousand calories, her internist and her psychiatrist took the steady loss of weight as a sure sign that Anne was not telling the truth.

That day Anne was seeing Dr. Myron Falchuk, a gastroenterologist. Falchuk had already gotten her medical records, and her internist had told him that Anne's irritable bowel syndrome was yet another manifestation of her deteriorating mental health. Falchuk heard in the doctor's recitation of the case the implicit message that his role was to examine Anne's abdomen, which had been poked and prodded many times by many physicians, and to reassure her that irritable bowel syndrome, while uncomfortable and annoying, should be treated as the internist had recommended, with an appropriate diet and tranquilizers.

But that is exactly what Falchuk did not do. Instead, he began to question, and listen, and observe, and then to think differently about Anne's case. And by doing so, he saved her life, because for fifteen years a key aspect of her illness had been missed.

This book is about what goes on in a doctor's mind as he or she treats a patient. The idea for it came to me unexpectedly, on a September morning three years ago while I was on rounds with a group of interns, residents, and medical students. I was the attending physician on "general medicine," meaning that it was my responsibility to guide this team of trainees in its care of patients with a wide variety of clinical problems, not just those in my own specialties of blood diseases, cancer, and AIDS. There were patients on our ward with pneumonia, diabetes, and other common ailments, but there were also some with symptoms that did not readily suggest a diagnosis, or with maladies for which there was a range of possible treatments, where no one therapy was clearly superior to the others.

I like to conduct rounds in a traditional way. One member of the team first presents the salient aspects of the case and then we move as a group to the bedside, where we talk to the patient and examine him. The team then returns to the conference room to discuss the problem. I follow a Socratic method in the discussion, encouraging the students and residents to challenge each other, and challenge me, with their ideas. But at the end of rounds on that September morning I found myself feeling disturbed. I was concerned about the lack of give-and-take among the trainees, but even more I was disappointed with myself as their teacher. I concluded that these very bright and very affable medical students, interns, and residents all too often failed to question cogently or listen carefully or observe keenly. They were not thinking deeply about their patients' problems. Something was profoundly wrong with the way they were learning to solve clinical puzzles and care for people.

You hear this kind of criticism — that each new generation of young doctors is not as insightful or competent as its forebears — regularly among older physicians, often couched like this: "When I was in training thirty years ago, there was real rigor and we had to know our stuff. Nowadays, well . . ." These wistful, aging doctors speak as if some magic that had transformed them into consummate clinicians has disappeared. I suspect each older generation carries with it the notion that its time and place, seen through the distorting lens of nostalgia, were superior to those of today. Until recently, I confess, I shared that nostalgic sensibility. But on reflection I saw that there also were major flaws in my own medical training. What distinguished my learning from the learning of my young trainees was the nature of the deficiency, the type of flaw.

My generation was never explicitly taught how to think as clinicians. We learned medicine catch-as-catch-can. Trainees observed senior physicians the way apprentices observed master craftsmen in a medieval guild, and somehow the novices were supposed to assimilate their elders' approach to diagnosis and treatment. Rarely did an attending physician actually explain the mental steps that led him to his decisions. Over the past few years, there has been a sharp reaction against this catch-as-catch-can approach. To establish a more organized structure, medical students and residents are being taught to follow preset algorithms and practice guidelines in the form of decision trees. This method is also being touted by certain administrators to senior staff in many hospitals in the United States and Europe. Insurance companies have found it particularly attractive in deciding whether to approve the use of certain diagnostic tests or treatments.

The trunk of the clinical decision tree is a patient's major symptom or laboratory result, contained within a box. Arrows branch from the first box to other boxes. For example, a common symptom like "sore throat" would begin the algorithm, followed by a series of branches with "yes" or "no" questions about associated symptoms. Is there a fever or not? Are swollen lymph nodes associated with the sore throat? Have other family members suffered from this symptom? Similarly, a laboratory test like a throat culture for bacteria would appear farther down the trunk of the tree, with branches based on "yes" or "no" answers to the results of the culture. Ultimately, following the branches to the end should lead to the correct diagnosis and therapy.

Clinical algorithms can be useful for run-of-the-mill diagnosis and treatment — distinguishing strep throat from viral pharyngitis, for example. But they quickly fall apart when a doctor needs to think outside their boxes, when symptoms are vague, or multiple and confusing, or when test results are inexact. In such cases — the kinds of cases where we most need a discerning doctor — algorithms discourage physicians from thinking independently and creatively. Instead of expanding a doctor's thinking, they can constrain it.

Similarly, a movement is afoot to base all treatment decisions strictly on statistically proven data. This so-called evidence-based medicine is rapidly becoming the canon in many hospitals. Treatments outside the statistically proven are considered taboo until a sufficient body of data can be generated from clinical trials. Of course, every doctor should consider research studies in choosing a therapy. But today's rigid reliance on evidence-based medicine risks having the doctor choose care passively, solely by the numbers. Statistics cannot substitute for the human being before you; statistics embody averages, not individuals. Numbers can only complement a physician's personal experience with a drug or a procedure, as well as his knowledge of whether a "best" therapy from a clinical trial fits a patient's particular needs and values.

Each morning as rounds began, I watched the students and residents eye their algorithms and then invoke statistics from recent studies. I concluded that the next generation of doctors was being conditioned to function like a well-programmed computer that operates within a strict binary framework. After several weeks of unease about the students' and residents' reliance on algorithms and evidence-based therapies alone, and my equally unsettling sense that I didn't know how to broaden their perspective and show them otherwise, I asked myself a simple question: How should a doctor think?

This question, not surprisingly, spawned others: Do different doctors think differently? Are different forms of thinking more or less prevalent among the different specialties? In other words, do surgeons think differently from internists, who think differently from pediatricians? Is there one "best" way to think, or are there multiple, alternative styles that can reach a correct diagnosis and choose the most effective treatment? How does a doctor think when he is forced to improvise, when confronted with a problem for which there is little or no precedent? (Here algorithms are essentially irrelevant and statistical evidence is absent.) How does a doctor's thinking differ during routine visits versus times of clinical crisis? Do a doctor's emotions — his like or dislike of a particular patient, his attitudes about the social and psychological makeup of his patient's life — color his thinking? Why do even the most accomplished physicians miss a key clue about a person's true diagnosis, or detour far afield from the right remedy? In sum, when and why does thinking go right or go wrong in medicine?

I had no ready answers to these questions, despite having trained in a well-regarded medical school and residency program, and having practiced clinical medicine for some thirty years. So I began to ask my colleagues for answers.* Nearly all of the practicing physicians I queried were intrigued by the questions but confessed that they had never really thought about how they think. Then I searched the medical literature for studies of clinical thinking. I found a wealth of research that modeled "optimal" medical decision-making with complex mathematical formulas, but even the advocates of such formulas conceded that they rarely mirrored reality at the bedside or could be followed practically. I saw why I found it difficult to teach the trainees on rounds how to think. I also saw that I was not serving my own patients as well as I might. I felt that if I became more aware of my own way of thinking, particularly its pitfalls, I would be a better caregiver. I wasn't one of the hematologists who evaluated Anne Dodge, but I could well have been, and I feared that I too could have failed to recognize what was missing in her diagnosis.

Of course, no one can expect a physician to be infallible. Medicine is, at its core, an uncertain science. Every doctor makes mistakes in diagnosis and treatment. But the frequency of those mistakes, and their severity, can be reduced by understanding how a doctor thinks and how he or she can think better. This book was written with that goal in mind. It is primarily intended for laymen, though I believe physicians and other medical professionals will find it useful. Why for laymen? Because doctors desperately

---

* I quickly realized that trying to assess how psychiatrists think was beyond my abilities. Therapy of mental illness is a huge field unto itself that encompasses various schools of thought and theories of mind. For that reason, I do not delve into psychiatry in this book.

need patients and their families and friends to help them think. Without their help, physicians are denied key clues to what is really wrong. I learned this not as a doctor but when I was sick, when I was the patient.

We've all wondered why a doctor asked certain questions, or detoured into unexpected areas when gathering information about us. We have all asked ourselves exactly what brought him to propose a certain diagnosis and a particular treatment and to reject the alternatives. Although we may listen intently to what a doctor says and try to read his facial expressions, often we are left perplexed about what is really going on in his head. That ignorance inhibits us from successfully communicating with the doctor, from telling him all that he needs to hear to come to the correct diagnosis and advice on the best therapy.

In Anne Dodge's case, after a myriad of tests and procedures, it was her words that led Falchuk to correctly diagnose her illness and save her life. While modern medicine is aided by a dazzling array of technologies, like high-resolution MRI scans and pinpoint DNA analysis, language is still the bedrock of clinical practice. We tell the doctor what is bothering us, what we feel is different, and then respond to his questions. This dialogue is our first clue to how our doctor thinks, so the book begins there, exploring what we learn about a physician's mind from what he says and how he says it. But it is not only clinical logic that patients can extract from their dialogue with a doctor. They can also gauge his emotional temperature. Typically, it is the doctor who assesses our emotional state. But few of us realize how strongly a physician's mood and temperament influence his medical judgment. We, of course, may get only glimpses of our doctor's feelings, but even those brief moments can reveal a great deal about why he chose to pursue a possible diagnosis or offered a particular treatment.

After surveying the significance of a doctor's words and feelings, the book follows the path that we take when we move through today's medical system. If we have an urgent problem, we rush to the emergency room. There, doctors often do not have the benefit of knowing us, and must work with limited information about our medical history. I examine how doctors think under these conditions, how keen judgments and serious cognitive errors are made under the time pressures of the ER. If our clinical problem is not an emergency, then our path begins with our primary care physician — if a child, a pediatrician; if an adult, an internist. In today's parlance, these primary care physicians are termed "gatekeepers," because they open the portals to specialists. The narrative continues through these portals; at each step along the way, we see how essential it is for even the most astute doctor to doubt his thinking, to repeatedly factor into his analysis the possibility that he is wrong. We also encounter the tension between his acknowledging uncertainty and the need to take a clinical leap and act. One chapter reports on this in my own case; I sought help from six renowned hand surgeons for an incapacitating problem and got four different opinions.

Much has been made of the power of intuition, and certainly initial impressions formed in a flash can be correct. But as we hear from a range of physicians, relying too heavily on intuition has its perils. Cogent medical judgments meld first impressions — gestalt — with deliberate analysis. This requires time, perhaps the rarest commodity in a healthcare system that clocks appointments in minutes. What can doctors and patients do to find time to think? I explore this in the pages that follow.

Today, medicine is not separate from money. How much does intense marketing by pharmaceutical companies actually influence either conscious or subliminal decision-making? Very few doctors, I believe, prostitute themselves for profit, but all of us are susceptible to the subtle and not so subtle efforts of the pharmaceutical industry to sculpt our thinking. That industry is a vital one; without it, there would be a paucity of new therapies, a slowing of progress. Several doctors and a pharmaceutical executive speak with great candor about the reach of drug marketing, about how natural aspects of aging are falsely made into diseases, and how patients can be alert to this.

Cancer, of course, is a feared disease that becomes more likely as we grow older. It will strike roughly one in two men and one in three women over the course of their lifetime. Recently there have been great clinical successes against types of cancers that were previously intractable, but many malignancies remain that can be, at best, only temporarily controlled. How an oncologist thinks through the value of complex and harsh treatments demands not only an understanding of science but also a sensibility about the soul — how much risk we are willing to take and how we want to live out our lives. Two cancer specialists reveal how they guide their patients' choices and how their patients guide them toward the treatment that best suits each patient's temperament and lifestyle.

At the end of this journey through the minds of doctors, we return to language. The epilogue offers words that patients, their families, and their friends can use to help a physician or surgeon think, and thereby better help themselves. Patients and their loved ones can be true partners with physicians when they know how doctors think, and why doctors sometimes fail to think. Using this knowledge, patients can offer a doctor the most vital information about themselves, to help steer him toward the correct diagnosis and offer the therapy they need. Patients and their loved ones can aid even the most seasoned physician avoid errors in thinking. To do so, they need answers to the questions that I asked myself, and for which I had no ready answers.

Not long after Anne Dodge's visit to Dr. Myron Falchuk, I met with him in his office at Boston's Beth Israel Deaconess Medical Center. Falchuk is a compact man in his early sixties with a broad bald pate and lively eyes. His accent is hard to place, and his speech has an almost musical quality. He was born in rural Venezuela and grew up speaking Yiddish at home and Spanish in the streets of his village. As a young boy, he was sent to live with relatives in Brooklyn. There he quickly learned English. All this has made him particularly sensitive to language, its nuances and power. Falchuk left New York for Dartmouth College, and then attended Harvard Medical School; he trained at the Peter Bent Brigham Hospital in Boston, and for several years conducted research at the National Institutes of Health on diseases of the bowel. After nearly four decades, he has not lost his excitement about caring for patients. When he began to discuss Anne Dodge's case, he sat up in his chair as if a jolt of electricity had passed through him.

"She was emaciated and looked haggard," Falchuk told me. "Her face was creased with fatigue. And the way she sat in the waiting room — so still, her hands clasped together — I saw how timid she was." From the first, Falchuk was reading Anne Dodge's body language. Everything was a potential clue, telling him something about not only her physical condition but also her emotional state. This was a woman beaten down by her suffering. She would need to be drawn out, gently.

Medical students are taught that the evaluation of a patient should proceed in a discrete, linear way: you first take the patient's history, then perform a physical examination, order tests, and analyze the results. Only after all the data are compiled should you formulate hypotheses about what might be wrong. These hypotheses should be winnowed by assigning statistical probabilities, based on existing databases, to each symptom, physical abnormality, and laboratory test; then you calculate the likely diagnosis. This is Bayesian analysis, a method of decision-making favored by those who construct algorithms and strictly adhere to evidence-based practice. But, in fact, few if any physicians work with this mathematical paradigm. The physical examination begins with the first visual impression in the waiting room, and with the tactile feedback gained by shaking a person's hand. Hypotheses about the diagnosis come to a doctor's mind even before a word of the medical history is spoken. And in cases like Anne's, of course, the specialist had a diagnosis on the referral form from the internist, confirmed by the multitude of doctors' notes in her records.

Falchuk ushered Anne Dodge into his office, his hand on her elbow, lightly guiding her to the chair that faces his desk. She looked at a stack of papers some six inches high. It was the dossier she had seen on the desks of her endocrinologists, hematologists, infectious disease physicians, psychiatrists, and nutritionists. For fifteen years she'd watched it grow from visit to visit.

But then Dr. Falchuk did something that caught Anne's eye: he moved those records to the far side of his desk, withdrew a pen from the breast pocket of his white coat, and took a clean tablet of lined paper from his drawer. "Before we talk about why you are here today," Falchuk said, "let's go back to the beginning. Tell me about when you first didn't feel good."

For a moment, she was confused. Hadn't the doctor spoken with her internist and looked at her records? "I have bulimia and anorexia nervosa," she said softly. Her clasped hands tightened. "And now I have irritable bowel syndrome."

Falchuk offered a gentle smile. "I want to hear your story, in your own words."

Anne glanced at the clock on the wall, the steady sweep of the second hand ticking off precious time. Her internist had told her that Dr. Falchuk was a prominent specialist, that there was a long waiting list to see him. Her problem was hardly urgent, and she got an appointment in less than two months only because of a cancellation in his Christmas-week schedule. But she detected no hint of rush or impatience in the doctor. His calm made it seem as though he had all the time in the world.

So Anne began, as Dr. Falchuk requested, at the beginning, reciting the long and tortuous story of her initial symptoms, the many doctors she had seen, the tests she had undergone. As she spoke, Dr. Falchuk would nod or interject short phrases: "Uh-huh," "I'm with you," "Go on."

Occasionally Anne found herself losing track of the sequence of events. It was as if Dr. Falchuk had given her permission to open the floodgates, and a torrent of painful memories poured forth. Now she was tumbling forward, swept along as she had been as a child on Cape Cod when a powerful wave caught her unawares. She couldn't recall exactly when she had had the bone marrow biopsy for her anemia.

"Don't worry about exactly when," Falchuk said. For a long moment Anne sat mute, still searching for the date. "I'll check it later in your records. Let's talk about the past months. Specifically, what you have been doing to try to gain weight."

This was easier for Anne; the doctor had thrown her a rope and was slowly tugging her to the shore of the present. As she spoke, Falchuk focused on the details of her diet. "Now, tell me again what happens after each meal," he said.

Anne thought she had already explained this, that it all was detailed in her records. Surely her internist had told Dr. Falchuk about the diet she had been following. But she went on to say, "I try to get down as much cereal in the morning as possible, and then bread and pasta at lunch and dinner." Cramps and diarrhea followed nearly every meal, Anne explained. She was taking anti-nausea medication that had greatly reduced the frequency of her vomiting but did not help the diarrhea. "Each day, I calculate how many calories I'm keeping in, just like the nutritionist taught me to do. And it's close to three thousand."

Dr. Falchuk paused. Anne Dodge saw his eyes drift away from hers. Then his focus returned, and he brought her into the examining room across the hall. The physical exam was unlike any she'd had before. She had been expecting him to concentrate on her abdomen, to poke and prod her liver and spleen, to have her take deep breaths, and to look for any areas of tenderness. Instead, he looked carefully at her skin and then at her palms. Falchuk intently inspected the creases in her hands, as though he were a fortuneteller reading her lifelines and future. Anne felt a bit perplexed but didn't ask him why he was doing this. Nor did she question why he spent such a long while looking in her mouth with a flashlight, inspecting not only her tongue and palate but her gums and the glistening tissue behind her lips as well. He also spent a long time examining her nails, on both her hands and her feet. "Sometimes you can find clues in the skin or the lining of the mouth that point you to a diagnosis," Falchuk explained at last.

He also seemed to fix on the little loose stool that remained in her rectum. She told him she had had an early breakfast, and diarrhea before the car ride to Boston.

When the physical exam was over, he asked her to dress and return to his office. She felt tired. The energy she had mustered for the trip was waning. She steeled herself for yet another somber lecture on how she had to eat more, given her deteriorating condition.

"I'm not at all sure this is irritable bowel syndrome," Dr. Falchuk said, "or that your weight loss is only due to bulimia and anorexia nervosa."

She wasn't sure she had heard him correctly. Falchuk seemed to recognize her confusion. "There may be something else going on that explains why you can't restore your weight. I could be wrong, of course, but we need to be sure, given how frail you are and how much you are suffering."

Anne felt even more confused and fought off the urge to cry. Now was not the time to break down. She needed to concentrate on what the doctor was saying. He proposed more blood tests, which were simple enough, but then suggested a procedure called an endoscopy. She listened carefully as Falchuk described how he would pass a fiberoptic instrument, essentially a flexible telescope, down her esophagus and then into her stomach and small intestine. If he saw something abnormal, he would take a biopsy. She was exhausted from endless evaluations. She'd been through so much, so many tests, so many procedures: the x-rays, the bone density assessment, the painful bone marrow biopsy for her low blood counts, and multiple spinal taps when she had meningitis. Despite his assurances that she would be sedated, she doubted whether the endoscopy was worth the trouble and discomfort. She recalled her internist's reluctance to refer her to a gastroenterologist, and wondered whether the procedure was pointless, done for the sake of doing it, or, even worse, to make money.

Dodge was about to refuse, but then Falchuk repeated emphatically that something else might account for her condition. "Given how poorly you are doing, how much weight you've lost, what's happened to your blood, your bones, and your immune system over the years, we need to be absolutely certain of everything that's wrong. It may be that your body can't digest the food you're eating, that those three thousand calories are just passing through you, and that's why you're down to eighty-two pounds."

When I met with Anne Dodge one month after her first appointment with Dr. Falchuk, she said that he'd given her the greatest Christmas present ever. She had gained nearly twelve pounds. The intense nausea, the urge to vomit, the cramps and diarrhea that followed breakfast, lunch, and dinner as she struggled to fill her stomach with cereal, bread, and pasta had all abated. The blood tests and the endoscopy showed that she had celiac disease. This is an autoimmune disorder, in essence an allergy to gluten, a primary component of many grains. Once believed to be rare, the malady, also called celiac sprue, is now recognized more frequently thanks to sophisticated diagnostic tests. Moreover, it has become clear that celiac disease is not only a childhood illness, as previously thought; symptoms may not begin until late adolescence or early adulthood, as Falchuk believed occurred in Anne Dodge's case. Yes, she suffered from an eating disorder. But her body's reaction to gluten resulted in irritation and distortion of the lining of her bowel, so nutrients were not absorbed. The more cereal and pasta she added to her diet, the more her digestive tract was damaged, and even fewer calories and essential vitamins passed into her system.

Anne Dodge told me she was both elated and a bit dazed. After fifteen years of struggling to get better, she had begun to lose hope. Now she had a new chance to restore her health. It would take time, she said, to rebuild not only her body but her mind. Maybe one day she would be, as she put it, "whole" again.

Behind Myron Falchuk's desk, a large framed photograph occupies much of the wall. A group of austerely dressed men pose, some holding derby hats, some with thick drooping mustaches like Teddy Roosevelt's; the sepia tinge of the picture and the men's appearance date it to the early 1900s. It seems out of phase with Falchuk's outgoing demeanor and stylish clothes. But it is, he says, his touchstone.

"That photograph was taken in 1913, when they opened the Brigham Hospital," Falchuk explained. "William Osler gave the first grand rounds." A smile spread across his face. "It's a copy. I didn't steal the original when I was chief resident." Osler was acutely sensitive to the power and importance of words, and his writings greatly influenced Falchuk. "Osler essentially said that if you listen to the patient, he is telling you the diagnosis," Falchuk continued. "A lot of people look at a specialist like me as a technician. They come to you for a procedure. And there is no doubt that procedures are important, or that the specialized technology we have these days is vital in caring for a patient. But I believe that this technology also has taken us away from the patient's story."

Falchuk paused. "And once you remove yourself from the patient's story, you no longer are truly a doctor."

How a doctor thinks can first be discerned by how he speaks and how he listens. In addition to words spoken and heard, there is nonverbal communication, his attention to the body language of his patient as well as his own body language — his expressions, his posture, his gestures. Debra Roter, a professor of health policy and management at Johns Hopkins University, works as a team with Judith Hall, a professor of social psychology at Northeastern University. They are among the most productive and insightful researchers studying medical communication. They have analyzed thousands of videotapes and live interactions between doctors of many types — internists, gynecologists, surgeons — and patients, parsing phrases and physical movements. They also have assayed the data from other researchers. They have shown that how a doctor asks questions and how he responds to his patient's emotions are both key to what they term "patient activation and engagement." The idea, as Roter put it when we spoke, is "to wake someone up" so that the patient feels free, if not eager, to speak and participate in a dialogue. That freedom of patient speech is necessary if the doctor is to get clues about the medical enigma before him. If the patient is inhibited, or cut off prematurely, or constrained into one path of discussion, then the doctor may not be told something vital. Observers have noted that, on average, physicians interrupt patients within eighteen seconds of when they begin telling their story.

Let's apply Roter's and Hall's insights to the case of Anne Dodge. Falchuk began their conversation with a general, open-ended question about when she first began to feel ill. "The way a doctor asks a question," Roter said, "structures the patient's answers." Had Falchuk asked a specific, close-ended question — "What kind of abdominal pain do you have, is it sharp or dull?" — he would have implicitly revealed a preconception that Anne

Dodge had irritable bowel syndrome. "If you know where you are going," Roter said of doctors' efforts to pin down a diagnosis, "then close-ended questions are the most efficient. But if you are unsure of the diagnosis, then a close-ended question serves you ill, because it immediately, perhaps irrevocably, moves you along the wrong track." The great advantage of open-ended questioning is that it maximizes the opportunity for a doctor to hear new information.

"What does it take to succeed with open-ended questions?" Roter asked rhetorically. "The doctor has to make the patient feel that he is really interested in hearing what they have to say. And when a patient tells his story, the patient gives cues and clues to what the doctor may not be thinking about."

The type of question a doctor asks is only half of a successful medical dialogue. "The physician should respond to the patient's emotions," Roter continued. Most patients are gripped by fear and anxiety; some also carry a sense of shame about their disease. But a doctor gives more than psychological relief by responding empathetically to a patient. "The patient does not want to appear stupid or waste the doctor's time," Roter said. "Even if the doctor asks the right questions, the patient may not be forthcoming because of his emotional state. The goal of a physician is to get to the story, and to do so he has to understand the patient's emotions."

Falchuk immediately discerned emotions in Anne that would inhibit her from telling her tale. He tried to put her at ease by responding sympathetically to her history. He did something else that Roter believes is essential in eliciting information: he turned her anxiety and reticence around and engaged her by indicating that he was listening actively, that he wanted to hear more. His simple interjections — "uh-huh, I'm with you, go on" — implied to Anne Dodge that what she was saying was important to him.

Judy Hall, the social psychologist, has focused further on the emotional dimension of the dialogue between doctor and patient: whether the doctor appears to like the patient and whether the patient likes the doctor. She discovered that those feelings are hardly secret on either side of the table. In studies of primary care physicians and surgeons, patients knew remarkably accurately how the doctor actually felt about them. Much of this, of course, comes from nonverbal behavior: the physician's facial expressions, how he is seated, whether his gestures are warm and welcoming or formal and remote. "The doctor is supposed to be emotionally neutral and evenhanded with everybody," Hall said, "and we know that's not true."

Her research on rapport between doctors and patients bears on Anne Dodge's case. Hall discovered that the sickest patients are the least liked by doctors, and that very sick people sense this disaffection. Overall, doctors tend to like healthier people more. Why is this? "I am not a doctor-basher," Hall said. "Some doctors are averse to the very ill, and the reasons for this are quite forgivable." Many doctors have deep feelings of failure when dealing with diseases that resist even the best therapy; in such cases they become frustrated, because all their hard work seems in vain. So they stop trying. In fact, few physicians welcome patients like Anne Dodge warmly. Consider: fifteen years of anorexia nervosa and bulimia, a disorder with a social stigma, a malady that is often extremely difficult to remedy. Consider also how much time and attention Anne had been given over those fifteen years by so many caregivers, without a glimmer of improvement. And by December 2004, she was only getting worse.

Roter and Hall also studied the effect a doctor's bedside manner has on successful diagnosis and treatment. "We tend to remember the extremes," Hall said, "the genius surgeon with an autistic bedside manner, or the kindly GP who is not terribly competent. But the good stuff goes together — good doctoring generally requires both. Good doctoring is a total package." This is because "most of what doctors do is talk," Hall concluded, "and the communication piece is not separable from doing quality medicine. You need information to get at the diagnosis, and the best way to get that information is by establishing rapport with the patient. Competency is not separable from communication skills. It's not a tradeoff."

Falchuk conducts an inner monologue to guide his thinking. "She told me she was eating up to three thousand calories a day. Inside myself, I asked: Should I believe you? And if I do, then why aren't you gaining weight?" That simple possibility had to be carried to its logical end: that she was actually trying, that she really was putting the cereal, bread, and pasta in her mouth, chewing, swallowing, struggling not to vomit, and still wasting away, her blood counts still falling, her bones still decomposing, her immune system still failing. "I have to give her the benefit of a doubt," Falchuk told himself.

Keeping an open mind was reflected in Falchuk's open-ended line of questioning. The more he observed Anne Dodge, and the more he listened, the more disquiet he felt. "It just seemed impossible to absolutely conclude it was all psychiatric," he said. "Everyone had written her off as some neurotic case. But my intuition told me that the picture didn't entirely fit. And once I felt that way, I began to wonder: What was missing?"

Clinical intuition is a complex sense that becomes refined over years and years of practice, of listening to literally thousands of patients' stories, examining thousands of people, and most important, remembering when you were wrong. Falchuk had done research at the National Institutes of Health on patients with malabsorption, people who couldn't extract vital nutrients and calories from the food they ate. This background was key to recognizing that Anne Dodge might be suffering not only from anorexia nervosa or bulimia but also from some form of malabsorption. He told me that Anne reminded him that he had been fooled in the past by a patient who was also losing weight rapidly. That woman carried the diagnosis of malabsorption. She said she ate heartily and had terrible cramps and diarrhea, and her many doctors believed her. After more than a month of evaluation, with numerous blood tests and an endoscopy, by chance Falchuk found a bottle of laxatives under her hospital bed that she had forgotten to hide. Nothing was wrong with her gastrointestinal tract. Something was tragically wrong with her psyche. Falchuk learned that both mind and body have to be considered, at times independently, at times through their connections.

Different doctors, as we will see in later chapters, achieve competency in remarkably similar ways, despite working in disparate fields. Primarily, they recognize and remember their mistakes and misjudgments, and incorporate those memories into their thinking. Studies show that expertise is largely acquired not only by sustained practice but by receiving feedback that helps you understand your technical errors and misguided decisions. During my training, I met a cardiologist who had a deserved reputation as one of the best in his field, not only a storehouse of knowledge but also a clinician with excellent judgment. He kept a log of all the mistakes he knew he had made over the decades, and at times revisited this compendium when trying to figure out a particularly difficult case. He was characterized by many of his colleagues as eccentric, an obsessive oddball. Only later did I realize his implicit message to us was to admit our mistakes to ourselves, then analyze them, and keep them accessible at all times if we wanted to be stellar clinicians. In Anne Dodge's case, Falchuk immediately recalled how he had taken at face value the statements of the patient at NIH who was secretly using laxatives. The opposite situation, he knew, could also apply. In either setting, the case demanded continued thought and investigation.

When Falchuk told me that "the picture didn't fit," his words were more than mere metaphor. Donald Redelmeier, a physician at Sunnybrook Health Sciences Centre in Toronto, has a particular interest in physician cognition and its relation to diagnosis. He refers to a phenomenon called the "eyeball test," the pivotal moment when a doctor identifies "something intangible yet unsettling in the patient's presentation." That instinct may, of course, be wrong. But it should not be ignored, because it can cause the physician to recognize that the information before him has been improperly "framed."

Doctors frame patients all the time using shorthand: "I'm sending you a case of diabetes and renal failure," or "I have a drug addict here in the ER with fever and a cough from pneumonia." Often a doctor chooses the correct frame and all the clinical data fit neatly within it. But a self-aware physician knows that accepting the frame as given can be a serious error. Anne Dodge was fitted into the single frame of bulimia and anorexia nervosa from the age of twenty. It was easily understandable that each of her doctors received her case in that one frame. All the data fit neatly within its borders. There was no apparent reason to redraw her clinical portrait, to look at it from another angle. Except one. "It's like DNA evidence at a crime," Falchuk explained. "The patient was saying 'I told you, I'm innocent.'" Here is the art of medicine, the sensitivity to language and emotion that makes for a superior clinician.

Falchuk almost rose from his chair when he showed me the pictures of Dodge's distorted small intestine taken through the endoscope. "I was so excited about this," he said. He had the sweet pleasure of the detective who cracks the mystery, a legitimate pride in identifying a culprit. But beyond intellectual excitement and satisfaction, he showed his joy in saving a life.

Intellect and intuition, careful attention to detail, active listening, and psychological insight all coalesced on that December day. It could have been otherwise. Anne Dodge, with her history of anorexia nervosa and bulimia, may then have developed irritable bowel syndrome. But Falchuk had asked himself, "What might I be missing in this case? And what would be the worst thing that could be missed?"

What if he had not asked himself these questions? Then Anne Dodge, her boyfriend, or a family member could have asked them — perhaps many years earlier. Of course, a patient or a loved one is not a doctor. They lack a doctor's training and experience. And many laymen feel inhibited about asking questions. But the questions are perfectly legitimate. Patients can learn to question and to think the way a doctor should. In the chapters and epilogue that follow, we will examine the kinds of errors in thinking that physicians can make, and the words that patients and their loved ones can offer to prevent these cognitive mistakes.

In Anne Dodge's case, it was Falchuk who asked simple but ultimately life-saving questions, and to answer them he needed to go further. And Anne Dodge needed to agree to go further, to submit to more blood tests and an invasive procedure. For her to assent, she had to trust not only Falchuk's skill but also his sincerity and motivations. This is the other dimension of Roter's and Hall's studies: how language, spoken and unspoken, can give information essential to a correct diagnosis, and persuade a patient to comply with a doctor's advice. "Compliance" can have a negative connotation, smacking of paternalism, casting patients as passive players who do what the all-powerful physician tells them. But according to Roter's and Hall's research, without trust and a sense of mutual liking, Anne Dodge probably would have deflected Falchuk's suggestions of more blood tests and an endoscopy. She would have been "noncompliant," in pejorative clinical parlance. And she would still be struggling to persuade her doctors that she was eating three thousand calories a day while wasting away.

My admiration for Myron Falchuk increased when we went on from Anne Dodge's case to discuss not his clinical triumphs but his errors. Again, every doctor is fallible. No doctor is right all the time. Every physician, even the most brilliant, makes a misdiagnosis or chooses the wrong therapy. This is not a matter of "medical mistakes." Medical mistakes have been written about extensively in the lay press and analyzed in a report from the Institute of Medicine of the National Academy of Sciences. They involve prescribing the wrong dose of a drug or looking at an x-ray of a patient backward. Misdiagnosis is different. It is a window into the medical mind. It reveals why doctors fail to question their assumptions, why their thinking is sometimes closed or skewed, why they overlook the gaps in their knowledge. Experts studying misguided care have recently concluded that the majority of errors are due to flaws in physician thinking, not technical mistakes. In one study of misdiagnoses that caused serious harm to patients, some 80 percent could be accounted for by a cascade of cognitive errors, like the one in Anne Dodge's case, putting her into a narrow frame and ignoring information that contradicted a fixed notion. Another study of one hundred incorrect diagnoses found that inadequate medical knowledge was the reason for error in only four instances. The doctors didn't stumble because of their ignorance of clinical facts; rather, they missed diagnoses because they fell into cognitive traps. Such errors produce a distressingly high rate of misdiagnosis. As many as 15 percent of all diagnoses are inaccurate, according to a 1995 report in which doctors assessed written descriptions of patients' symptoms and examined actors simulating patients with various diseases. These findings match classical research, based on autopsies, which shows that 10 percent to 15 percent of all diagnoses are wrong.

I can recall every misdiagnosis I've made during my thirty-year career. The first occurred when I was a resident in internal medicine at the Massachusetts General Hospital; Roter's and Hall's research explains it. One of my patients was a middle-aged woman with seemingly endless complaints whose voice sounded to me like a nail scratching a blackboard. One day she had a new complaint, discomfort in her upper chest. I tried to pin down what caused the discomfort — eating, exercise, coughing — to no avail. Then I ordered routine tests, including a chest x-ray and a cardiogram. Both were normal. In desperation, I prescribed antacids. But her complaint persisted, and I became deaf to it. In essence, I couldn't think in a different way. Several weeks later, I was stat paged to the emergency room. My patient had a dissecting aortic aneurysm, a life-threatening tear of the large artery that carries blood from the heart to the rest of the body. She died. Although an aortic dissection is often fatal even when discovered, I have never forgiven myself for failing to diagnose it. There was a chance she could have been saved.

Roter's and Hall's work on liking and disliking illuminates in part what happened in the clinic three decades ago. I wish I had been taught, and had gained the self-awareness, to realize how emotion can blur a doctor's ability to listen and think. Physicians who dislike their patients regularly cut them off during the recitation of symptoms and fix on a convenient diagnosis and treatment. The doctor becomes increasingly convinced of the truth of his misjudgment, developing a psychological commitment to it. He becomes wedded to his distorted conclusion. His strong negative feelings about the patient make it harder for him to abandon that conclusion and reframe the clinical picture differently.

This skewing of physicians' thinking leads to poor care. What is remarkable is not merely the consequences of a doctor's negative emotions. Despite research showing that most patients pick up on the physician's negativity, few of them understand its effect on their medical care and rarely change doctors because of it. Rather, they often blame themselves for complaining and taxing the doctor's patience. Instead, patients should politely but freely broach the issue with their doctor. "I sense that we may not be communicating well," a patient can say. This signals the physician that there is a problem in compatibility. The problem may be resolvable with candor by a patient who wants to sustain the relationship. But when I asked other physicians what they would do if they, as patients, perceived a negative attitude from their doctor, each one flatly said he or she would find another doctor.

CHAPTER I

Flesh-and-Blood Decision-Making

O N A SWELTERING MORNING in June 1976, I put on a starched white coat, placed a stethoscope in my black bag, and checked for the third time in the mirror that my tie was correctly knotted. Despite the heat, I walked briskly along Cambridge Street to the entrance of the Massachusetts General Hospital. This was the long-awaited moment, my first day of internship — the end of play-acting as a doctor, the start of being a real one. My medical school classmates and I had spent the first two years in lecture halls and in laboratories, learning anatomy, physiology, pharmacology, and pathology from textbooks and manuals, using microscopes and petri dishes to perform experiments. The following two years, we learned at the bedside. We were taught how to organize a patient's history: his chief complaint, associated symptoms, past medical history, relevant social data, past and current therapies. Then we were instructed in how to examine people: listening for normal and abnormal heart sounds; palpating the liver and spleen; checking pulses in the neck, arms, and legs; observing the contour of the nerve and splay of the vessels in the retina. At each step we were closely supervised, our hands firmly held by our mentors, the attending physicians.

Throughout those four years of medical school, I was an intense, driven student, gripped by the belief that I had to learn every fact and detail so that I might one day take responsibility for a patient's life. I sat in the front row in the lecture hall and hardly moved my head, nearly catatonic with concentration. During my clinical courses in internal medicine, surgery, pediatrics, obstetrics and gynecology, I assumed a similarly focused posture. Determined to retain everything, I scribbled copious notes during lectures and after bedside rounds. Each night, I copied those notes onto index cards that I arranged on my desk according to subject. On weekends, I would try to memorize them. My goal was to store an encyclopedia in my mind, so that when I met a patient, I could open the mental book and find the correct diagnosis and treatment.

The new interns gathered in a conference room in the Bulfinch Building of the hospital. The Bulfinch is an elegant gray granite structure with eight Ionic columns and floor-to-ceiling windows, dating from 1823. In this building is the famed Ether Dome, the amphitheater where the anesthetic ether was first demonstrated in 1846. In 1976, the Bulfinch Building still housed open wards with nearly two dozen patients in a single cavernous room, each bed separated by a flimsy curtain.

We were greeted by the chairman of medicine, Alexander Leaf. His remarks were brief — he told us that as interns we had the privilege to both learn and serve. Though he spoke in a near whisper, what we heard was loud and clear: the internship program at the MGH was highly selective, and great things were expected of us during our careers in medicine. Then the chief resident handed out each intern's schedule.

There were three clinical services, Bulfinch, Baker, and Phillips, and over the ensuing twelve months we would rotate through all of them. Each clinical service was located in a separate building, and together the three buildings mirrored the class structure of America. The open wards in Bulfinch served people who had no private physician, mainly indigent Italians from the North End and Irish from Charlestown and Chelsea. Interns and residents took a fierce pride in caring for those on the Bulfinch wards, who were "their own" patients. The Baker Building housed the "semi-private" patients, two or three to a room, working- and middle-class people with insurance. The "private" service was in the Phillips House, a handsome edifice rising some eleven stories with views of the Charles River; each room was either a single or a suite, and the suites were rumored to have accommodated valets and maids in times past. The very wealthy were admitted to the Phillips House by a select group of personal physicians, many of whom had offices at the foot of Beacon Hill and were themselves Boston Brahmins.

I began on the Baker service. Our team was composed of two interns and one resident. After the meeting with Dr. Leaf, the three of us immediately went to the floor and settled in with a stack of patient charts. The resident divided our charges into three groups, assigning the sickest to himself.

Each of us was on call every third night, and my turn began that first evening. We would be on call alone, responsible for all of the patients on the floor as well as any new admissions. At seven the following morning, we would meet and review what had happened overnight. "Remember, be an ironman and hold the fort," the resident said to me, the clichés offered only half jokingly. Interns were to ask for backup only in the most dire circumstances. "You can page me if you really need me," the resident added, "but I'll be home sleeping, since I was on call last night."

I touched my left jacket pocket and felt a pack of my index

cards from medical school. The cards, I told myself, would provide the ballast to keep me afloat alone. I spent the better part of the day reading my patients' charts and then introducing myself to them. The knot in my stomach gradually loosened. But it tightened again when my fellow intern and supervising resident signed out their patients, alerting me to problems I might encounter on call.

A crepuscular quiet settled over the Baker. There were still a few patients I had not met. I went to room 632, checked the name on the door against my list, and knocked. A voice said, "Enter."

"Good evening, Mr. Morgan. I am Doctor Groopman, your new intern." The appellation "Doctor Groopman" still sounded strange to me, but it was imprinted on the nameplate pinned to my jacket.

William Morgan was described in his chart as "a 66-year-old African-American man" with hypertension that was difficult to control with medications. He had been admitted to the hospital two days earlier with chest pains. I called up from my mental encyclopedia the fact that African Americans have a high incidence of hypertension, which could be complicated by cardiac enlargement and kidney failure. His initial ER evaluation and subsequent blood tests and electrocardiogram did not point to angina, pain from coronary artery blockage. Mr. Morgan shook my hand firmly and grinned. "First day, huh?"

I nodded. "I saw in your chart that you're a letter carrier," I said. "My grandfather worked in the post office too."

"Carrier?"

"No, he sorted mail and sold stamps."

William Morgan told me that he had started out that way, but was a "restless type" and felt better working outside than inside, even in the worst weather.

"I know what you mean," I said, thinking that right now I too would rather be outside than inside — alone, in charge of a floor of sick people. I updated Mr. Morgan on the x-ray tests done earlier in the day. A GI series showed no abnormality in his esophagus or stomach.

"That's good to hear."

I was about to say goodbye when Mr. Morgan shot upright in bed. His eyes widened. His jaw fell slack. His chest began to heave violently.

"What's wrong, Mr. Morgan?"

He shook his head, unable to speak, desperately taking in breaths.

I tried to think but couldn't. The encyclopedia had vanished. My palms became moist, my throat dry. I couldn't move. My feet felt as if they were fixed to the floor.

"This man seems to be in distress," a deep voice said.

I spun around. Behind me was a man in his forties, with short black hair, dark eyes, and a handlebar mustache. "John Burnside," he said. "I trained here a number of years ago and was by to see some old friends. I'm a cardiologist in Virginia."

With his handlebar mustache and trimmed hair, Burnside looked like a figure from the Civil War. I remembered that a famous general of that name had fought in that conflict. Burnside deftly took the stethoscope from my pocket and placed it over Mr. Morgan's chest. After a few short seconds, he held the bell of the instrument over Mr. Morgan's heart and then removed the earpieces from his ears. "Here, listen."

I heard something that sounded like a spigot opened full blast, then closed for a moment, and opened again, the pattern repeated over and over. "This gentleman just tore through his aortic valve," Burnside said. "He needs the services of a cardiac surgeon. Pronto."

Dr. Burnside stayed with Mr. Morgan while I raced to find a nurse. She told another nurse to stat page the surgery team and ran back with me, the resuscitation cart in tow. Dr. Burnside quickly inserted an airway through Mr. Morgan's mouth and the nurse began to pump oxygen via an ambu bag. Other nurses arrived. The cardiac surgery resident appeared. Together we rushed Mr. Morgan to the OR. Dr. Burnside said goodbye. I thanked him.

I returned to the Baker and sat for several minutes at the nurses' station. I was in a daze. The event seemed surreal — enjoying a first conversation with one of my patients, then, like an earthquake, Mr. Morgan's sudden upheaval, then the *deus ex machina* appearance of Dr. Burnside. I felt the weight of the cards in my pocket. Straight A's when I was a student, play-acting. Now, in the real world, I gave myself an F.

I forced myself to go about my chores through the rest of the evening: checking the potassium level of a patient with diarrhea; adjusting the insulin dose for a diabetic whose blood sugar was too high; ordering another two units of blood to be transfused for an elderly woman with anemia. Between each task, my thoughts returned to what had happened with Mr. Morgan. In medical school physiology lectures I learned the relevant formulas for cardiac output and gas exchange in the lungs; in pharmacology class, the actions of various medications on heart muscle. On bedside rounds, I had spent hours listening to the sounds of patients' hearts. But I had no idea what I was hearing in Mr. Morgan's chest, or what to do about it. My high grades were meaningless. The MGH selection committee had made a mistake offering me an internship. After all the years of preparation, I ended up with an empty head and my feet fixed to the floor.

Mercifully, the rest of the night was uneventful. Three patients were admitted, but none was very ill, and most of their evaluation had been completed in the ER before they were transferred upstairs to the Baker service. Around 3 A.M., I called the OR. I heard that Mr. Morgan had survived open heart surgery, a prosthetic valve firmly in place. My shoulders slumped in relief.

That first night of internship showed me that I needed to think differently from how I had learned to think in medical school — indeed, differently from the way I had ever thought seriously in my life. This was despite my having met patients like Mr. Morgan before. During medical school we had studied what are called paper cases, patients in the form of written data. The attending physician would hand out a detailed description that would begin something like this: "A 66-year-old African-American retired postal worker with a history of poorly controlled hypertension presented to the hospital with the chief complaint of worsening chest pain over several weeks. Initial evaluation ruled out angina. On the third day of the hospital stay, he developed acute respiratory distress." The attending would then give more details on Mr. Morgan — the range of his elevated blood pressure, the medications that failed to control it in the past — and lead us through a systematic analysis of the problem. First, the chief complaint, here acute shortness of breath. Second, the history of the present illness, angina having been ruled out. Third, the medical history, notably poorly controlled hypertension. Fourth, the physical examination. At that point, the attending would elaborate on what was heard through the stethoscope: breath sounds described as "rales," indicating fluid in the lungs; another heart sound, an "S3," indicating cardiac failure; and the crescendo/decrescendo murmur of aortic regurgitation — blood being pumped out through the left ventricle into the aorta but then flowing back into the heart.

Hands would shoot up in the classroom as students offered their ideas about what was wrong. Our mentor would take these hypotheses and write them on the board, creating a "differential diagnosis," a laundry list of possible causes of sudden shortness of breath in a man with this medical history and these physical findings. From this differential diagnosis, he would point to the right answer and then enumerate the measures taken to restore respiratory and cardiac function until the patient was placed on heart-lung bypass in the OR.

In the last two years of medical school, when we saw patients on bedside rounds, the attending physician modeled a similar intellectual strategy for us. He would lead us through a calm, deliberate, and linear analysis of the clinical information and how to treat the malady.

As Robert Hamm of the Institute of Cognitive Science at the University of Colorado, Boulder, contends, the irony is that our mentor, the senior attending physician, does not think this way when he actually encounters a patient like William Morgan. At such moments, Hamm writes, it is not evident that any "reasoning" is being used at all. Studies show that while it usually takes twenty to thirty minutes in a didactic exercise for the senior doctor and students to arrive at a working diagnosis, an expert clinician typically forms a notion of what is wrong with the patient within twenty seconds. According to Hamm and other researchers on physician cognition, if I had asked John Burnside what was going on in his head, he would have been hard-pressed to describe it. It simply happened too fast.

Dr. Pat Croskerry, an emergency room doctor in Halifax, Nova Scotia, began his academic career as a developmental psychologist and now studies physician cognition. He explained to me that "flesh-and-blood decision-making" pivots on what is called pattern recognition. The key cues to a patient's problem — whether from the medical history, physical examination, x-ray studies, or laboratory tests — coalesce into a pattern that the physician identifies as a specific disease or condition. Pattern recognition, Croskerry told me, "reflects an immediacy of perception." It occurs within seconds, largely without any conscious analysis; it draws most heavily on the doctor's visual appraisal of the patient. And it does not occur by a linear, step-by-step combining of cues. The mind acts like a magnet, pulling in the cues from all directions.

On that first night of internship I also learned that thinking is inseparable from acting. Donald A. Schön, a professor at the Massachusetts Institute of Technology, studied types of cognition in various professions. Medicine, he contended, involves "thought-in-action," unlike, say, economics. Economists work by first assembling a large body of data, then analyzing it meticulously, and only after the assembly and analysis do they draw conclusions and make recommendations. Physicians at the bedside do not collect a great deal of data and then leisurely generate hypotheses about possible diagnoses. Rather, physicians begin to think of diagnoses from the first moment they meet a patient. Even as they say hello they take the person's measure, registering his pallor or ruddiness, the tilt of his head, the movement of his eyes and mouth, the way he sits down or stands up, the timbre of his voice, the depth of his breathing. Their notions of what is wrong continue to evolve as they peer into the eyes, listen to the heart, press on the liver, inspect the initial set of x-rays. Research shows that most doctors quickly come up with two or three possible diagnoses from the outset of meeting a patient — a few talented ones can juggle four or five in their minds. All develop their hypotheses from a very incomplete body of information. To do this, doctors use shortcuts. These are called heuristics.

Croskerry said that heuristics flourish when a physician assesses unfamiliar patients, or when he must work quickly, or when his technological resources are limited. Shortcuts are the doctor's response to the uncertainty and demands of the situation. They are the essential working tools of clinical medicine, where a doctor must combine thought and action. As Croskerry puts it, they are "fast and frugal," the core of flesh-and-blood decision-making.

The problem is that medical schools do not teach shortcuts. In fact, you are discouraged from using them, since they deviate sharply from the didactic exercises in classrooms or on bedside rounds conducted by the attending physician. In our paper case of a patient like Mr. Morgan, after we systematically analyzed all the components of his problem, we would be asked to reflect on the underlying basic science of acute heart failure. An animated discussion of the contractile changes in the heart's muscle and the pressure fluxes across the torn valve would follow. Of course, a doctor must know physiology and pathology and pharmacology. But he should also be schooled in heuristics — in the power and necessity of shortcuts, and in their pitfalls and dangers.

Further on in this book, we will explore how heuristics serve as the foundation of all mature medical thinking, how they can save lives, and how they also can lead to grave errors in clinical decision-making. Importantly, the right shortcuts have to be employed at an optimal emotional temperature. The doctor has to be aware of which heuristics he is using — and how his inner feelings may influence them.

The effects of a doctor's inner feelings on his thinking get short shrift in medical training and in research on decision-making. "Most people assume that medical decision-making is an objective and rational process, free from the intrusion of emotion," Pat Croskerry said to me. Yet the opposite is true. The physician's internal state, his state of tension, enters into and strongly influences his clinical judgments and actions. Croskerry spoke of the Yerkes-Dodson law on task performance, developed by psychologists studying psychomotor skill. It is expressed as a bell-shaped curve.

The vertical axis represents a person's "performance," the horizontal axis his level of "arousal" — meaning the level of tension, driven by adrenaline and other stress-related chemicals. Before the ascent, at the base of the bell, there is very little, if any, tension.

"You want to be just at the peak, where you think and perform the best," Croskerry said. This point he termed "productive anxiety," an optimum level of tension and anxiety that sharply focuses the mind and triggers quick reactions.

Thirty years after that harrowing episode in Mr. Morgan's room, I watched three medical students in similarly extreme anxiety. They were caring for a man in his forties named Stan, who had come to the emergency room with severe abdominal pain. He had a low fever and his blood pressure was falling. As the students began to examine him, he cried out to them to alleviate his suffering. "Please," Stan demanded, "please stop the pain." The students looked frantic. One picked up a syringe with morphine and delivered it through an intravenous line in Stan's arm. Within a minute, Stan stopped breathing. The students called for help performing cardiopulmonary resuscitation.

Fortunately, Stan is not a living patient, despite the pliant texture of his skin, the authentic timbre of his voice, and the palpable pulse in his wrists. He is a high-tech mannequin. He can be programmed to show either normal physiology or the signs of various diseases, and to respond authentically to treatments. Dr. Nancy Oriol, the dean of students at Harvard Medical School, said the three students that day were like all the other novices who had cared for Stan: every group missed the correct diagnosis. Stan's blood pressure was falling because he had an acute inflammation of the pancreas. The students failed to give him the right kind of therapy for this condition and did not order the correct type and amounts of intravenous fluids to restore his blood pressure. In response to Stan's cries of pain and pleas for action, several students injected a possibly lethal dose of morphine. "What happened to you, Jerry, in Mr. Morgan's room is what happened to the students with Stan," Dr. Oriol said. "It is as if everything that you learn in school is erased."

Simulations with Stan are designed to act as a bridge between analytical learning in classrooms and pattern recognition performed at the peak of the Yerkes-Dodson curve. But, as Oriol and others readily admit, there still will come that first moment when the novice can no longer be a novice, when he is the one who must take responsibility for a living, breathing patient in need.

Extreme arousal happens not only during the first encounter with a William Morgan, but throughout internship and residency. During this training, young doctors gradually learn how to move themselves back from the edge of the Yerkes-Dodson curve toward points of effective performance. My internship group did so largely, as interns still do, by following the maxim "See one, do one, teach one." In the emergency room or in the intensive care unit or on the wards, you saw "one," which might be a massive heart attack, or a pulmonary embolism, or a brain hemorrhage, or a grand mal seizure. If you were lucky and it was during the day, the senior resident would not be at home sleeping but would be called to the scene and would rapidly assess the situation, issue orders, and work to save the patient. As the intern "seeing one," you pitched in, starting, in part, to "do one" by following the resident's instructions as you listened to the heart and lungs or examined the widened pupils or inserted an airway into a clenching mouth. You listened closely to what the senior resident ordered, the measures he initiated to supply oxygen to an injured lung or stabilize blood pressure with a failing heart or stanch a hemorrhage or arrest the electrical discharges of a seizing brain. If you were very lucky, despite the rush of the moment, the senior resident might offer a few explicit words, explaining the tricks he used to pass a breathing tube into the trachea and not mistakenly into the esophagus, how to adjust the dose of an anticoagulant for a pulmonary embolism, which drug he preferred to try to restore falling blood pressure or stop a seizure. The next time, you were more ready to imitate him. You were beginning to think and act simultaneously.

It took Dr. Burnside some fifteen seconds to figure out what was wrong and what to do for William Morgan. Physicians had fifteen years to ponder Anne Dodge's case. Anne Dodge was dying a slow death from malnutrition; William Morgan would have died quickly from acute heart failure. Anne Dodge's condition called for the withdrawal of a single dietary component, gluten; William Morgan's demanded complex intervention, opening his heart and inserting a new valve. Given these contrasts, you might imagine that a doctor thinks differently with an Anne Dodge than with a William Morgan. Certainly, time and task determine how much deliberate analysis is called for versus how much rapid intuitive thinking is required. But I would argue that important similarities outweigh any differences. In both cases Myron Falchuk and John Burnside recognized a clinical pattern. And in both cases they had to modulate their inner emotions. Falchuk had to avoid the negative feelings that physicians have for patients labeled as "psychiatric," seeing such people as neurotic, cloying, deranged, and generally delusional, a burden because they do not tell the truth, their physical complaints not worth taking seriously because their symptoms originate not in the chest or bowels or bones but in the mind. A wealth of research shows that patients thought to have a psychological disorder get short shrift from internists and surgeons and gynecologists. As a result, their physical maladies are often never diagnosed or the diagnosis is delayed. The doctor's negative feelings cloud his thinking. Burnside faced a different challenge: to lower his level of arousal so he could think and act quickly and effectively. In each case, correctly adjusting the emotional temperature saved a life. Cognition and emotion are inseparable. The two mix in every encounter with every patient, obviously in a clinical catastrophe like William Morgan's, more subtly in a drawn-out chronic case like Anne Dodge's.

The importance of a physician's insight into his inner state came into sharp focus when I told colleagues what had happened in William Morgan's room. My fear and anxiety were familiar to them. But what I and my colleagues rarely recognized, and what physicians still rarely discussed as medical students, interns, residents, and indeed throughout their professional lives, is how other emotions influence a doctor's perceptions and judgments, his actions and reactions. I long believed that the errors we made in medicine were largely technical ones — prescribing the wrong dose of a drug, transfusing a unit of blood matched for another person, mislabeling an x-ray of an arm as "right" instead of "left." But as a growing body of research shows, technical errors account for only a small fraction of our incorrect diagnoses and treatments. Most errors are mistakes in thinking. And part of what causes these cognitive errors is our inner feelings, feelings we do not readily admit to and often don't even recognize.

CHAPTER 2

Lessons from the Heart

O N A SPRING AFTERNOON several years ago, Evan Mc-
Kinley was hiking in the woods near Halifax, Nova Scotia, when a pain in his chest stopped him in his tracks.
McKinley was a forest ranger in his early forties, trim and extremely fit, with straw-blond hair and chiseled features. He had
had a growing discomfort in his chest for the past few days, but
nothing as severe as this. He wasn't sweating or lightheaded, and
didn't feel feverish. But each time he took a breath, the pain got
worse. McKinley slowly made his way back through the woods to
the shed that housed his office. He sat and waited for the pain to
pass, but it didn't. As a forest ranger, he was used to muscle aches
from scaling a steep rocky trail or jogging with a loaded pack on
his back. But this was different, and he decided he should see a
doctor immediately.

As it happened, Dr. Pat Croskerry was working in the emergency department that day. He took McKinley's measure: a wiry,
muscular man wearing the distinctive bright olive bomber jacket
and pants, much like an American park ranger's uniform. McKinley's face was ruddy, as would be expected of someone who spends
most of his day working outdoors, and his brow was free of per-

spiration. Croskerry listened intently as McKinley described how his chest pains had increased over the past few days and how they had worsened today. Croskerry questioned him further to get a more precise description of his symptoms. McKinley said the pains stayed in the center of his chest but did not move down his arms, into his neck, or through to his back. The pain got no worse if he changed position, and even taking a really deep breath didn't make him feel faint.

Croskerry went over a checklist of risk factors for heart and lung disease. McKinley had never smoked and had no family history of heart attack, stroke, or diabetes. He laughed, as Croskerry did, when Croskerry used the term "sedentary lifestyle." McKinley added that he felt under no particular stress, his family life was fine and he loved his job, and he had never been overweight. Croskerry then did a physical examination. First he verified that the vital signs recorded by the triage nurse were correct. McKinley's blood pressure was 110 over 60, his pulse 60 and regular, as would be expected of an athletic man. Croskerry listened with particular care to McKinley's lungs and heart, especially when he took a deep breath, but everything sounded fine. His muscles were well developed, and when Croskerry pressed on the junction between McKinley's ribs and breastbone, McKinley felt no pain. There was no swelling or tenderness in his calves or thighs. Finally, the doctor ordered an electrocardiogram, a chest x-ray, and blood work that would include tests for oxygen level and cardiac enzymes that indicate heart damage. As he expected, all of these were normal.

"I'm not at all worried about your chest pain," Croskerry told McKinley. "You probably overexerted yourself in the field and strained some muscle. My suspicion for this coming from your heart is about zero." Deeply reassured, the forest ranger went home.

The next morning, Croskerry was off duty, and read part of a novel that he was keen to finish. He is an avid athlete and rowed on Canada's 1976 Olympic crew in Montreal. He stays in shape, and that day he had jogged four miles around the Halifax harbor. When he arrived in the emergency department in the early evening, he bumped into a colleague. "Very interesting case, that man you saw yesterday," the doctor said. "He came in this morning with an acute myocardial infarction."

Croskerry was stunned. He reviewed his notes on the emergency room chart. The colleague tried to reassure him. "If I had seen this guy, I wouldn't have gone as far as you did in ordering all those tests." But Croskerry found this cold comfort. It was not because he expected to be infallible. Rather, he recognized that he had made a common cognitive error that could have cost the forest ranger his life. "Clearly, I missed it," Croskerry told me after recounting McKinley's case. "And why did I miss it? I didn't miss it because of any egregious behavior or negligence. I missed it because my thinking was overinfluenced by how healthy this man looked." Croskerry's voice faltered for a moment. "Happily, he didn't die."

Chest pain is the second most common reason for a patient to visit an emergency room (abdominal pain is number one). Each year in the United States and Canada there are more than six million evaluations in the ER of patients like McKinley. But despite its frequency, chest pain is one of the most challenging symptoms for the clinician to unravel. In retrospect, Croskerry realized that when he saw Evan McKinley, the ranger was in the midst of unstable angina — a crescendo of chest pain, caused by coronary artery disease, that usually prefigures a heart attack. "The unstable angina didn't show on the EKG, because fifty percent of such cases don't," Croskerry said in a voice that sounded to me as if he were lecturing himself. "His unstable angina did not show up on the cardiac enzymes because there wasn't yet injury to the heart muscle, and it didn't show up on the chest x-ray because the heart had not yet begun to fail to pump blood, so there was no fluid backup into the lungs."

The mistake Croskerry made is called a representativeness error: your thinking is guided by a prototype, so you fail to consider possibilities that contradict the prototype and thus attribute the symptoms to the wrong cause. Croskerry told me how his eyes had fixed on McKinley's trim frame and his elegant olive uniform, and how the ranger's physique and chiseled features reminded him of a young Clint Eastwood — all strong associations with health and vigor. Yes, there were unusual aspects to McKinley's angina; his pain was not typical of coronary artery disease, nor did the physical examination and tests point to the heart. But, Croskerry emphasized, that was precisely the point: "You have to be prepared in your mind for the atypical and not so quickly reassure yourself, and your patient, that everything is okay." When Croskerry now teaches students and interns about such errors, he uses Evan McKinley as an example.

More commonly, doctors make what are called attribution errors when patients fit a negative stereotype. Dr. Donald Redelmeier of the University of Toronto, who, like Croskerry, studies physician cognition, told me about a case he had recently seen on rounds. Charles Carver was in his seventies, retired from the merchant marine and living by himself in a small apartment. Over the past months, he had felt fatigued and his belly had begun to swell. When Carver came into the ER, the intern noticed alcohol on his breath, and Carver readily told him that he enjoyed a glass of rum each evening. His legs and feet, as well as his abdomen, were swollen. Carver was unshaven; his clothes were old and frayed. The intern wondered to himself how many days it had been since he bathed.

The initial presentation to Dr. Redelmeier on rounds was terse. "Charles Carver, a seventy-three-year-old retired merchant mariner, with a long history of alcohol ingestion, presents with increasing fatigue and fluid retention." The intern palpated Carver's liver and told Redelmeier that it was enlarged, hard, and nodular. Redelmeier began to quiz the intern about Carver's problem. It soon became apparent that the trainee had in mind one and only one possible diagnosis: alcoholic cirrhosis. Redelmeier asked the medical team to offer other explanations for Carver's problems. He could see in their eyes that they felt burdened, that he was wasting precious time on rounds when they could be discussing much more interesting cases than that of an old, foul-smelling, rum-swilling sailor. "The intern's plan was to have this boozer sleep it off, give him some mild diuretics, and send him home as quickly as possible," Redelmeier told me.

"You are filled with a sense of disgust," Redelmeier said when we discussed the kinds of feelings that a man like Charles Carver summons in a doctor. That disgust pushes you away from him. Of course, as a doctor, it is your job to diagnose and treat him properly, but, consciously or subconsciously, you want to get the job over with and send such a man on his way. In particular, doctors consider people who seem not to be caring for themselves — alcoholics with cirrhosis, heavy smokers with end-stage emphysema, massively obese people with diabetes — as to some degree less deserving of their time and attention. Or, as in the stereotype of psychiatric patients that cloaked Anne Dodge, people who are not to be believed when they say they are following the doctor's orders. Physicians like to succeed in their treatment, and an essential ingredient for that success is a patient's cooperation. One doctor told me that patients who don't care for themselves made him feel like Sisyphus.

Redelmeier himself is prone to that visceral sense of disgust. He has taught himself to recognize the feeling and, as he put it, "plant a red flag in my mind." So, on rounds that day, Redelmeier didn't back down. He pushed the interns and residents to come up with alternative hypotheses for Carver's liver disease. He insisted on tests for unusual conditions, like alpha-1 antitrypsin deficiency, an inherited malady that can cause lung and liver disease, and Wilson's disease, another inherited disorder, in which copper deposits damage the liver and brain.

To everyone's surprise, including Redelmeier's, Charles Carver had Wilson's disease. "They said I was a brilliant clinician," Redelmeier recalled with a chuckle. "But it wasn't really brilliance. It was just forcing myself not to make an attribution error and dismiss the case out of hand as one more scuzzy alcoholic." Redelmeier added that, in fact, Carver was not an alcoholic. He enjoyed his glass of rum a day, but it really was only one glass, as Carver's daughter confirmed. Now, along with his evening drink, Carver takes copper chelators, drugs that remove the excess metal from his tissues.

Croskerry's prototypical error illustrates the opposite pole of emotion from disgust. Croskerry embodies many of Evan McKinley's characteristics himself: both are energetic, passionate men who love their work and for whom outdoor exercise is a major part of life. Powerful positive feelings about a patient are generally held to be good, the cornerstone of humanistic medicine. We all want to feel that our physician really likes us, sees us as special, and is emotionally moved by our plight, attracted not so much by the fascinating biology of our disease but by who we are as people. Usually such positive feelings enhance our relationship with our doctor and the quality of care we receive. But not always.

Doctors must be wary of "going with your gut" when what's in your gut is a strong emotion about a patient, even a positive one. Physicians understandably care deeply about their patients and want a good outcome, which can cause them to underinvestigate problems. Doctors may make decisions that stack the deck so that they draw what seems to be a winning hand for a patient they especially like, admire, or identify with. Croskerry chose to rely on the very first set of data — the normal EKG, chest x-ray, and blood tests — all of which indicated a favorable diagnosis for Mc-Kinley. He didn't arrange for follow-up testing.

We all tend to prefer what we hope will happen to the less appealing alternatives; this natural tendency is termed "affective error." We also lull ourselves into thinking that what we wish for will occur when we get the first inkling, however fragmentary, that our wish may come true. In short, we value too highly information that fulfills our desires. This kind of error can affect even a consummate clinician like Pat Croskerry.

The case of Evan McKinley brought me back to my conversation with Dr. Myron Falchuk. After Falchuk told me about Anne Dodge, I asked him if he had misdiagnosed a patient recently. His face fell for a moment. Then he told me about an elderly Jewish man he had seen earlier that year. "He was a wonderful, delightful character from the old country," Falchuk said. Joe Stern was in his late eighties but still spry, driving himself around Brookline and taking adult education classes. Stern complained of indigestion, specifically heartburn, for several weeks. Such symptoms are common; a general practitioner or internist usually treats them. But Falchuk knew the Stern family, and so took Joe on as his own patient. Over the course of four months, he treated him with antacids and other medications. The treatments gave him only slight relief.

Falchuk found himself enjoying Joe Stern's company so much that he ran over the allotted time at each visit. "He had a great sense of humor, and we kibitzed together in Yiddish," Falchuk recalled. "We really connected. I said to myself, Do I really have to put him through invasive tests? So I just kept adjusting his medications over four months." Falchuk paused. "Then he came in saying he felt faint and exhausted, and it was clear that something was different. He had become anemic." Falchuk performed an upper endoscopy, the same procedure he had done on Anne

Dodge, snaking a fiberoptic instrument down Stern's throat and into his esophagus and stomach. What he saw was not subtle: large growths with the characteristic pleated appearance of gastric lymphoma. A biopsy confirmed the diagnosis. The cancer clearly had been there all the time, and accounted for Stern's persistent indigestion and acid reflux.

"It's a treatable cancer," Falchuk said, "but I kicked myself over and over again. I just didn't want to subject someone of this age, whom I liked so much, to the discomfort and the strain of the procedure. And because of that, I missed the diagnosis." Fortunately, as with Evan McKinley, the ultimate outcome was good. The delay in diagnosis did not harm Joe; he went into remission. After Falchuk finished, I told him of a case of my own from many years ago: the case of Brad Miller.

Ever since he was a little boy, Brad Miller loved to run. His mother joked that it didn't matter when or where, even if he didn't have sneakers on. Growing up in Southern California, he would jog three miles to school, and on weekends he'd take the bus from Culver City west to the beach and sprint in the warm sand. Brad went east for college. He was undeterred by the sleet and broken sidewalks of New Haven, running each day in a wide arc from the university to the train station and back. Brad never joined the college track team, and doubted that his speed was sufficient to compete at the varsity level. But that didn't matter, because running just seemed to be a part of him. All through the stresses of college and graduate school, Brad used running as his tonic. He returned to Los Angeles with his doctorate in hand, his dissertation a meticulously footnoted study of ancient and contemporary female archetypes that influenced James Joyce's work. As a new English professor at a local college, he felt his life had taken a strong start out of the blocks.

"You look familiar," Brad said to me the first day I entered his hospital room at the UCLA Medical Center. It was the early winter of 1979, and I was in my fellowship training in hematology and oncology. I studied Brad, but his face did not register.

"I see you running with two or three friends around the university," he said. "I'm a runner too — or at least was."

Nearly every evening, a pack of young doctors ran the hills of Westwood. The incline along Highland Avenue was particularly steep, from the hospital to the apex of the campus. It tested my stamina. "I must have been the one gasping for breath," I said. "Perhaps that's why I stuck in your mind."

Brad's smile was brief.

"We'll do everything possible to get you back running," I said. "The chemotherapy is difficult, I won't minimize that, but it can make all the difference."

About six weeks earlier, Brad had noted an ache in his left knee. At first he thought it was simply due to his intense training schedule for an upcoming marathon. But the ache did not go away with rest and anti-inflammatory medication. He saw a sports medicine physician, who examined the leg and recommended stretching and wearing a knee brace when he ran. Brad dutifully followed this advice, but the ache only seemed to get worse, the leg stiffer. The physician ordered an x-ray. He told Brad that it showed some kind of growth around the end of the femur, just above the knee. He said the problem was outside his area and that Brad should see a specialist. The doctor couldn't hide the gravity of what he saw with euphemisms.

The growth in Brad's leg was an osteosarcoma, a bone cancer. The surgical oncology department at UCLA, among the best in the country, had pioneered an experimental program for these types of sarcomas. In the past, people like Brad would have had the leg amputated, but a new chemotherapy drug, Adriamycin, had been developed that often shrank the tumor. Oncologists had nicknamed it "the red death" because of its cranberry color and its terrible toxicity. Not only did it cause severe nausea, vomiting, blistering of the mouth, and reduced blood counts, but repeated doses could injure cardiac muscle, resulting in heart failure. Patients had to be monitored closely, since once the heart was damaged, there was no good way to restore its pumping capacity. The experimental strategy at UCLA involved treating patients with multiple doses of Adriamycin in the hope that the cancer would shrink enough to be surgically removed without amputation.

We began the treatment that afternoon. Despite medication to stave off vomiting, Brad spent several hours retching uncontrollably. Within a week, his white blood cell count had fallen precipitously. Because of this decline in his immune defenses, Brad was at great risk for an infection. To try to prevent this, we isolated him; he was visited only by people wearing a mask, gown, and gloves. His diet was changed to reduce exposure to bacteria in raw foods.

"Not to your taste," I observed, eyeing the untouched meal on his tray.

"My mouth hurts," Brad whispered. He had multiple oral ulcers from the chemotherapy. "And even if I could chew, it looks pretty tasteless."

We were giving Brad a special anesthetic mouthwash to try to alleviate the pain, but it clearly was not helping much. I agreed that the food looked dismal.

"What is to your taste? Fried kidney?"

Brad looked knowingly at me.

"Nothing like Joyce to lift the spirit."

I had told him when we met that I'd studied *Ulysses* in a freshman seminar. The professor had explained the relevant Irish history, especially Parnell and the Easter Rebellion; the subtle references to Catholic liturgy; and a host of other allusions that otherwise would have passed most of the class by. In the book, Leopold Bloom savors fried kidneys.

Brad was my favorite patient on the ward. Each morning when I made rounds with the residents and students, I would take an inventory of his symptoms, examining him to check on the medical team's findings and reviewing his laboratory results. Then I would linger, trying to raise his spirits and distract him from the misery of the therapy.

The protocol called for a CT scan after the third cycle of Adriamycin. If the cancer had shrunk sufficiently, the surgery would proceed. If it hadn't, or if the cancer had grown despite the chemotherapy, then there was little to be done short of amputation. And even after amputation, patients still live under a cloud, since the cancer can metastasize to the lungs or other organs.

Three cycles of chemotherapy took their toll on Brad. He became listless, difficult to engage in conversation. Then, one morning, he developed a low-grade fever of 100.2° F. The residents told me on morning rounds that they had already gotten blood and urine cultures, and that his physical examination was "nonfocal," medical jargon meaning that they had found no clear origin for an infection. People undergoing chemotherapy often get low-grade fevers after their white blood cell count falls; if the fever has no identifiable cause, a physician must use his judgment about when to begin a course of antibiotics.

"So you feel even more wiped out?" I asked Brad.

He nodded. I reviewed again a list of symptoms that might identify a source of infection: Did he have a headache, difficulty with vision, pressure in his sinuses, a sore throat, problems breathing? He answered no to each. Was he bringing up any sputum? No again. Any pain in his abdomen, diarrhea, burning on urination? None at all.

Brad said he was too exhausted to sit up on his own, so a resident took one shoulder and a student another and propped him up in bed. Brad had the body of a long-distance runner, tall and lean. Adriamycin dosages are based on body surface area rather than weight, so with the large surface area of a person of his physique, Brad had been getting high doses. His remaining wisps of black hair were matted with sweat, and he was ashen.

I examined his eyes, ears, nose, and throat, and found nothing of note except some small ulcers on his inner cheeks and under his tongue, side effects of his treatment. Brad worked hard to take deep breaths when I examined his lungs — they were clear — and his heart sounds were strong, without a "gallop" indicating heart failure. His abdomen was soft, and there was no tenderness over his bladder.

"Enough for today," I said. Brad looked so peaked that it seemed wise to let him rest. He nodded his thanks.

Later that day, I was in the hematology lab, looking at the bone marrow biopsy of a patient with leukemia, when my beeper went off with a stat page. "Brad Miller has no blood pressure," the resident reported when I called. "His temperature is up to 104, and we're moving him to the ICU."

Septic shock. When bacteria spread through the bloodstream, they can shut down the circulation. This can be fatal even in people who are otherwise healthy, but patients with impaired immunity, like Brad, whose white blood cell count has been lowered by chemotherapy, often die.

"Do we have a source?" I asked.

"He has what looks like an abscess in his left buttock," the resident said.

Patients who lack the white cells to fight bacteria are prone to infections at sites that are routinely soiled, like the area between the buttocks.

I fell silent as I replayed in my mind the scene on rounds with Brad that morning. The abscess had certainly been there a few hours before. "Enough for today," I had said. *Not enough at all.* I had failed to ask him to roll over so I could examine his buttocks and rectum.

"We repeated his cultures and began broad-spectrum antibiotics," the resident said. "The ICU team will take over."

"Okay. Good job." As I hung up the phone, I berated myself further. *Bad job. Sloppy job.*

My heart had ached for Brad, and that deep feeling had caused me to break discipline. Normally, I had a system that I followed with every immune-deficient patient every day, beginning at the crown of their head and working down to the tip of their toes, examining every cleft and fold and orifice and organ. I had not wanted to add further to Brad's discomfort. I left the bedsheets on him. That could prove to be a fatal mistake.

I attended to the day's remaining tasks and rushed to the ICU as soon as I was free. Brad was on a respirator and opened his eyes wide to signal "hello." In addition to saline, he was receiving pressors, drugs that increase the contraction of the heart and the tone of the vessels to try to sustain the blood pressure. His heart was holding up now despite all the Adriamycin. His platelet count had fallen, as often happens in septic shock, and he was receiving platelet transfusions. The senior doctor in the ICU had already told Brad's parents how serious his situation was. I saw them sitting in a room next to the ICU, their heads bowed. At first I considered walking by, since they had not seen me, but I forced myself to go in and offer a few words of encouragement. They thanked me for my care of their son.

After a restless night, I arrived early the next morning before the residents on the ward to review all the charts of my patients. Rounds lasted an hour longer than usual, as I checked and double-checked every bit of information the team offered. I could see them growing restless, but I needed to reclaim my balance and this was the only way I knew how.

Brad Miller survived. Slowly his white blood cell count increased, and the infection was resolved. After he left the ICU, I told him that I should have examined him more thoroughly that morning, but I did not explain why I failed to. His CT scan showed that the sarcoma had shrunk enough for him to undergo surgery without amputation. But a large portion of his thigh muscle had to be removed along with the tumor. After his surgery, running was too demanding. Occasionally I would see Brad riding his bicycle on campus, and I gave silent thanks each time I did.

One of the most celebrated statements in clinical medicine comes from a lecture delivered by Dr. Francis Weld Peabody of Harvard Medical School in 1925: "The secret of the care of the patient is in caring for the patient." This is undoubtedly true, but less obvious than it may seem. Peabody cautioned doctors about the way their training conditions them. Of necessity, we learn to suppress our emotions, to block our natural reactions to many of the awful things we see and the brutal things we must do.

Consider what happens in the ER when we try to save the life of a person smashed by a car or burned in a fire. If a doctor thought too much about the person before him, he couldn't insert his gloved hands into a hemorrhaging abdomen or maneuver a breathing tube past charred flesh. Even in less desperate circumstances — giving chemotherapy to a young woman with widespread breast cancer, say, or inserting a dialysis shunt into the arm of a blind diabetic whose kidneys have failed — we have to detach ourselves from anguish that could impede our work. But to become immune to feeling, as Peabody indicated, is to diminish the full role of the physician as a healer and relegate him to a single dimension of his job, that of a tactician. If we feel our emotions deeply, we risk recoiling or breaking down. If we erase our emotions, however, we fail to care *for* the patient. We face a paradox: feeling prevents us from being blind to our patient's soul but risks blinding us to what is wrong with him.

I asked Dr. Karen Delgado about this paradox. Delgado is an

acclaimed specialist in endocrinology and metabolism at a large urban teaching hospital who cares for patients with hormonal and metabolic disorders such as diabetes, infertility, and hypothyroidism. To my mind, she is the very model of a doctor, deeply knowledgeable about medical science and compassionate, empathetic, and generous with her patients. When I asked Delgado whether she had ever made an attribution error, she readily recalled a patient from her training in the 1970s. A young man was brought to the emergency ward of the hospital in the wee hours. The police had found him sleeping on the steps of a local art museum. He was unshaven, his clothes were dirty, and he was uncooperative, unwilling to rouse himself and respond with any clarity to the triage nurse's questions. Dr. Delgado was busy that night attending to other patients, so she "eyeballed" him and decided that he could stay on a gurney in the corridor, another homeless hippie who would be given breakfast in the morning and returned to the streets. Some hours later, she felt a nurse tugging at her sleeve. "I really want you to go back and examine that guy," the nurse said. Delgado was reluctant, but she had learned to respect an ER nurse who felt that something was really wrong with a patient.

"His blood sugar was sky-high," Delgado told me. The young man was on the brink of a diabetic coma. He had fallen asleep near the art museum because he was weak and lethargic and unable to make it back to his apartment. It turned out that he was not a vagrant but a student, and his difficulties giving the police and the triage nurse information reflected the metabolic changes that typify out-of-control diabetes.

"The hardest thing about being a doctor," Delgado said, "is that you learn best from your mistakes, mistakes made on living people." Chastened by the experience, she conjured up the picture of that young man whenever she was called to the ER to evaluate other disheveled and uncooperative people. But, Delgado continued, that was a single experience corresponding to a single stereotype. "It is impossible to catalog all of the stereotypes that you carry in your mind," she said, "or to consistently recognize that you are fitting the individual before you into a stereotypical mold. But you don't want to have to make a mistake to learn with each stereotype." Rather, Delgado believes, patients and their families should be aware that a doctor relies on pattern recognition in his work and, understandably, draws on stereotypes to make decisions. With that knowledge, they can help him avoid attribution errors.

Is this really possible? I asked.

"Sure, it's not easy for laypeople to do," Delgado said, "because patients and their families are especially reluctant to question a doctor's thinking when their questioning suggests his thinking is colored by personal prejudice or bias." Still, Delgado thinks laypeople can diplomatically direct a doctor's attention to his reliance on stereotypes, because one of her patients had done this with her.

Ellen Barnett had recently sought out Dr. Delgado for help with a multitude of vexing symptoms. Many people who see Delgado have symptoms that are difficult to pin down — low energy, for example, or abrupt weight gain — and assume they have a hormonal or metabolic imbalance. Usually they don't. Ellen Barnett had already consulted five physicians and felt all five had shunned her. "I'm having what I call explosions, feeling hot all over, which make my skin crawl. I mean really crawl, like ants all over, and sometimes they come with terrible headaches," she told Delgado. "Really, it's like a bomb going off in my body. I know I am in menopause, and all five doctors told me that that's the cause of my problems. And two told me that I'm crazy. And, frankly, I *am* a little crazy," Barnett said with a wry smile. "Okay, I know menopausal women have hot flashes. But I think this is something else, that what I'm feeling is more than just menopause."

As Delgado listened, she recognized how easy it would be to

make an attribution error with a persistently complaining, melodramatic menopausal woman who quite accurately describes herself as kooky. So she stopped herself from casting Ellen Barnett as a stereotype and assumed for a minute that her patient was telling her something important, something meaningful, that these "explosions" were indeed different from run-of-the-mill menopausal hot flashes and hormonal migraines.

"I evaluated her very extensively," Delgado said, "and it turned out that, yes, she was menopausal, and yes, she was a strange person with lots of weird ideas, but what turned up in her urine was not from menopause or being kooky. Her catecholamine levels were through the roof. A CT scan showed a pheochromocytoma above her left kidney." A pheochromocytoma is a relatively rare endocrine tumor that produces catecholamines, chemicals like adrenaline that can cause wild swings in blood flow and blood pressure. The changes in circulation may mimic menopausal hot flashes and precipitate severe migraine-like headaches. The catecholamines can also cause psychological symptoms such as anxiety, despair, and even aggression. If untreated, the patient may have a stroke or heart or kidney failure.

"She had surgery and the tumor was removed. Now her hot flashes are much less severe, as are her headaches, at the level you would expect during menopause," Delgado said. "But Ellen is still kooky, by her own admission."

Delgado believes that patients or family members can adopt Ellen Barnett's approach. With a disarming sense of humor, she communicated that she understood she fit a certain social stereotype, and that stereotype had caused her doctors to fail to fully consider her complaints. "I didn't feel like Ellen was being obnoxious or patronizing," Delgado said, "and I didn't react and become alienated or annoyed with her. What she said enhanced her credibility and helped me avoid an attribution error."

Negative feelings that patients like Ellen Barnett trigger in a physician are usually close to the surface. But positive feelings, like the ones Croskerry had for Evan McKinley, Falchuk had for Joe Stern, and I had for Brad Miller, are more difficult to recognize as dangerous. Since Delgado is a physician who has genuine affection for many of her patients, I asked whether she had ever fallen into that trap, the trap of affective error. She thought she had. "I had an elderly patient with thyroid cancer and considered treating him with radioactive iodine. There are difficult logistics involved with the therapy, and it really can disrupt the person's life. I was just about to refrain from treating this man when he said to me: 'Don't save me from an unpleasant test just because we're friends.'" At best, in severe circumstances, the family or friends of patients who realize that a doctor's affection may stay his hand at times can address this concern by saying: "You should know how deeply we appreciate how much care you show. Please know also that we understand you may need to do things that cause discomfort or pain."

Only a layman aware of how such feelings can color a doctor's judgment in subtle but significant ways could make such a remark. In pondering Delgado's vignette, I realized it would have been impossible for Brad Miller to muster the energy to think about our prior interactions and warn me this way when I saw him that morning on rounds. It was my job to be complete in my exam, and my charge to monitor my feelings when they might break my discipline.

Patients and their loved ones swim together with physicians in a sea of feelings. Each needs to keep an eye on a neutral shore where flags are planted to warn of perilous emotional currents.

CHAPTER 3

Spinning Plates

TUBA CITY, ARIZONA, lies 3,246 miles west of Halifax, Nova Scotia. Halifax was the first British town in Canada, founded in 1749; most of its 360,000 inhabitants still trace their roots to the British Isles. Tuba City has a population of just 6,000, but it serves as the central town for more than 100,000 members of the Navajo and Hopi nations. Modern glass-and-steel skyscrapers ring the Halifax harbor, and a sharp northern light reflects off the sea. Tuba City sits on high mesa, the surrounding country highlighted by scrub and the soft pastels of ancient sedimentary rock. Halifax's Dalhousie University Medical School is renowned for its academic departments and cadres of researchers. The hospital in Tuba City is a cluster of low-slung dun-colored buildings housing the Indian Health Service; the nearest MRI scanner is an hour's drive away. Despite these differences in geography, size, resources, and culture, an emergency room physician in Tuba City, like Dr. Harrison Alter, has to recognize the same clinical patterns and avoid the same cognitive errors as a counterpart in Halifax like Pat Croskerry.

Alter, who is forty-three, did not initially see himself as a physician. He studied comparative literature at Brown and only four years later attended medical school at the University of California at Berkeley. Following his residency at Highland Hospital in Oakland, he went to the University of Washington in Seattle as a Robert Wood Johnson scholar to study medical decision-making. After two years on the faculty at UW, he wanted to work with dedicated doctors in an underserved community, so he moved with his wife and three young children to a small yellow stucco house in Tuba City.

One day in April 2003, while Alter was working in the emergency department, an ambulance brought in a ten-year-old boy named Nathan Talumpqewa from the local Hopi school. The fourth graders had just ended recess and were lining up to return to class when another student jumped on his back, expecting a piggyback ride. Nathan was a hefty boy, four feet eight inches tall and 140 pounds, and reveled in rough-and-tumble play. But this time he screamed in pain and fell to the ground. "Nathan came in on a backboard in full spinal immobilization," Alter recalled, describing how a patient is kept in a fixed supine position to prevent any stress on potentially injured nerves. "He was terrified, sobbing and moaning." Alter quickly took the history and asked Nathan several key questions. "He said that he could move his arms and legs, that there was no tingling or electric shocks going down his spine or into his buttocks, only that he had this terrible pain in the middle of his back." Alter concluded that it was safe to move the child off the backboard onto a bed.

When Alter examined him and pressed on the lower thoracic spine, Nathan cried out. "I sent him off for x-rays, and, sure enough, right at the tender spot he had a wedge compression fracture of the tenth thoracic vertebra. This was a ten-year-old boy with the kind of fracture that I am accustomed to seeing in an eighty-year-old woman. And I thought to myself, This just isn't supposed to happen."

Alter told me that with each patient he recites the ABCs he learned during his training. (In fact, the alphabet of emergency care includes D and E as well.) "*A* stands for airway, meaning that the mouth, throat, trachea, and bronchi are all open; *B* is breathing, that the patient's lungs are able to get enough oxygen and pass it into the bloodstream; *C* is circulation, that the heart is pumping, the blood pressure is adequate for the blood to reach vital organs like the liver, kidneys, and brain. *D* stands for disability, a reminder to check neurological function, not only muscle strength and reflexes but also mental responses; and finally, *E* is for exposure, not to neglect any part of the body just because you are focusing on a problem in one area." In Nathan's case, he concluded, each letter was satisfactory.

Alter ordered tests, including a complete blood count, calcium level, and bone enzymes. All were normal. He then went further and got a CT scan, which was transmitted digitally to a bone radiologist at the University of Arizona. Shortly, a report came back to the emergency department: "Normal, except for a compression fracture at the tenth thoracic vertebra." Alter still was uneasy. He put Nathan in an ambulance and transported him for an MRI scan to Flagstaff, an hour and a half away. Later that day, Alter learned that an MRI confirmed what the CT scan showed: the single collapsed vertebra and no other abnormalities.

Alter called a local pediatrician. The specialist reassured him that nothing serious was going on, nothing to be concerned about. "We just see this sometimes," the pediatrician assured him. "I had to accept the data," Alter said, but still was worried. He made sure the pediatrician saw Nathan a few days later. At that appointment, Nathan was feeling better, with only minor discomfort in his back. The pediatrician told the family not to worry; it was just a freakish playground accident.

In Seattle, Alter had been trained in Bayesian analysis, a mathematical approach to making decisions in the face of uncertainty.

When he sees a patient, he calculates a numerical probability for each possible diagnosis. In Nathan's case, he was at a loss to assign such a probability. There simply was no database to refer to for a compression fracture of the tenth thoracic vertebra in an overweight but otherwise healthy ten-year-old Hopi boy. So Alter tried to approach the problem not by sophisticated mathematics but by common sense. "The event was nothing," Alter said, "a student jumping on Nathan for a piggyback ride, and it didn't seem enough to explain the injury." But the pediatrician seemed to think looking for another answer was unnecessary. "I was at a loss," Alter told me. "This was a specialist talking to me. I should bow to his authority."

I heard a familiar resonance in Nathan's story, not because I trained in emergency medicine or take care of children, but because I've heard specialists say, "We see this sometimes." It has the ring of confidence, a statement based on long experience, and is meant to lift the burden of further investigation off everyone's shoulders. But it should be said only after an exhaustive search for an answer and ongoing monitoring of a patient. If said glibly, it shows worrisome ignorance instead of representing reassuring knowledge. It means that everyone should stop thinking.

Alter had no choice but to move on. He had done the best he could, more than most would have done in evaluating Nathan. But he couldn't stop thinking about him. He was forced to wait until, in clinical jargon, the problem would "declare itself."

That declaration took place some weeks later when Nathan got out of bed and immediately collapsed in pain. He was rushed back to the ER. Alter examined him and confirmed that D was in order: that Nathan's legs were not weak and his reflexes were intact. He ordered another set of x-rays. Now there were four wedge fractures of the spine. Alter transferred Nathan to a hospital in Phoenix. An orthopedic surgeon there performed a bone biopsy and sent it to the pathology laboratory. Peering into the microscope, the pathologist in Phoenix saw sheets of large round cells inside the bone; each cell resembled the next, dark blue with a convoluted nucleus. Special tests identified the enzymes within the cells and the proteins on their surface. The diagnosis soon was clear: Nathan had acute lymphoblastic leukemia. The leukemia had so weakened the vertebra that it had collapsed with a piggy-back ride. Now the case made sense. As Alter had surmised, what the pediatrician had said did not. "No one — no doctor, no patient — should ever accept, as a first answer to a serious event, 'We see this sometimes,'" Alter said. "When you hear that sentence, reply, Let's keep looking until we figure out what is wrong or know the problem has passed."

One winter day in the same year that Nathan Talumpqewa fell ill, a Navajo woman in her sixties named Blanche Begaye came to the emergency department because she was having trouble breathing. Mrs. Begaye was a compact woman with slate-gray hair gathered in a bun who worked in a grocery store on the reservation. Over the past few weeks, a nasty virus had been moving through the close-knit community, and scores of patients like Blanche Begaye had come to the hospital with viral pneumonia. Mrs. Begaye said that she first thought she had just "a bad head cold." So she had drunk lots of orange juice and tea and taken a few aspirin, but the symptoms worsened and now she felt terrible.

Alter noted that she was running a low-grade fever, 100.2° F, and her respiratory rate was almost twice normal. He examined her lungs and heard the air rapidly moving in and out, but none of the harsh sounds, called rhonchi, that are caused by accumulated mucus. Alter obtained blood tests. Blanche Begaye's white blood cell count was not elevated, but her electrolytes showed that the acid-base balance of her blood had tipped toward acid, not uncommon in someone with a major infection. Her chest x-ray did not show the characteristic white streaks of viral pneumonia.

Alter made the diagnosis of "subclinical viral pneumonia." He told Mrs. Begaye that she was in the early stages of the infection, subclinical, so that the footprints of the microbe were not yet evident on her chest x-ray. Like many other patients with pneumonia whom he had seen recently, she should be admitted to the hospital and given intravenous fluids and medicine to keep her fever down. At her age, he said, viral pneumonia can tax the heart and sometimes cause it to fail, so it was prudent to keep her under observation.

Alter handed off the case to an internist on the staff and began evaluating another patient, a middle-aged Navajo man who also had fever and shortness of breath. A few minutes later, the internist approached Alter and took him aside. "That's not a case of viral pneumonia," he said. "She has aspirin toxicity."

Even years later in retelling the story, Alter groaned. "Aspirin poisoning, bread-and-butter toxicology," he said, "something that was drilled into me throughout my training. She was an absolutely classic case — the rapid breathing, the shift in her blood electrolytes — and I missed it. I got cavalier."

As there are classic clinical maladies, there are classic cognitive errors. Alter's misdiagnosis resulted from such an error, the use of a heuristic called "availability." Amos Tversky and Daniel Kahneman, psychologists from the Hebrew University in Jerusalem, explored this shortcut in a seminal paper more than two decades ago. Kahneman won the Nobel Prize in economics in 2002 for work illuminating the way certain patterns of thinking cause irrational decisions in the marketplace; Tversky certainly would have shared the prize had he not died an untimely death in 1996.

"Availability" means the tendency to judge the likelihood of an event by the ease with which relevant examples come to mind. Alter's diagnosis of subclinical pneumonia was readily available to him because he had seen numerous cases of the infection over recent weeks. As in any environment, there is an ecology in medical clinics. For example, large numbers of patients who abuse alcohol populate inner-city hospitals like Cook County in Chicago, Highland in Oakland, or Bellevue in Manhattan; over the course of a week, an intern in one of these hospitals may evaluate ten trembling alcoholics, all of whom have DTs — delirium tremens, a violent shaking due to withdrawal. He will tend to judge it as highly likely that the eleventh jittery alcoholic has DTs because it readily comes to mind, although there is a long list of diagnostic possibilities for uncontrolled shaking. DTs is the most available hypothesis based on his most recent experience. He is familiar with DTs, and that familiarity points his thinking that way.

Alter experienced what might be called "distorted pattern recognition," caused by the background "ecology" of Begaye's case. Instead of integrating all the key information, he cherry-picked only a few features of her illness: her fever, her rapid breathing, and the shift in the acid-base balance in her blood. He rationalized the contradictory data — the absence of any streaking on the chest x-ray, the normal white blood cell count — as simply reflecting the earliest stage of an infection. In fact, these discrepancies should have signaled to him that his hypothesis was wrong.

Such cognitive cherry-picking is termed "confirmation bias." This fallacy, confirming what you expect to find by selectively accepting or ignoring information, follows what Tversky and Kahneman referred to as "anchoring." Anchoring is a shortcut in thinking where a person doesn't consider multiple possibilities but quickly and firmly latches on to a single one, sure that he has thrown his anchor down just where he needs to be. You look at your map but your mind plays tricks on you — confirmation bias — because you see only the landmarks you expect to see and neglect those that should tell you that in fact you're still at sea. Your skewed reading of the map "confirms" your mistaken assumption that you have reached your destination. Affective error resembles confirmation bias in selectively surveying the data. The former is driven by a wish for a certain outcome, the latter driven by the expectation that your initial diagnosis was correct, even if it was bad for the patient.

After the internist made the correct diagnosis, Alter replayed in his mind his conversation with Blanche Begaye. When he asked whether she had taken any medication, including over-the-counter drugs, she replied, "A few aspirin." He heard this as further evidence for his anchored assumption that she had a viral syndrome that began as a cold and now had blossomed into pneumonia. "I didn't define with her what 'a few' meant," Alter said. It turned out to be several dozen.

The irony is that Alter had suspended judgment about Nathan Talumpqewa's diagnosis, had not anchored his thinking at all, because he could not estimate a probability for a particular disease or identify a biological mechanism causing a vertebra to collapse. This had held him back from accepting the pediatrician's glib assurance. Yet he jumped to a conclusion with Blanche Begaye, assigning a probability of 100 percent to her case. "I learned from this to always hold back, to make sure that even when I think I have the answer, to generate a short list of alternatives." That simple strategy is one of the strongest safeguards against cognitive errors.

Imagine that you are an emergency physician like Harrison Alter or Pat Croskerry. In most instances, you don't know the patients you see. So you have to rely on a snapshot view of their illness — unlike an internist in his office, who is familiar with his patients and their families, knows their character and their behavior, and can observe the evolution of a clinical problem over time. Imagine that it is a typically busy evening, and the triage nurse has assigned three patients to you over a half-hour period. Each patient has a host of complaints. Pat Croskerry told me that at moments like this he feels as if he is "plate-spinning on sticks," like a circus performer using sticks to spin plates without letting them slow down or fall.

Actually, it's harder than spinning plates, because plate-spinning requires a single rotary motion and all the plates are of similar size and weight. Each patient, of course, is different, and for each you may have to go through different motions quickly to reach a working diagnosis, treat any urgent problems, and then decide on the safest disposition: admission to the hospital, transfer to another institution, or discharge to home. Now consider what you must do to meet these goals of diagnosis, treatment, and disposition. First you have to figure out the main reason each patient has come for emergency care. While that may seem straightforward, it is not. Patients may give a triage nurse or a doctor a reason that is tangential to the real, more serious underlying problem, or they may offer the symptoms that bother them most but may be unrelated to their underlying disease. All doctors work under time constraints, and this is especially true in the emergency department. So, as we saw with Alter, the questions you choose to ask and how you ask them will shape the patient's answers and guide your thinking. You may go off on a tangent if you try to elicit a history too quickly, but you will neglect your other tasks if you take too long to hear what is wrong.

I recall an elderly man who arrived at the ER complaining of pain in his ankle after tripping on the street. All he wanted was to be reassured it wasn't broken and be given a painkiller. Everyone focused on his ankle. No one thought about why he might have tripped. Only much later we learned that he'd fallen because he was weak from an undiagnosed anemia. The cause of his anemia turned out to be colon cancer. To compound matters, patients may not remember key aspects of their past medical history, and without a hospital chart or office record, you lack any independent source to help fill in the gaps. This is especially true with regard to medications. "I take a blue pill and a pink pill for my heart," a dizzy patient may say, but he doesn't recall the names and doses of the pills, and you are at a loss to assess whether his nausea and dizziness are related to his therapy.

After you determine your patient's primary complaint, you must then decide what blood tests and x-rays to order, if any. Harrison Alter returned to Oakland's Highland Hospital after three years in Tuba City. He told me that he emphasizes to his interns and residents in the emergency department there that they should not order a test unless they know how that test performs in a patient with the condition they assume he has. That way, they can properly weigh the result in their assessment. This is not as easy as it may sound. Take, for example, Pat Croskerry's encounter with Evan McKinley, the forest ranger whose chest pain was not typical of angina. As Croskerry's colleague pointed out, he went the extra mile in ordering tests on McKinley, not only an EKG and a chest x-ray but also a test for cardiac enzymes. For each, Croskerry had to judge whether the result was normal, abnormal, or spurious. Laboratory, x-ray, and EKG technicians make mistakes. I recall when I incorrectly placed the EKG leads on a patient's chest and, not realizing my mistake, concluded he had a serious problem with the electrical conduction pathways of his heart. He had no such thing; the EKG was an artifact generated by my mistake. Other errors can be more subtle, like taking a chest x-ray when the patient has not held his breath. This can cause white streaking in the lower lungs, a sign of pneumonia.

For each patient, you are making scores of decisions about his symptoms, physical findings, blood tests, EKG, and x-rays. Now, multiply all of those decisions you made for each patient by three assigned in thirty minutes by the triage nurse; the total can reach several hundred. The circus performer spins only a handful of plates. A more accurate analogy might be to stacks of plates, one on top of another, and another, and another, all of different shapes and weights. Add to these factors the ecology of an emergency department, the number of people tugging at your sleeve, interrupting and distracting you with requests and demands as you spin your plates. And don't forget you are in an era of managed care, with limited money, so you have to set priorities and allocate resources parsimoniously: it costs less if you can take several plates off their sticks, meaning if you limit testing and rapidly send the patient home.

Perhaps you breathe a sigh of relief when the triage nurse sends you a patient you have seen before. People who repeatedly visit the emergency department are called "frequent flyers." Instead of a single page of a new patient sheet, the frequent flyer has a hefty chart with ample past history and testing that would seem to simplify things. Except, of course, when it complicates them.

Maxine Carlson was a single woman in her early thirties working as an office secretary in Halifax. Two years earlier, she had developed sharp pains in her right lower abdomen. She told her primary care physician that it was different from the pain she had as a child with appendicitis or the postoperative pain of the appendectomy. The doctor examined her but found nothing of concern. Over the next few months, on some days Maxine Carlson was constipated and on other days her bowel movements came with great urgency. Her doctor suggested she eat a more balanced diet, including fiber every day, but this had little effect on the pains. Maxine finally was referred to a gastroenterologist. At first the specialist wondered whether she might have an inflammatory bowel disease, like ulcerative colitis or Crohn's. But the doctor didn't find anything abnormal after an extensive evaluation that included numerous blood tests, x-rays, and both upper and lower endoscopy, which visualized her esophagus, stomach, duodenum, and colon. The gastroenterologist confirmed that she had irritable bowel syndrome and emphasized the importance of a high-fiber diet. A psychiatrist also evaluated her and prescribed antianxiety medications to relieve the stress that can exacerbate irritable bowel syndrome.

A year after the onset of the sharp pains in her right abdomen, Maxine Carlson felt discomfort in her pelvis. At first her primary care physician said it was just her irritable bowel disease, but Maxine insisted it was different, a squeezing, persistent ache rather than the familiar sharp, fleeting pains. She was referred to a gynecologist, who performed an internal examination and then ordered an ultrasound of her uterus and ovaries. He, too, found nothing abnormal.

Maxine's pelvic aches waxed and waned and then eventually disappeared. Then, two weeks before she came to the emergency department, the regular pains in her right abdomen became more intense. It was August and her primary care physician was away, so Maxine went to the hospital. The doctors in the emergency department had the two volumes of her medical records. They examined her, obtained blood tests, and told her that nothing was wrong. It was just a flare-up of her irritable bowel disorder.

Dr. Pat Croskerry was working in the emergency department when Maxine Carlson returned for the third time in seven days. "The triage nurse was rolling her eyes when she told me about the case," Croskerry recalled. "That this was a young woman with no tangible problem, that she had been worked up extensively by her primary care physician, her gastroenterologist, and her gynecologist, and she carried a functional diagnosis." The euphemism "functional" means psychosomatic in clinical medicine. "She is really woolly," the nurse told Croskerry. "And she won't stop coming in."

It was very busy in the emergency department, and Croskerry was caring for several patients with urgent problems. When he finally entered Maxine's room, he saw how agitated and distraught she was. She bitterly complained that the pains just wouldn't go away. He found no new symptoms when he asked Maxine Carlson what prompted her visit that evening. As he examined her, he later told me, he felt "consoled" upon seeing the appendectomy scar, since Maxine's pain was in her right lower abdomen.

"I'm coming up with nothing," Croskerry told the triage nurse. Nonetheless, he said he was sending off blood and urine tests. This was met by considerable resistance. "Why are you doing this?" the nurse asked. "She's already been worked up." Croskerry told me he felt "palpable" pressure because it was hectic in the emergency department and the nurse needed Maxine's bed for another patient. But he insisted. About an hour later, her test results were in hand, all normal. "I reassured her that this seemed to be her irritable bowel acting up," Croskerry said. "I went over again issues about proper diet and stress management. I also emphasized to her not to be reluctant to come back." Croskerry has learned from experience never to discourage patients from seeking follow-up care.

"She broke into tears, crying that no one believed her, that no one was able to come to a diagnosis," he recalled. "She kept saying that the pain was getting worse, that it was much worse than it had been even a week before.

"How can you not be moved by a patient's tears?" Croskerry asked me rhetorically. Still, he sent Maxine home. A short time later, she was rushed by ambulance back to the ER. "She collapsed while walking home," Croskerry said. She was bleeding internally and on the verge of shock. She was rushed to the OR, where a surgeon found that Maxine had a ruptured ectopic pregnancy. "It had been missed three times. I was the third miss," Croskerry told me.

Yes, Maxine Carlson did suffer from irritable bowel syndrome. She had been extensively evaluated by her many doctors. That evaluation had ultimately exhausted the options of her physicians, even the most astute, like Pat Croskerry. During my training, we used a euphemism, "worked up the gazoo," to refer to a patient who had been examined by every conceivable specialist, had had every imaginable blood test, x-ray, and procedure, and there seemed to be nothing left to do for them. In Halifax ER parlance, Maxine Carlson had been worked up the "yin-yang" and then was "out." "The physician tells himself that he can't throw any light on the dark place where a diagnosis might be hiding," Croskerry said. "You go through a checklist of all the avenues that have been explored, and it seems that each was a dead end, and you have no new direction to go in." Croskerry refers to the failure to think of a new direction, because you assume all have been explored, as the "yin-yang out" mistake.

The ecology of an emergency department includes not only patients, their families, and, of course, nurses, but also other doctors. At Highland Hospital not long ago, Alter was the attending physician when a resident in training evaluated a man in his thirties complaining of a sore throat. "It's an open-and-shut case of strep," the resident told Alter — an "uncomplicated" patient. Alter had the sense that the resident wanted to move quickly to his next patient. Alter asked for details. "He has an exudative pharyngitis, pus near the tonsils, and painful lymph nodes," the resident said. Alter insisted that he wanted to meet the man himself. The resident sighed in frustration.

Alter peered into the patient's throat and saw no signs of pus. He ran his fingers along the sides of the man's neck and felt small, soft lymph nodes that were not tender. Alter pressed more firmly on them. Still no reaction from the patient. The resident had already given him a large dose of an antibiotic and a prescription for more.

Alter led the resident into the corridor and told him that it didn't at all look like strep, that it was most certainly a virus causing the sore throat, and that prescribing antibiotics unnecessarily could have serious consequences. "Our hospital is overrun with MRSA," Alter told the resident, using the acronym for methicillin-resistant staphylococcus aureus. This type of staph infection has become the bane of modern medicine; it is the direct result of promiscuous prescribing of penicillin, and extremely difficult to eradicate. "I questioned the resident's automaticity," Alter said, "how he just wanted to dispose of the case, and the easiest way was to label it strep, give a slug of antibiotic, and be done with it."

A short time later, another man came in with a sore throat. "Go to room 23 and start with the patient," Alter instructed the resident. After Alter had sutured the arm of a man with a knife wound, he made his way back to room 23. "He's fine," the resident said curtly. "Another one of your favorite viruses."

Alter didn't just sign off on the resident's assessment. As he interviewed the patient, he saw that he was restless, moving around on the examining table, unable to find a comfortable position to rest his head. When Alter peered into his mouth, he saw nothing abnormal. The man was breathing easily, and there was no stridor, no harsh sounds suggesting an obstruction in the upper airway. But Alter was concerned about the patient's restlessness and his fever of 101° F. He lingered awhile, thinking.

"Like I said, it's a viral pharyngitis, and at Highland Hospital we don't give these people antibiotics," the resident said with dripping sarcasm. Alter ignored the baiting tone. He again moved his fingers down the sides of the man's neck, marching meticulously, this time pressing inch by inch. When he was about halfway down, the man winced in pain.

"I want a CT scan of his neck," Alter told the resident. For a long moment the junior doctor said nothing, but then he left and ordered the scan. The call later from the radiologist did not surprise Alter: the man had an abscess in his neck. "This is the kind of infection that can kill you," Alter said. "If it's not treated quickly with intravenous antibiotics, it can block the upper airway and you'll suffocate."

There were sixteen attending physicians and forty residents

working in the Highland Hospital emergency department at the time. Most of them were dedicated, serious, honest, and emotionally balanced. But not all. As Alter explained it to me, the resident's behavior was "payback" for the earlier criticism for prescribing antibiotics when they weren't appropriate. The resident wanted the second patient's diagnosis to be viral pharyngitis so he could needle Alter, and that desire led to an inadequate physical examination. That kind of incomplete care and immature acting out could have resulted in the man's death had Alter not been the kind of attending who double-checks everything the residents say and do. As in every place, ecology is determined in part by atmosphere. Here, the emotional temperature had risen dangerously high.

Most people believe that decisions in the ER must be made instantly, but Alter said that "is a misperception that we doctors in part foster." In order to think well, especially in hectic circumstances, you need to slow things down to avoid making cognitive errors. "We like the image that we can handle whatever comes our way without having to think too hard about it — it's kind of a cowboy thing." As if being swift and decisive saves lives. But as Alter put it, he works with "studied calm," consciously slowing his thinking and his actions with each patient in order not to be distracted or pressed by the hectic and sometimes chaotic atmosphere.

Alter also emphasized that laypeople should realize the limitations of emergency medicine and have realistic expectations. "We are diagnosticians, but not comprehensive diagnosticians. Often whatever is bothering a patient, it's flying below the level of our clinical radar. Like with Nathan, the last thing I want is a patient to leave the ER and say, 'The doctor said there is nothing wrong with me.' What we try to establish to our comfort, and the patient's comfort, is that what is bothering them is not going to kill them in the next three days."

An ER doctor's "studied calm" should be apparent to a patient or his family. If the physician is distracted, frequently interrupted by other doctors, nurses, social workers, or the administrative staff as he interviews or examines you, the steady flow of his thinking may be diverted in the wrong direction. There is similar cause for concern if the physician seems rushed or breaks in as you answer a question, so that you feel he is not letting you tell him everything about your symptoms. Being quick and shooting from the hip are indications of anchoring and availability. These are the two most frequent cognitive biases in the emergency department, and often they are all a doctor needs to hit the mark, to make a correct diagnosis and recommend an effective therapy. But they also can veer wide of the mark.

So a fair question to ask an ER physician is: What's the worst thing this can be? That question is not a sign of neurosis or hypochondria; in fact, residents are trained to keep it in mind with each patient they see. But it can easily slip from the forefront of thinking in the intense environment of emergency care. By asking that question, a patient, friend, or family member can slow down the doctor's pace and help him think more broadly. You can prompt him to consider lifting his anchor from the most available harbor. You might also cause the rare doctor who is acting out of pique, like the resident we just saw, to stop in his tracks and revert to a professional form of behavior.

Twice in Pat Croskerry's career he made a dazzling diagnosis in the emergency department. In each instance, a triage nurse had diagnosed a middle-aged man with a kidney stone. It was a fair first assessment. The usual hallmarks were present: the onset of acute pain in the flank, so severe that the patient vomited, followed by blood in the urine. Treatment with painkillers and intravenous fluids until the stone passes is almost always successful. But Croskerry recalled the importance of the worst-case scenario. "I found that it wasn't a kidney stone at all," he told me, "but a dissecting abdominal aortic aneurysm." The aorta, the large vessel that carries blood from the heart through the chest and into the abdomen, had a tear on one side, accounting for the acute pain. Blood was leaking through the vessel into the kidney and being passed in the urine. Croskerry told me he didn't think the diagnosis was brilliant at all, but I felt otherwise. I imagined myself not in relaxed conversation with him but in the midst of evaluating four or five sick people at once under all the stresses of the ER environment.

Another way that laypeople can focus a doctor's attention is to ask: What body parts are near where I am having my symptom? This sounds elementary, but this query can help avoid "yin-yang out" errors. "Yes, I know that I have irritable bowel syndrome," Maxine Carlson might have said, "and that I've been here many times and been told that it's my chronic condition. But if the pain is something new, on top of that long-standing problem, what body part might be causing the symptom?" Enumerating the tissues and organs in the lower abdomen could have steered the discussion to the reproductive tract, and then on to recent intercourse and missed periods.

It may seem presumptuous to expect a patient short of breath like Blanche Begaye or in pain like Maxine Carlson to help a doctor think. But what we say to a physician, and how we say it, sculpts his thinking. That includes not only our answers but our questions.

CHAPTER 4

Gatekeepers

IMAGINE WATCHING A TRAIN go by. You are looking for one face in the window. Car after car passes. If you become distracted or inattentive, you risk missing the person. Or, if the train picks up too much speed, the faces begin to blur and you can't see the one you are seeking. "That's what primary care medicine is like," Victoria Rogers McEvoy told me. McEvoy is a tall, lean woman in her fifties with short-cropped blond hair and steady eyes. She practices general pediatrics in a town west of Boston. "It's much harder than the proverbial needle in a haystack, because the haystack is not moving. Each day there is a steady flow of children before your eyes. You are doing well-baby checks, examinations for school, making sure each one is up to date on his vaccinations. It can become rote, and you stop observing closely. Then you have the endless number of kids who are cranky and have a fever, and it's almost always a virus or a strep throat. They can all blur. But then there is that one time it's meningitis.

"The blessing of pediatrics, but also its curse, is that almost all of the children who come to the office turn out to be healthy or have a minor problem," McEvoy elaborated. A blessing, of course, that the kids are fine, but a curse because you can become lulled by the monotony of the mundane. With that in mind, she asks herself one pivotal question each time she sees a child, in essence the same question Pat Croskerry and Harrison Alter ask about each patient in the ER: Does he or she have a serious problem? "Every pediatrician should consider that as soon as the child comes into the room." And because many of the patients are infants and toddlers who can't communicate what they are feeling, "your powers of observation have to be particularly acute."

Essentially the doctor gets all of the information from the parents, which means she has to consider both the parents' degree of familiarity with their child and their subconscious or emotional reaction to the possibility that something is wrong. This reaction can be extreme: some parents deny the existence of a serious problem; others exaggerate what is normal because of their anxiety. Parents have reported that their child was lethargic and not eating, information that would trigger a high level of concern in the doctor; but with one glance she would see the child playing happily on the examining table and grinning. "The story was completely overblown, and you knew immediately that the kid was not seriously sick." Then there was the corollary, where a mother said that her baby felt a little warm but was otherwise okay. McEvoy was stunned to see the child breathing rapidly and lying limp in the mother's arms. The child had pneumonia. McEvoy, like all pediatricians, looks for certain key features: Does the child smile, play with toys, actively walk or crawl, or is she passive, not resisting when a foreign instrument like a stethoscope is placed on her chest?

Pattern recognition in pediatrics begins with behavior. And the art of pediatrics, then, is to further study the child while simultaneously interpreting what the parents report. This melding of data, McEvoy said, is not a skill set that comes from a textbook, because it requires a level of self-awareness by the doctor about his own feelings toward the family. While first impressions are often right, you have to be careful and always doubt your initial response. "It's a foolish pediatrician who does not listen closely to the parents and take seriously what they are saying," McEvoy said. "But you need to filter what they say with the child's condition." I told her the story of my first child, Steven. My wife, Pam, and I had returned from living in California to the East Coast. It was the July Fourth weekend, and we stopped in Connecticut to visit her parents. Steven was then nine months old, and had been irritable and not feeding well during the cross-country flight. When we arrived at Pam's parents' house, he was restless in the crib and then had a dark, malodorous stool that was different from his usual bowel movements. We took him to an older pediatrician in town; the doctor glanced at Steve and quickly dismissed Pam's worries that he was seriously ill. "You're overanxious, a first-time mother," the pediatrician told her. "Doctor parents are like this." By the time we arrived in Boston, Steve was grunting and drawing his legs up to his chest. We rushed him to the emergency room of the Boston Children's Hospital. He had an intestinal obstruction requiring urgent surgery. Pam and I could only conclude that despite his many years in practice, the pediatrician in Connecticut had made a snap judgment — that Pam was neurotic about her firstborn, not a reliable reporter of a meaningful change in her baby's behavior and condition.

The pediatrician in Connecticut watched the train go by, hour after hour, day after day, year after year after year. I asked McEvoy, who had also been in practice for decades, "How do you keep your eyelids open?"

"I prepare myself mentally before each session," she replied, just as she used to prepare herself mentally before a competitive tennis match. In 1968, when she was in college, McEvoy was ranked third in the nation in tennis, and played at Wimbledon. As an athlete, she learned to focus her mind, to anticipate the unexpected spin, and not to be lulled into complacency despite her expertise. But beyond the skills from sports, "you simply have to control the volume," she said. "And the truth is that most pediatricians stay afloat by seeing large numbers of children each day."

Before McEvoy took her current job, she worked in a busy group practice in another Boston suburb. At the time, she had four children of her own at home. She spent each day tending to dozens of patients and their parents. "But it was the night call that was killing me," she said. She was paged every twenty or thirty minutes, and the calls continued into the next morning. If there was serious concern based on the telephone contact, then McEvoy returned to the office and saw the child, regardless of the hour. "After doing this for a few years, I was beginning to burn out. I just couldn't stand it." McEvoy found herself becoming irritable and bitter. "I was so exhausted from this brutal schedule that at times I said things to parents that were curt and sharp, and later regretted saying them," she told me. "Pediatrics was no longer fun. Most worrisome, it impaired my thinking. I would immediately assume that the parent was telephoning inappropriately. I was just so exhausted."

McEvoy's story of relentless work and sleep deprivation reminded me of the worst moments of my own internship and residency. There were times when I was so spent, and yet still pulled in so many directions by patients in need and nurses demanding action, that all I wanted to do was deflect their requests. Subconsciously, I found myself minimizing the severity of a symptom or assuming that an aberrant laboratory result was an artifact rather than a sign of a serious problem. "As soon as the pager went off, I was angry," McEvoy confessed. "The great danger is that you stop caring. The goal of each day and each night was simply to move everyone through, to clear the decks, rather than to deliberately and expertly care for those who needed care and reassure those who did not."

McEvoy left that practice. In the course of a day, a full-time pediatrician may see two dozen or more children. Now she limits the number of patients she will see in any single session, despite the pressure to schedule brief visits and maintain a high volume. Many doctors who provide primary care do this because they feel they simply cannot function properly otherwise. Some suffer a fall in income. Others have set up so-called concierge practices, charging a premium over the insurance reimbursement and limiting the number of patients they see. Still others move into administrative roles, seeing fewer patients but sustaining their income. McEvoy chose this last path. Her group is associated with Partners Healthcare and the Massachusetts General Hospital. This linkage largely remedied the problem of relentless night calls; the Partners group hired experienced pediatric nurses who take the phone calls at night. These nurses offer advice to the parents, but if a family insists on speaking directly to the doctor, then the doctor will be paged. "This is the only way to maintain one's sanity," McEvoy said. "And the care is much better, because the doctors are not burned out."

McEvoy devotes half days to direct clinical care, seeing about a dozen children; she spends the rest of the day largely on aftercare: the forms that must be filled out, the documentation of visits, the review of records, the preparation of letters of referral to specialists, and — most trying — the negotiations with insurers about expensive tests like MRIs. Recently, McEvoy published an article in the *Harvard Medical Alumni Bulletin* that received wide notice. It was titled "The Incredibles" and argued that to fully function as a primary care provider in today's environment requires the superhuman powers found only in comic-book heroes:

> . . . Docs of Steel! Faster than a speeding bullet, yet with no stone left unturned. Paperwork? Bring it on! . . . As we draw our capes around us and prepare to plunge into the next pit of human suffer-

ing, we pause only to check schedules, to ensure that productivity remains on target. Juggling BlackBerries, cell phones, electronic medical records, notes from specialists, lab results, patient phone calls, referrals, radiology requests, beepers, handheld formularies, patient-satisfaction surveys, color-coded preferred-drug charts from insurers, and quality report cards from HMOs, we forge on, as our patients wait, shivering expectantly . . . The superhuman demands of our specialty have either morphed us into steely-eyed combatants or reduced us to blithering, overwhelmed, white-coated globs of jelly. We now practice triage medicine — surrendering time-honored bedside roles to hospitalists; slicing face time with patients; retreating to administrative roles; appending MBA, Esq., or MPH to our names to shield us from the line of fire.

Alas, serving as a gatekeeper to limit access is not what most doctors envisioned when they chose primary care. "Frankly, now what really sustains me is the relationships with the family," McEvoy said. Many of the families that McEvoy cares for are immigrants. Her practice is located in a town where many Mandarin and Farsi speakers live. "Determining a child's verbal development is a key challenge for the pediatrician," McEvoy said, "and it is made even more difficult with families where the language is not English." Effectively extracting accurate information from parents about their child's milestones is often quite difficult. "Again, it can go both ways," McEvoy said. "Some parents are absolutely hysterical that their child is not developing quickly enough, and fear that it's an early sign of autism. Other parents sugarcoat the difficulties their children are having because they are terrified that their kids aren't intelligent enough." In today's culture there is tremendous pressure even on toddlers to develop the skills to succeed; parents meet any apparent deviation from a path of achievement with grave concern. This is no longer restricted to the middle or upper classes; it is widely recognized that education is the route forward in our society, and abilities in science and technology are particularly prized among a child's talents.

Recently, McEvoy had been "burned" by initially taking at face value the report of the Yazdans, an Iranian family who spoke Farsi at home. Their daughter, Azar, was a curly-haired toddler who averted her large brown eyes when McEvoy greeted her and did not speak at all during the visit. When McEvoy pursued these observations with Mrs. Yazdan, she said, "Oh, yes, Azar talks quite a bit at home." On a later visit, McEvoy again observed that Azar did not speak. This time, she investigated the issue further and contacted the girl's school, and discovered that Azar was not talking and no one was speaking to her. The teachers assumed that, because of the language difference, Azar did not understand enough English to respond verbally. "The little girl was autistic," McEvoy said. But it took nearly a year before this diagnosis was confirmed. "It is all made difficult because a pediatrician has such limited time during a visit," she said, "so you might be misled by thinking that this is just a shy little kid and you don't speak her language."

McEvoy, thinking out loud with me, also wondered whether delays in diagnosis reflect a wish to avoid snap judgments. "The last thing you want to do is plant the seed of doubt with parents," she said. "It's devastating for a loving parent to think that their child may not be normal. And the range of what is normal at different ages can be quite large." The mother or father, McEvoy continued, immediately concludes that the child will be placed in a special school and has no chance at an excellent college.

"This is one of the great tests of a pediatrician," McEvoy said, "how you play this balance between raising unnecessary fears and ignoring what may be a serious developmental issue." A seasoned pediatrician has to finesse this particular terrain, McEvoy said, bringing up the need for more observation and perhaps testing without unduly alarming the family. She does this by taking time to explain to the parents that, indeed, some intelligent children may not learn to read as early as others; that some are shy while others are gregarious; that some smile readily with strangers and others are reticent. "I begin by saying that there is a very wide range of what is normal and emphasize that everything may turn out to be okay." Despite this cautious introduction, "some parents take their eighteen-month-old to five different specialists if the child is not speaking much," McEvoy said. The parents who have raised children already are usually more relaxed, and say, "Okay, so she is a late talker."

"It's often a shoot-the-messenger scenario," McEvoy said. Even when she gingerly approaches the question of a developmental disorder with a family, she braces herself for a strong and some-times angry reaction. "This is when patients have left me," she said, "families that just didn't want to hear that there may be au-tism or some other serious problem."

Moreover, McEvoy is leery about attaching a label to a child, because once that label is fixed, "it's as though the child is changed forever," she said. "It almost borders on cruelty to raise the idea of a serious problem that might not be there." For that reason, she doesn't begin by introducing a specific diagnosis to the family; rather, she might say, "I am not sure, but this may just be the way your child is developing and will soon catch up. So let's schedule the next visit sooner. That will give me the opportunity to see him again." When to follow up is a judgment call. "You don't want to have the visit too soon, because it's like watching the grass grow," she said. "So you may see the kid in two or three months instead of six months," and then assess the child again for language and interpersonal interaction. This time frame also is a signal to the parents that the doctor does not believe the situation is an emer-gency.

The process of assessing developmental milestones is compli-cated by narrowing definitions of what is psychologically normal: moodiness is labeled as depression, shyness as social affective disorder, a drive to precision as obsessive-compulsive disorder. "There are so many diagnoses put on children these days," she said. "But all of human behavior is a continuum." For that reason, again, she refrains from raising a psychiatric issue with the family until she has had an adequate opportunity to observe the child herself and navigate the shoals of parental overconcern and parental denial. "Psychiatric labels can be shattering," McEvoy said, "so I try to move the parents away from focusing on the label and tell them that the key is to take an activist approach, to figure out what kind of learning style and social environment is best for their child."

McEvoy's approach reminded me of Jane Holmes-Bernstein, a neuropsychologist at Boston's Children's Hospital whom I met several years ago. Holmes-Bernstein emphasizes that what is normal or abnormal is highly related to the context of the behavior. She assiduously refrains from fixing ready rubrics to a child's condition, and instead seeks to describe the ways she gathers and assesses information through cognitive testing and play. Holmes-Bernstein develops a descriptive profile of how the child functions in different settings. She can then customize her recommendations for how to overcome particular obstacles, whether they be difficulties in decoding written text, organizing speech and language, or controlling emotional and antisocial behaviors.

Of course, some children do suffer well-recognized psychological syndromes. McEvoy bemoaned the current difficulty in referring such children for psychiatric evaluation. Pediatric psychiatrists generally have long waiting lists, and much of their work has been reduced to a relatively brief evaluation followed by the prescription of a psychotropic medication. This is because insurers reimburse poorly for psychotherapy.

Many primary care physicians find their practices taking on a similar frenetic quality, and for similar reasons. Insurance companies seriously underreimburse doctors for primary care, a legacy of the period when surgeons headed the medical societies that negotiated with insurers about what was a "customary" payment for services. A specialist who performs a procedure — a bronchoscopy, say, or a surgical operation — gets a substantial payment from the insurance carrier. But if a pediatrician or another primary care provider, a general practitioner or internist, spends an hour with a complex set of medical problems trying to arrive at a diagnosis, or probing the emotional fallout from an illness or its treatment, the payment is meager. For this reason, many general pediatricians "feel like they are running up a hill of sand," McEvoy said.

In fact, a recent study showed that over the past decade, taking inflation into account, the incomes of physicians like pediatricians have fallen. Many doctors have reacted by truncating visits to ten or fifteen minutes and increasing the volume of patients they see in a given day. This speeds up the train and fosters the kinds of errors that Pat Croskerry and Harrison Alter fear when the ER doctor is spinning plates. Working in haste can not only increase cognitive mistakes but impair the communication of even the most basic information about treatment. A study of 45 doctors caring for 909 patients found that two thirds of the physicians did not tell the patient how long to take a new medication or what side effects it might cause. Nearly half of the doctors failed to specify the dose of the medication and how often it should be taken.

Sometimes the frenetic pace overwhelms the doctor and estranges the patient and family. Friends of mine who live in a Dallas suburb had adored their pediatrician until they came to feel that she was not paying close attention during routine visits. "She had four rooms going at once," the mother told me, with the doctor and her nurses shuttling among them. Often my friends' visit was interrupted by a nurse entering to ask the doctor a question about another child. Then, one evening after a yearly checkup, the pediatrician called my friends at home. "She apologized and told us that she had injected saline and forgotten to mix in the vaccine." My friends took their children in the next day for the vaccination and then decided to find another doctor. "We really liked her, but she just became too busy and too distracted, and we worried that she would miss something important about the kids."

My wife and I searched for, and found, a pediatrician who, despite a busy practice, focuses squarely on our children during their visits. We met him first on the sidelines of a soccer field where both of our children were playing. He had a warm and outgoing manner, as many pediatricians do. We asked colleagues their opinion of him, and each said he was highly competent. Pam found some fellow mothers who were not doctors, and again heard notes of praise. His waiting room is usually packed, but his secretary and nurses know our children by name. Sometimes we sit awhile in the waiting room, but we know he is running late because another family has needs that take longer than the allotted time. He often thinks out loud as he ponders our questions, and raises issues that we did not consider. He doesn't talk to us while typing his note on his computer. His eyes engage ours, not the clock.

Years ago, the mother of one of my patients said, "I want you to take care of my son like he is the only one in your practice." At first I was taken aback by what seemed a selfish demand. But then I realized what she meant: that my mind should be entirely on his case when we are together. That required me to manage my time so I could hear his problems and consider them. It also prompted me to encourage him to organize his concerns in advance of his visits. But one day, after going through his list and preparing to end the appointment, he mentioned in passing that he had a "stitch" in his groin. It was probably nothing, he continued, since he had been rearranging the furniture in his apartment and probably just pulled the muscle. But we went back to the examining room and I found a large, hard lymph node that heralded the return of his lymphoma.

Lists are useful, and like algorithms can make care more efficient in certain circumstances, yet they also pose the same risks, that the doctor will not ask the kinds of open-ended questions that Debra Roter and Judith Hall had shown in their research as yielding the most information. In addition, as McEvoy pointed out about developmental disorders, and as I saw with my patient with lymphoma, we often push from our minds the concern that is most frightening. In pediatrics, parents may ask themselves in advance what it is that scares them the most about their child's condition. This question is an echo of the one that we posed before: What is the worst diagnosis that this could be? If fear still inhibits a parent's or patient's mind from recognizing this, then the pediatrician should budget time to allow the concern to come to the surface, drawn out through a dialogue.

A good physician learns how to manage time. Symptoms that are straightforward can be accurately defined and explained to a patient and loved ones in clear and accessible language within a twenty-minute visit. Families leave the office feeling informed and satisfied. Complicated problems cannot be solved so quickly. A discerning doctor will recognize when more time is needed to ask questions and explain his thinking. In such instances, the appointment may need to be extended or a follow-up visit scheduled as soon as feasible. Cogent thinking and clear communication cannot be conducted like a race being run. Despite all the pressures to limit time in managed care and the pursuit of putative efficiency, doctors and patients should push back. Finding the right answer often takes time. Haste makes cognitive errors.

Dr. JudyAnn Bigby is also a gatekeeper. We met some thirty years ago when she was a student and I was a resident. She is an internist and the director of Community Health Programs and the Center for Excellence in Women's Health at Boston's Brigham and Women's Hospital. She divides her time between caring for patients as their general internist and administering the hospital's program, which tries to improve care in underserved communities, mainly among African-American and Latino women. After her internship and residency, Bigby took a fellowship in general internal medicine, and during that period received didactic instruction in certain forms of clinical decision-making. "We learned how to be critical, particularly how to apply Bayesian analysis when considering different tests and procedures." The curriculum was meant to teach young doctors how best to use resources like sophisticated imaging techniques, and how far to pursue a particular diagnosis given a set of initial findings. Bigby was not taught about different modes of cognition and the various types of cognitive errors that physicians can make. I wondered how much of this theoretical grounding she applies in her day-to-day clinical practice. "I don't use Bayesian analysis routinely," she told me, "but I do use it at times to help explain to patients why I think a particular test that they want won't really help them. In my mind, I see the probabilities and try to translate them into language that a patient will understand."

The day we spoke, Bigby had seen one of her longtime patients, a healthy middle-aged white man. He wanted to have an exercise test as a part of his routine yearly physical. "We talked about what value it would add, based on its prediction of cardiac disease in his case," she said. "And he got it. He understood that the test wasn't valuable for him." She recalled another patient, an African-American woman in her eighties, who had coronary artery disease and renal failure and had had numerous negative mammograms over the past decades. In this instance, she used probabilities to explain to the woman why another mammogram was unnecessary, given how unlikely it was that further screening would find an abnormality. Even if a tumor were found, she told the patient, it would take so long to develop that it would probably never threaten her.

JudyAnn Bigby is a compact woman with a round face, alert eyes, and a lilting, almost musical voice that often breaks into laughter. She was raised in Hempstead, Long Island. When she was a child, hers was one of the first African-American families in town; by the time she graduated from high school, Bigby told me, the school was more than 80 percent black. Her father worked as a mechanic for United Airlines, and only later in life did her mother, a homemaker, return for a high school equivalency degree.

Although Bigby devotes only about a third of her time to direct clinical care, she is not immune to the pressures that all primary care physicians now feel. "We are supposed to see patients every fifteen minutes," she told me. "And I probably don't meet my target numbers. That's largely because I put blocks in my schedule. I simply cannot see patients every fifteen minutes." She doesn't like to keep patients waiting, and because many of the people she cares for require extended thinking about their problems, she has set her schedule to accommodate this style of practice. "I have to have some leeway in each clinical session," she said. I asked whether anyone from the hospital administration ever expressed disapproval of this leeway, which is, of course, not reimbursed by insurance and would be considered unproductive by a bean counter. She laughed. "Not anymore," she said. "I think if I were a full-time clinician, someone might. But I've reached a point in my career where this is simply the way I want to doctor.

"A lot of primary care is about getting people to recognize and change certain behaviors," she said. Whether it be smoking, overeating, failing to exercise, or missing a mammogram appointment, Bigby tries to think about how to make her patients' behavior healthier given their particular social context.

For example, two weeks before we spoke, Gloria Manning, a

seventy-four-year-old African-American woman, was admitted to the hospital. Manning had diabetes, hypertension, and coronary artery disease, in addition to advanced rheumatoid arthritis. Her rheumatologist had been seeing her as an outpatient, and Manning had told him that her ankles were increasingly painful and swollen. She had been treated with a number of medications for her arthritis, including methotrexate and Plaquenil. The rheumatologist decided to give her Remicade, a new antibody used in autoimmune diseases like rheumatoid arthritis that works by blocking an inflammatory protein called TNF. When Bigby examined Manning, she had gained more than twenty pounds and was tired and short of breath. "It was clear that she was in heart failure," Bigby told me, "all the weight being retained water." And, Bigby suspected, the Remicade therapy could have made her condition worse.

Years before, Manning had been admitted to the Brigham and Women's Hospital with poorly controlled hypertension and bouts of angina. "At that time, she was labeled as noncompliant," Bigby said — that term we saw earlier, fraught with meaning for both doctors and patients. Physicians dislike patients who don't follow their advice. During a hospitalization, it is not easy to determine the optimal dose of medications to control blood pressure, facilitate blood flow to the atherosclerotic vessels of the heart, and keep blood sugars within an acceptable range, and then discharge such a patient with a regimen that will sustain the progress made during her hospitalization. When a patient after discharge seems to be ignoring the prescribed diet and not reliably taking her medicines — being noncompliant — physicians, as Toronto's Donald Redelmeier said, react with anger and disgust. "She had been lectured time and again by other doctors that she was not taking her medications, and that's why she kept being readmitted to the hospital," Bigby continued.

It was at this admission that Bigby met Manning and recognized what the other physicians had overlooked. "An African-American woman of her age, from Mississippi — you have to consider the high likelihood that she never learned to read or write. The reason that Gloria Manning could not take her medications correctly was not a matter of being noncompliant but was explained by her inability to read the labels on the medicine bottles." So Bigby made sure that Manning's daughter, who works as a manager at a local corporation, was present when her mother was discharged and the outpatient plan was presented. "I just saw her in clinic yesterday," Bigby said. "She has lost seven more pounds, which is great, because so often people put back the weight and retain fluid after they leave the hospital. Everything is in order, and the daughter, this time, is making sure that the medications are being taken properly."

Bigby is trying to relay this sort of thinking about context to the interns and residents at the Brigham and Women's Hospital. That institution is one of the premier academic centers in the country and boasts cutting-edge technologies in fields like cardiology and surgery. It resembles the hospitals where I trained as a student, resident, and fellow. But I cannot recall a single instance when an attending physician taught us to think about social context. When an elderly patient was noncompliant, you generously considered whether this was a sign of early dementia or psychological depression, not a reflection of the severe disadvantages of being a black woman in the rural Mississippi of the 1930s.

Bigby, like all clinicians who have practiced for decades, made a diagnosis that had been missed by others and, in a moment, reversed the apparent fortunes of a patient. She recalled the case of Constance Gardner, who had developed a persistent cough and went to a local emergency room where a chest x-ray was ordered. The ER physician told Mrs. Gardner that she had metastatic cancer, since her lungs were studded with multiple masses. "I saw her the next day," Bigby said. After listening to her story and examining her, Bigby reviewed the chest x-ray. "I don't think this is metastatic cancer," she said to Mrs. Gardner. "It looks like a rare autoimmune disease called Wegener's granulomatosis." This malady can cause inflammatory masses in the lungs as well as other parts of the respiratory system. "It wasn't that brilliant, really," Bigby said, "just a matter of developing a complete differential diagnosis and thinking beyond the immediate possibility."

And, like all doctors after years in practice, Bigby had a patient who stopped coming to see her. Harriet West was an elderly African-American woman whom Bigby had cared for over several years and with whom she felt she had a good relationship. West had long-standing hypertension and heart disease and came to the emergency room at the Brigham and Women's Hospital complaining of shortness of breath. "She was in heart failure," Bigby said. Fluid was backing up in her lungs because her heart could not pump effectively. Harriet West had no evidence of an infection, Bigby continued, no fever, and no elevation of her white blood cell count. Nonetheless, Bigby recounted, "someone decided to obtain blood cultures." This was done to rule out a systemic infection, particularly one called endocarditis, which can affect the valves of the heart and contribute to heart failure.

Not only was the test unnecessary, it started a chain of events that led to West's leaving Bigby's practice. "One of the three blood cultures grew out staph epidermidis," Bigby said. This bacterium is commonly found on skin and usually has no significance if it appears in a single blood culture. "In a spirit of full disclosure, one of the residents said to Mrs. West, 'Oh, one of your blood cultures grew out this bacteria, but don't worry. It was contaminated.'"

After West's heart failure was treated in the hospital, she went to see Bigby, to follow up as an outpatient. West was very agitated. "I want to know *exactly* what my medical records say," she said to Bigby, who was taken aback by this change in her demeanor. "After many, many conversations and much back-and-forth, I still couldn't figure out what was the matter," Bigby said. "She couldn't remember the exact words that the resident had said in the ER. But finally I realized that she thought she had been told that she had 'bad blood.'" "Bad blood" is an old euphemism, particularly in the South, where West was raised, for syphilis. West was convinced that the resident had asserted this, and, understandably, she was very insulted. "I was married for more than forty years, and now I am a widow, and I am a churchgoing woman," West told Bigby. "What does this say about me, a Christian woman?" She demanded that it be removed from her medical records. "I attempted to explain to her what 'contaminated' meant in this setting, that when he took the blood, the resident contaminated it." But West was not consoled. In fact, she then concluded that the resident in the emergency room had put a contaminated needle into her vein, and so had tainted her.

"It was the biggest divide in communication that I've experienced," Bigby said. "It was as though the two of us were speaking a completely different language. And that was the last time I ever saw her." Bigby now uses this case in teaching young doctors. "The irony was that it was a set of blood cultures that she didn't need," Bigby told me. "She was insulted, deeply insulted, by the institution."

Bigby is familiar with the work of Roter and Hall on doctor-patient communication, and emphasized to me that sensitivity to language, while particularly important with patients like Harriet West, should be considered with every patient. This is a challenge for the primary care physician, since so much of what she deals with is labeled routine in medicine. "One woman I cared for had knee pain," Bigby said. Her x-rays showed degenerative changes, common findings as we age. "I called her up and told her that she had osteoarthritis. I was ready to go on with my next phone call, but then I realized that she was devastated. To me it seemed to be no big deal, and I stated the x-ray findings in a matter-of-fact way. But to her, arthritis meant severe pain and being crippled."

Pediatricians like McEvoy learn how to talk to parents about the possibility of a developmental or psychological disorder, and general internists like Bigby craft phrases to deliver clearly bad news, such as a cancer diagnosis. But both McEvoy and Bigby emphasized to me that in the hurly-burly of primary care, a physician must not lose sight of the fact that what may seem mundane to the doctor can strike the patient as tragic.

Several years ago, I was speaking at medical grand rounds at Tufts–New England Medical Center when the chairman of the Department of Medicine, Dr. Deeb Salem, posed a difficult question for which I had no easy answer. I'd been discussing the importance of compassion and communication in the art of doctoring, and Salem asked the following: There are primary care physicians in every hospital who speak with great sensitivity and concern, and their longtime patients love them, but clinically they are incompetent — how is a patient to know this?

Salem's words resonated with me. There had been a cadre of such doctors who practiced on Beacon Hill and admitted their patients only to the Phillips House at the Massachusetts General Hospital when I was a resident there in the 1970s. A few of them were highly skilled, but several were, at best, marginal in their clinical acumen. Nonetheless, their patients were devoted to them. It was the job of the residents to plug the holes in these marginal doctors' care. "Just as a physician has to be wary of his first impression of a patient's condition, as a patient you have to be careful of your first impression of a physician," I said, particularly in choosing who will coordinate your care, or your children's care. Thankfully, fewer students are admitted to medical school now because of social standing and family connections than at the time of my training. America has become more of a meritoc-racy in the professions. Medical school admissions committees no longer accept a record of gentlemen's C's at an Ivy League college. At best, I said to Salem, a layman should inquire of friends and, if possible, other physicians as well as nurses about the clinical qual-ity of a doctor beyond his personality. His credentials can be found on the Internet or by contacting the local medical board. Ultimately, I realized that Salem's query required a much more comprehensive answer, which I hope this book will help provide.

Dr. Bigby has experienced the flip side of a patient's positive first impression. "As a black woman, I have had patients arrive, take one look at me, and walk out of my waiting room," she said. Bigby mentors many residents, and has a special message for those who are African American or Latino. "I tell them, Always wear your white coat, always wear your name badge, and always have a stethoscope visible in your pocket," she said. "Despite all that, they will still sometimes be asked if they have come to take the meal tray. People focus on your being black and don't pay atten-tion to the uniform that indicates you are a doctor."

Bigby, who covers weekend call with several prominent physi-cians on the staff, has also experienced situations when their pa-tients looked askance at her when she entered the hospital room on a Saturday morning. Not subtly, they quizzed her about her credentials. "Wellesley College, Harvard Medical School, Mass General," she recites. Although there has been a significant in-crease in the number of women in medicine — now more than 50 percent in many parts of the country — as well as in the number of minorities, prejudice remains. Bigby believes this prejudice fac-tors into her doctoring. She still feels, some thirty years after her residency, that she has to prove herself as a black woman, that she has to strive to be flawless, because some people still assume that she arrived at her senior post because of affirmative action and po-litical correctness. "I . . . ," she said, her voice faltering briefly, "feel that I have to do everything better just to be judged as okay. It is something I wish I could let go of. It's something that I wish just wasn't there."

In 1997, Dr. Eric J. Cassell wrote an insightful and illuminating book, *Doctoring: The Nature of Primary Care Medicine.* Cassell is a clinical professor of internal medicine at Weill Medical College of Cornell University in New York and has a thriving Manhattan practice. In the 1990s, the train had begun to pick up considerable speed, because its controls had been increasingly taken over by insurance companies, HMOs, and hospital-based administrators. Cassell believed that many of the practice guidelines put forth by these organizations were designed to foster cost control rather than the best interests of the patient. "From this perspective . . . physicians themselves can be seen as interchangeable commodities in a marketplace."

This statement reminded me of a remark by an eminent academic physician-scientist who led a department around that time: "Anyone can take care of patients." His arrogance, like much arrogance, was a product of narrow vision and ignorance. University hospitals and medical schools prize research most highly, because it brings attention from medical journals and money from grants. Similar arrogance and ignorance about medical care persist among the businesspeople who design and enforce many of the healthcare delivery constraints that dictate the fifteen-minute office visit. "A common error in thinking about primary care is to see it as entry-level medicine . . . and, because of this, rudimentary medicine — for mostly (say) the common cold and imaginary illnesses. This is a false notion," Cassell writes. The great challenge is not only identifying serious illness but often being unable to decide if something is serious or not. "Everyone knows, however, that knowing when you don't know requires sophisticated knowledge . . . From the perspective of training physicians and the knowledge bases required for adequate performance, the higher we go on the scale of a specialist training, the *less* complex the medical problem becomes."

This conclusion, Cassell acknowledges, is the opposite of that usually drawn. "One should not confuse highly technical, even complicated, medical knowledge — special practical knowledge about an unusual disease, treatment (complex chemotherapy, for example), condition, or technology — with the complex, many-sided worldly-wise knowledge we expect of the best physicians." Moreover, "The narrowest subspecialist, the reasoning goes, should also be able to provide this range of medical services. This naïve idea arises, as do so many other wrong beliefs about primary care, because of the concept that doctors take care of diseases. Diseases, the idea goes on, form a hierarchy from simple to difficult. Specialists take care of difficult diseases, so, of course, they will naturally do a good job on simple diseases. Wrong. Doctors take care of people, some of whom have diseases and all of whom have some problem. People used to doing complicated things usually do complicated things in simple situations — for example, ordering tests or x-rays when waiting a few days might suffice — thus overtreating people with simple illnesses and overlooking the clues about other problems that might have brought the patient to the doctor."

Recently, patient templates were proposed as a solution to organizing clinical information so that data are not overlooked. These templates, like clinical algorithms, are based on a typical patient with a typical disease. All that is required of the doctor is to fill in the blanks. He types in the patient's history, physical examination, lab tests, and the recommended treatment.

Not long ago, one of my neighbors told me that she had returned from a visit to her internist, who is a member of a large practice in a Boston hospital. I know the internist, and he recounted to me that he had recently been instructed by the practice's administrator to cut thirty-minute visits for follow-up to fifteen minutes, and sixty-minute appointments for new patients down to forty. When the doctor protested, the administrator told him that there was an electronic solution to make this all possible — a template would be on his computer screen. As he spoke with a patient, he would fill in the form. This would help, the administrator added, not only in economizing his time but also maximizing his revenue, since it would make it easier for the billing office to submit invoices to insurance companies based on his template documentation of the history, physical exam, and treatment recommendations.

"I really like him as my doctor," the neighbor told me, "but for the first time in all these years he sat at his desk with one eye on the clock and one eye on the computer screen, only occasionally turning his head to look at me."

Electronic technology can help organize vast clinical information and make it more accessible, but it can also drive a wedge between doctor and patient when used in this way to increase "efficiency." It also risks more cognitive errors, because the doctor's mind is set on filling in the blanks on the template. He is less likely to engage in open-ended questioning, and may be deterred from focusing on data that do not fit on the template.

Eric Cassell expands on the danger that clinical care is being squeezed by the efficiencies of the marketplace: "In healthcare planning, it is natural that each service might be seen as a commodity or product. The calculus involved in determining the cost of providing the service, the factors affecting reimbursement, the required number of such services, and other factors all promote the commodity view . . . Medical care — in all of medicine, not just primary care — is a human interaction between patient and doctor within a context and in a social system. As such it is not a commodity."

Every aspect of medicine can be challenging, but, like Cassell, I have come to believe that the most difficult type of doctoring is primary care. Although there are complex decisions that specialists like myself make, we usually know what underlying problem we are addressing. Similarly, in surgery, while there are important nuances in both approach and technique, once he has begun an operation, a competent surgeon can pursue the abnormalities he sees. Again, the problems are largely apparent. On the other hand, as Victoria Rogers McEvoy said, practicing primary care is like trying to find that one distinct face in the passing train. The difficulty is all the greater, research shows, because nearly all of the complaints patients describe to their primary care physician, such as headache, indigestion, and muscle pain, are of no serious consequence.

And now insurers are packing the trains with so many passengers it feels like standing room only. Delivering high-quality care day after day to hundreds, if not thousands, is no easy feat. Currently, the bean counters are generating metrics to judge a physician's "quality," but many of these are trivial, simply scorecards to ensure that the blood sugar was measured and a flu shot given. "Quality" in primary care means much more. It means thinking broadly, because any and every problem of human biology can present itself; it means making judicious decisions with limited data about children and adults, neither overreacting nor being blasé; it means wielding one's words with precision and with a profound appreciation of the social context of the patients. It means, as a gatekeeper, knowing where to guide us. One of those portals opens to the intensive care unit.

CHAPTER 5

A New Mother's Challenge

THE FLIGHT FROM VIETNAM to Los Angeles seemed endless. Rachel Stein held Shira, her infant daughter adopted just days before in Phu Tho, on her lap, but neither slept. The infant had a cough and refused to take even a few sips from the bottle. Rachel walked up and down the narrow aisles, rocking Shira and singing in an effort to calm her enough to drink and then sleep. But the playful notes of Rachel's favorite Cole Porter tunes were of no comfort.

Rachel Stein originally had set her sights on business: she got an MBA and quickly climbed the corporate ladder in finance. But in her early thirties, when she had reached a high rung, she stalled. A sense of emptiness weighed her down. Every time she thought about the next step, she felt she lacked the energy and balance to reach it. So instead of looking up, Rachel looked back. And what she saw she didn't like at all.

Business, Rachel concluded, was daily conflict. The single measure of success was money. Rachel wanted her life to be grounded in something else. She came from a family that did not observe many traditions, but did encourage personal prayer. For months, Rachel questioned God about what to do with her life. Then she realized the answer was the conversation itself. She would study religious concepts and commandments, and seek to live a life in which generosity and caring were paramount. She quit the board-room for the classroom.

Rachel entered a seminary, and over time her faith took form. She emerged an ordained rabbi, but realized that the pulpit was not for her. Instead, she became a manager at an institution of higher Jewish learning and applied her financial skills to its suc-cess.

As Rachel approached fifty, she felt another void in her life. Her pursuit of God, she realized, had left her little opportunity to pur-sue marriage and family. She was an attractive woman with jet-black hair and deep-set amber eyes. But in the congregation where she prayed and the institution where she worked, there were few single men of her age. After much thought, she decided to adopt a child and build a family as a single mother. Women like Rachel face formidable difficulties in adopting newborns. Agencies typi-cally seek two-parent families. Moreover, since most birth moth-ers are themselves unmarried, they reject the idea of another single woman receiving their baby. Only two countries readily allow as-signment of infants to middle-aged single women: Vietnam and Guatemala.

In January 2001, Rachel completed the detailed supporting documents and sent them to Vietnam. The agency in the United States coordinating her application said that her "assignment" might come in March or April. But these months passed without a response, and her spirits began to sag. Then, in early June, she was informed that a baby girl, born on April 26 in the town of Phu Tho, some fifty miles north of Hanoi, was available.

Rachel was eager to learn more about the child. The American agency cautioned that getting information usually took many weeks, but within a few days a small folder arrived. In it was some information about the baby, Hoang Thi Ha, and a photograph.

The infant had a nest of black hair and high cheekbones, and she looked robust and content. Rachel was told to plan a trip to Vietnam in September, when the child would be six months old. But in July, out of the blue, she got word that she should be in Hanoi in two weeks. Although the Vietnamese authorities had not yet finished processing the last of the paperwork, the orphanage wanted Rachel to come anyway. Rachel flew first to Los Angeles, joined up with her sister-in-law, and then both traveled to Taipei and finally Hanoi.

It was a mercilessly hot morning when Rachel emerged from the plane. Veils of thick vapor cloaked the tarmac. Rachel was met by an agency representative in a small white Peugeot who drove her into the city. Along the streets, vendors cooked fish and vegetables in large woks, and laborers in conical hats carried loads on bamboo poles balanced across their shoulders. As the car entered downtown Hanoi, it was surrounded by hundreds of people on bicycles on their way to work. Rachel thought of herself as a pebble carried in a fast-flowing stream to its destiny.

Although prospective parents usually rested upon arrival, Rachel's adrenaline would not let her relax. She had to meet her daughter. The orphanage was housed in a low white concrete building set back from a dusty road. Six to eight metal-frame cots filled each room. The green-painted walls were cracking, and the linoleum floors were worn. But, Rachel observed, the surfaces were clean, and the women attending the children treated them with care.

A woman in white nurse's garb pointed to a baby with spindly limbs in one of the cots. "Ha," the nurse said. Rachel was unsure what she meant. The baby was thin and didn't, at first glance, resemble the infant in the photo. "Ha?" Rachel replied. The nurse picked up the child. "Ha," she said again, and pressed the baby to Rachel.

Rachel held the child. For three years she had imagined this moment with tingling anticipation. But the expected joy did not appear. Rather, she found herself distracted by the lingering impression that the baby she was holding didn't quite resemble the one in the photograph. And the infant was congested, coughing as she rocked her in her arms. Rachel was reassured by the staff that this was the same child originally assigned to her, and that runny noses were the norm in the orphanage.

The next day, Rachel returned, picked up the baby, took her back to the hotel, and began to prepare for the trip north to Phu Tho. There, along with several other prospective parents, a formal meeting with local government officials would occur, culminating in the signing of the adoption papers. The event was called "the ceremony for entrusting the child to the adoptive parents." Rachel placed the infant on the hotel bed to dress her for the ceremony. As she took her thin arm and guided it into the sleeve, the soft touch seemed to radiate through her. Rachel slowly lifted the baby and pressed her against her breast. She could feel the rapid fluttering of the infant's heart against her own. Tears flowed freely from her eyes. Rachel loved music, especially song. Her baby's intended name, Shira, meant "song" in Hebrew. Rachel sang in her rich alto voice a Psalm of thanksgiving, a song to God.

Phu Tho was some two hours' drive north of Hanoi. Along the way, peasants harvested rice in paddies and yoked oxen pulled crude plows through rocky fields. In the distance were high mountains thick with vegetation.

The mayor of Phu Tho was a middle-aged man in a white shirt and gray slacks. He said that the children of Vietnam were a national treasure, precious and to be guarded. These treasures were now being shared with people who had pledged to preserve them. After the ceremony, it typically took three weeks to complete the adoption process. But the officials in Phu Tho told Rachel they were expediting her paperwork. She and Shira left four days later.

By the time they landed, Rachel worried that Shira might be

dehydrated. She had family in Los Angeles, and so got off there to take the baby to a local doctor. The doctor agreed Shira was sick, but a chest x-ray was clear; an antibiotic was prescribed for presumed sinusitis. Rachel, reassured, arrived in Boston on Monday evening, July 30. During the six-hour trip from Los Angeles, Shira took only two ounces of formula.

Rachel was spent from the journey. Shortly after putting the baby to sleep, she collapsed in her bed. On awakening the next day, the first thing Rachel did was to try to get Shira to drink. But hours of coaxing were useless. Rachel's sister in California, a pediatrician, called in the early evening to check on the baby. "She's at risk for dehydration. You have to take her to an emergency room." So, as midnight approached, with nothing more than a diaper bag, Rachel took Shira to Boston's Children's Hospital, assuming she would be given fluids in the ER and they would soon return home.

The Children's Hospital ER has a triage system that rapidly directs the sickest children, like trauma victims, into examining or procedure rooms. The less sick, those with ear infections, diarrhea, and other common problems, sit in a waiting area while the urgent cases are seen. Rachel sat with Shira for five hours before they were called. A young resident looked at Shira's eyes, ears, and throat, listened to her chest, palpated her belly. He then drew blood for tests and ordered a chest x-ray.

Two hours later, the results were in. The resident began by explaining that Shira's fontanelle, the soft spot at the crown of an infant's skull where the bones have not yet fused, was sunken, a sure sign of dehydration. But, he said gravely, the cause was more than simple sinus congestion. Shira's mouth was covered with fungus, and although this sometimes happened as the result of taking the antibiotic started in Los Angeles, it also could be a sign of an immune deficiency.

Rachel's stomach tightened as the young doctor gave her more bad news: an x-ray showed pneumonia involving both lungs. "First we'll put an IV in, to give fluids. Once she gets hydrated, maybe she'll perk up."

Rachel stood in numb silence. A nurse held Shira down on the examining table as the resident began to thread a thin needle into a vein. But within seconds, the infant's face turned dusky and her skin mottled. The resident's eyes widened with alarm.

"She's de-tuning," he said to the nurse.

All at once, a frenzy of activity engulfed the child. Blood was drawn, a mask fitted over her face, and a large ambu bag attached to the mask to force air into her lungs. "Her pressure is falling. Give her a bolus of IV fluid," the resident ordered.

Rachel didn't know what a "bolus" was, or what "de-tuning" meant, or why holding down her baby for a few seconds had precipitated a crisis. Another nurse soon entered the room with the results from the blood tests. "Her O_2 saturation is seventy," she said.

The resident explained to Rachel that Shira's pneumonia was so severe that it was preventing her from getting enough oxygen to cope with even the most minor stress, like fussing while being held. "She needs to be in the ICU."

Rachel felt as if she were on one of those amusement park rides that spins you around in circles, turns you upside down, then flings you to the edge of the rail so your eyes blur, your stomach heaves, and your mind goes blank. "I . . . I . . . don't under-stand . . ."

The resident placed the chest x-ray on the light box attached to the wall. "This is the heart," he said, tracing a white shape in the center of the chest that looked like a giant teardrop. "Around the heart are the lungs. They should be black on the x-ray, be-cause normally they are filled with air and the x-ray beam passes through." Rachel looked at the lungs. They were almost as opaque as the heart. She felt her throat tightening. "Instead, the lungs are what we call 'ground glass' in appearance." Rachel wasn't sure whether the lungs resembled ground glass or a snowstorm. What she needed to know was what it meant for her baby.

"We'll cover her broadly with multiple antibiotics and add an antifungal agent because of what we found in her mouth," the resident said. "And for now, we'll give her oxygen via prongs that fit in her nose."

"What could it be?" Rachel asked.

"It could be anything," the resident replied. "Something common, like a virus, or something unusual, from Vietnam."

Over the next twenty-four hours, the pneumonia moved through Shira's lungs like fire through dry brush. Her thin chest, not much bigger than the width of Rachel's open hand, heaved desperately in the quest for more air. "We can't sustain her oxygen with the nasal prongs," the resident told Rachel. "We need to put her on a respirator. You probably want to leave the room when we place the tube down her trachea."

Rachel looked plaintively at the young doctor. She knew that she could not leave her daughter's side even for a moment. Whatever needed to be done, no matter how harrowing, she wanted to be there. Rachel explained this to the resident. He nodded kindly and said he understood.

Rachel stepped aside as the ICU team began to work on Shira. A nurse firmly held the baby's shoulders while another braced her legs. The resident tilted up her chin and deftly inserted a metal instrument to depress her tongue and illuminate the back of her throat. "I can see the cords," he said. The tube had to be passed beyond the vocal cords into the trachea. A few millimeters off this trajectory and the tube would go into the esophagus, blocking the infant's airway. It took several attempts until the tube was correctly placed. Rachel felt as if a fist were clenched around her heart, and with each try, it tightened. She fought to maintain her composure.

Normally, the air we breathe is 20 percent oxygen and the remainder largely nitrogen with a small amount of carbon dioxide. Our lungs are built like a honeycomb, and the sacs in this honeycomb are called alveoli. The oxygen we inhale passes through the thin wall of these alveoli into the bloodstream. When bacteria and mucus fill the lungs, as in pneumonia, it is difficult for oxygen to pass through the clogged sacs and into the blood. Without oxygen, of course, we cannot live. At reduced oxygen levels, tissues struggle to perform their functions. Over time, some of the oxygen-starved tissues weaken and die. This can have debilitating complications — like heart or brain damage. Preventing tissue loss and organ damage in cases like Shira's would seem simple: set the respirator to deliver pure oxygen through the tube and literally push the gas under pressure through the muck in the lungs. But this approach has limits. Raising the concentrations of oxygen to high levels is toxic to the alveoli, worsening inflammation and risking permanent scarring of the delicate tissue. And high pressure exerted to force the oxygen through the clogged alveoli can rupture them, causing the lungs to collapse. Still, there is little choice in cases like Shira's. The risks of high pressure and high concentrations of delivered oxygen have to be taken.

Throughout the day, the ICU team set and reset the respirator, delivering 60 percent, 70 percent, 80 percent, and then 90 percent oxygen. Simultaneously, the team dialed up the pressure to force the gas through. Finally, in desperation, Shira was given 100 percent oxygen at maximum pressure.

Still, not enough oxygen was reaching her bloodstream. A repeat chest x-ray showed that the "ground glass" was more opaque, meaning the infection was spreading. Bactrim was added to the initial set of antibiotic and antifungal agents. The resident explained to Rachel that Bactrim was the best treatment for Pneumocystis pneumonia. The examination of sputum and the chest x-ray picture were consistent with it. The disease is common in AIDS patients: AIDS was very prevalent in Southeast Asia.

Shira had been tested for HIV in Vietnam. The authorities assured Rachel the test had been negative. Could the unusual pace of the adoption — the rapid processing of the application, the call to appear in Vietnam soon thereafter, the permission to leave in days rather than a month — mean that the orphanage knew something was wrong with this baby? That her mother had AIDS?

Through her years in the business world, Rachel had learned to read people with a clear and discerning eye. Without that skill you were defeated in your deals. Someone was always ready to take advantage. Rachel didn't want to believe that was the case here. The gentleness and care with which the people at the orphanage handled each infant, the elaborate ceremony during which Shira and the other babies were "entrusted" as "treasures," did not suggest deceit. Perhaps, Rachel thought, the unusual efficiency and speed of the adoption were simply the work of a bureaucrat eager to clear a stack of papers off his desk during the steamy summer months. Or perhaps it was God trying to give this infant every possible chance to survive, knowing that Rachel would deliver her to one of the best pediatric hospitals on earth.

It was evening, and a somber quiet settled over the ICU. The oxygen level in Shira's blood was still low. "We'll try Hi-Fi," the ICU doctor told Rachel. Hi-Fi stood for high-frequency ventilation. Essentially, a machine would now push the oxygen into Shira's lungs at an even faster pace. It was the best any respirator could do.

Some hours later, Rachel left Shira's side to call her sister, the pediatrician. As she was talking, the ICU doctor walked over. His eyes were downcast. "It's not working," he said. "Even the Hi-Fi can't get her oxygen up."

Rachel relayed this news to her sister.

"She's critical," her sister said. Rachel's chest tightened.

"She's deteriorating quickly," the doctor said. "We may lose her."

Rachel acknowledged the reality but could not accept it. She believed with all her heart that God had meant for her to have a child, this child. Nothing that had happened had been regular. Yes, she had to admit, it *was* possible that the orphanage in Vietnam knew something was wrong with this baby, that the usual slow grinding of the bureaucracy had somehow flown like a well-oiled wheel, propelling this new life into her arms. But even if true, it no longer mattered. Because now Rachel, the mother, had to do everything she could to stop death from wrenching her daughter away.

Rachel had not slept for days, had eaten little. She had been cast into the ocean of illness, a vortex of calamity sucking her down deeper and deeper. In Los Angeles it seemed to be simple sinusitis, then in the ER more serious dehydration, then pneumonia, then in the ICU the respirator, and now Hi-Fi. But the child's oxygen kept falling, and Rachel saw in her mind's eye a dead baby — if not dead, then functionally dead, so brain-damaged that she could not speak or see or hear, that she would be incapable of love.

Rachel called her family in Los Angeles for advice. With her sister's voice in one ear, the ICU doctor's in the other, bracketing the image of a lifeless Shira, she finally broke. Rachel started to shake. Her jaw clenched, her throat constricted, her breath came fast and short. Then her knees started to buckle.

God, help me.

Rachel struggled to hold on. The shaking intensified, and she felt she would shatter into a thousand pieces.

God, where are You?

Rachel knew what was happening. It had happened twice before, when a person she loved was lost to her. She had fallen apart, unable to function for weeks. Straining, she summoned fragments of Psalms, silently pressing her mind onto each phrase.

In distress . . . I call . . . unto You.

When . . . my foot . . . slips . . . God supports me . . .

But her tremors continued. They seemed to move out from her bones and explode through her skin. Rachel felt outside of her body, as if watching a film in which she was being blown apart. She focused all of her force on steadying her limbs and slowing her breath.

God, give me strength.

The young doctor was standing before her. "Are you okay?"

He gently took Rachel's hand and guided her to a chair. He held her arms as she slowly lowered herself into the seat. She raised her head. She looked at the young doctor with her own eyes, from within her body.

"I'm . . . I'm . . . okay."

"There is one last resort," the ICU doctor told Rachel. "ECMO."

Rachel's thoughts moved slowly. "What is ECMO?" she asked in a whisper.

ECMO, he explained, stands for extracorporeal membrane oxygenation. It is a process whereby Shira's blood would be freshened with oxygen outside her body — thus "extracorporeal" — via a specialized machine. First an incision would be made in her neck and a large catheter inserted to drain the blood out of her veins into the machine. Inside the apparatus, the blood is percolated over a broad porous membrane. Then oxygen is pumped up through the membrane into the blood. At the exit, a pump returns the oxygen-enriched blood to the body. In essence, ECMO acts like an artificial lung and heart.

Rachel strained to assimilate all this information. She asked the resident to repeat what he said. He did. Then he said there were risks and complications to the procedure. Clear in its purpose, elegant in its engineering, ECMO nonetheless has limitations. Inserting catheters into large vessels and passing blood through a machine opened the door to infections despite the best precautions. Infections seeded in the blood could be fatal. Moreover, the artificial membrane in the machine cannot be made perfectly smooth. Small clots could form on the membrane's imperfections. Pumped back into the patient, these tiny clots could clog the arteries, causing brain or heart or kidney damage. ECMO was a stopgap measure. A person could not stay alive on ECMO forever. Eventually, the lungs had to recover.

Rachel knew what had been left unsaid. If the lungs did not recover, the person was disconnected, and died. Rachel looked at the clock. It was nearly 11 P.M. The resident handed her a consent form with Shira's name on the top. Rachel read the document. It reiterated what the resident had just said. She looked at his eyes. They said Shira was nearing the end.

A nurse readied Shira to be moved from the ICU to the ECMO suite. She disconnected the tube in Shira's mouth from the Hi-Fi respirator and immediately reconnected it to a large ambu bag that resembled a football. Pure oxygen flowed into the ambu bag at one end, and the nurse squeezed it by hand to move the oxygen out the other end into Shira's lungs. Two orderlies arrived to wheel the bed and the accompanying army of instruments — the intravenous lines with antibiotics and saline solution, the cardiac monitor charting the rate and rhythm of the heart, the oximeter displaying in large red digits the level of blood oxygen.

"What's going on?" the resident asked.

The nurse lifted her head as she kept pumping the ambu bag. Rachel looked nervously at the doctor. Now what was wrong?

"Look at the oximeter!" he exclaimed.

The nurse and Rachel simultaneously gazed at the neon readout of Shira's blood oxygen. The digits were increasing. Each squeeze of the ambu bag inched the number up, like a climber scaling a sheer cliff by dint of will.

"Put her back on the respirator," the resident told the nurse. "Let's give her another chance."

Rachel put her pen down, the consent form unsigned. She closed her eyes. A verse from Psalm 27 came into her mind.

Hope in God.

Strength and courage will be in your heart . . .

Shira was reattached to the Hi-Fi. Rachel stood for a long time at the bedside, hypnotized by the metronomic back-and-forth of the machine. Her child had gone to the very edge of existence. And then a bridge, in the form of an ambu bag, squeezed by a nurse's hand, had unexpectedly led her back.

Rachel realized then what all doctors and nurses should know, that every clinical event has a core of uncertainty. No outcome is ever completely predictable. Rachel prayed for the courage to engage that uncertainty. She would learn everything possible about Shira's case, and, respectfully, question each and every assumption about the diagnosis and treatment. It wasn't because Rachel didn't appreciate the skill and devotion of the doctors or the hospital; this was an extraordinary ICU team in an extraordinary institution. It was because God did not make people omniscient.

Rachel Stein lived near the synagogue I attended, and came there to pray on Saturdays when she didn't make the long walk to her regular congregation. We spoke occasionally, and I knew she was in the process of adoption. That mid-August Sabbath in synagogue, after the service concluded, I heard that her child was in the ICU. I decided to visit the first chance I could.

Children's Hospital is a short three blocks from my lab, surrounded by a warren of towering research buildings. It was a stifling afternoon, and the heat radiated from the concrete in waves. I took the large lumbering elevator to the pediatric ICU, introduced myself to the head nurse, and asked for Rachel Stein. "She's with the doctors. They're in the middle of a procedure on her child. I'll tell Ms. Stein you're here."

I surveyed the ICU, the focused faces of doctors and nurses. I had a special admiration for them. In medical school my pediatrics course was divided between a morning outpatient clinic and afternoon rounds in the inpatient ward. In the morning clinic, I saw scores of children with ear infections, strep throats, eczema, and other common problems. It was fun to amuse the kids and talk with the parents while remedying these minor ailments. But the ward was a different matter. At the end of each afternoon, after attending to the ward's children with terrible diseases — deformed hearts that hardly pumped, cystic fibrosis crippling lungs and intestines, tumors that grew despite radiation and chemotherapy — I returned to my dorm room sick with despair. I did not have the emotional reserve to witness and absorb the suffering of these children or to comfort their anguished parents. I had found my limits as a doctor. Since that time, I have viewed those who care for children with a special respect and awe.

"I'm sorry to keep you waiting," Rachel said. Her face was a mask of worry, her eyes puffy, the lines in her brow deeply drawn.

It was no problem, I replied, and took her hand in mine.

Rachel explained she had insisted on knowing every detail of Shira's condition, so the ICU doctors and nurses invited her to make rounds with them, sharing what they knew and what they didn't. Pediatricians, as Victoria McEvoy emphasized, try to partner with parents, and Rachel said she was made to feel she wasn't a burden. After rounds, Rachel went on the Internet or called her sister the pediatrician to pursue further the particular issues the doctors and nurses discussed. But at the end of each day, an unanswered question loomed over the doctors and Rachel: Why was

Shira's immune system so weak that it could not prevent Pneumocystis, a life-threatening pneumonia?

"The HIV tests came back negative," Rachel told me. Shira
definitely did not have AIDS. While Shira's T-cell count was
somewhat low, Rachel continued, the major problem was that
they weren't working. Her T cells couldn't muster the slightest response when challenged by microbes in the test tube. This paraly-
sis of her immune system made her susceptible to a multiplicity of
devastating infections.

In addition to the Pneumocystis, the cultures from Shira had
shown cytomegalovirus, or CMV. This highly destructive virus
not only can infest the liver, lung, and bone marrow, causing
hepatitis, pneumonia, and a reduction in blood counts, but also
can grow in the retina, risking blindness. Next was Klebsiella.
This bacterium causes widespread inflammation in the lungs.
The sputum it generates is called "currant jelly," because it is so
viscous and bloody. Then there was Candida albicans, the fungus
seen in Shira's mouth in the ER. Now it was growing in other
orifices.

I counted in my mind four deadly microbes: Pneumocystis,
CMV, Klebsiella, and Candida. Then Rachel told me of a fifth:
parainfluenzae. The doctors informed her there was little they
could do — no specific therapy existed against this virus. "The
working hypothesis is that Shira has an unusual, atypical form of
SCID," Rachel said. SCID is an acronym for severe combined
immunodeficiency disorder. It is a rare inherited disease caused by
the absence of a key part of the machinery of the T cells. This results in low numbers of T cells, and even those remaining do not
work effectively. The gene for the disorder is carried on the X
chromosome. Because males have one X chromosome, inherited
from their mother, the disease is mostly seen in boys. Girls, who
are XX, with one X chromosome donated from each parent,

would have to inherit two defective genes. In Shira's case, it would require that both her father and her birth mother carry the trait. The doctors said it was rare for a girl to have SCID. The fact that Shira's T-cell count was only somewhat low made her an "atypical" case.

"You haven't seen Shira yet," Rachel said. "Come, you'll meet her. She's a beautiful baby." At the entrance to the room, we put on sterile gowns, gloves, and masks to limit the transfer of microbes from our hands, clothes, and mouths to the defenseless infant. The bed was surrounded by machines and equipment — the Hi-Fi respirator, cardiac monitor, oximeter, intravenous pumps. On a small table was a pile of books. During the rare quiet times of the day, Rachel read to Shira.

I gazed down at the infant. She was turned on her side to accommodate the stiff tube in her mouth, which was attached to a large corrugated hose that led to the Hi-Fi respirator. The settings showed that the machine was delivering the maximum concentration of oxygen under the highest possible pressure. I looked at the red numbers on the oximeter and saw that this was barely enough to sustain her blood oxygen. "She's a beautiful child," I said. And she was. Looking beyond the tubes and catheters that entangled her, she had fine sculpted features, unblemished skin, and delicate limbs.

Rachel nodded. "Shira is going to live," she said. "I can feel it inside of me."

Glancing again at the numbers on the oxygen monitor, I said nothing.

Every morning and every evening, Rachel told me she stood next to Shira's bed and prayed. She read from a pocket-sized prayer book, well worn from daily use. Years ago, she had inserted a prayer of her own. It spoke to what she personally sought from God:

Dear Lord,
Having been created in Your image
I am full of unrealized potential
The realization of which
Depends upon my acknowledgment of the potential,
My recognition of all the gifts from You with which I am
    endowed,
And my exploitation of the opportunities that lie open
    before me.
Please Lord, help me rise to meet the challenge.
Let me use those gifts for the benefit of all people.
Dear Lord,
For all that I am
And all that I can be
I thank You.

Never before did Rachel pray with such fervor for help to "rise to meet the challenge."

"What could cause a baby to have so many infections other than AIDS or SCID?" Rachel asked.

"I'm not sure. I'm not an expert in this area."

Rachel trained her amber eyes on mine. "I know you're not. Neither am I." But she explained she had been looking on the Web, and after learning about SCID and talking with affected families online, she was growing convinced that Shira had something else. "I think it's a nutritional problem causing her immune system to not function."

When Rachel had raised this idea, one of the residents mentioned reports of malnourished infants whose immune systems collapsed and who developed Pneumocystis. Several cases occurred in Tehran in the early 1960s, and in Vietnam between 1974 and 1976, when the country was in the final throes of war and food was scarce. But, the resident emphasized, while Shira was a slim baby, she did not fit the picture of severe malnutrition — essentially skin and bones — described in those reports. He dismissed the possibility.

I reiterated that I really didn't know enough to offer opinions about children. My understanding was that in adults, the immune system collapsed only in cases of extreme starvation.

"Since the consensus is atypical SCID," Rachel said, "there's talk of doing a bone marrow transplant."

Bone marrow transplantation is the most extreme measure in medicine to cure a disease. In essence, a person is given lethal doses of radiation and chemotherapy, doses that destroy the blood and immune system. Into this void, stem cells from the bone marrow of a compatible donor are seeded. These marrow stem cells have extraordinary biological potential. They grow and mature into all of the elements that have been destroyed: red blood cells, neutrophils, monocytes, platelets, T cells, and B cells. As the donor stem cells grow and mature, they begin to perform the chores that immune cells are programmed to do. Primary among these is to recognize foreign invaders, like microbes, and to purge them. That was precisely what Shira needed at this point: cells that could recognize, confront, and destroy Pneumocystis and Klebsiella and CMV and Candida and parainfluenzae.

Yet within this promise of biological resurrection was also the potential for biological rebellion. Immune cells are also programmed to recognize foreign tissues as well. The patient's new immune system can perceive the surrounding body as foreign. The transplanted T cells then go on the attack against vital organs like liver and skin and bowel. This is so-called graft-versus-host disease, because the grafted donor cells are pitted against the recipient host tissue. If the donor and patient are genetically closely matched, like siblings, graft-versus-host disease is mild. If they are genetically disparate, however, it can be severe. In that case, after a successful transplant, just when life seems to be restored, the very procedure that renewed life spirals into debility and death.

After I left, Rachel decided to proceed on parallel tracks. She would continue to pointedly question the diagnosis of SCID while helping prepare for its treatment. She e-mailed the agency in Vietnam and informed them of Shira's need for a donor. The next day, the officials replied that the birth mother had readily agreed to be genetically typed. Blood would be drawn to see how closely her cells matched Shira's. The doctors were pleased, but Rachel found little comfort in this reply.

Shira struggled to live. There were hours when she seemed to improve, her oxygen level rising. Then, for no apparent reason, she would deteriorate, the neon numbers on the oximeter plummeting. At each downward turn, Rachel felt trembling in her bones and the pace of her breathing quicken. She closed her eyes and prayed intensely, and the feelings gradually subsided.

Then, slowly over the course of the next week, Shira's oxygen level began to rise consistently. A chest x-ray showed that the ground glass was receding; a black penumbra surrounded the heart like the night sky around a pulsating star. "It looks like we can try to wean her," the resident said cautiously.

Rachel could not believe her ears. Weaning here did not refer to the breast, of course, but to the life support of the respirator. Every few hours, the ICU team dialed down the pressure and the level of oxygen. Then they waited, observed Shira, rechecked her blood oxygen. All the while, Rachel sang. She sang show tunes, Cole Porter, children's songs — playful, lilting, carefree melodies. And when Shira struggled, her chest heaving, her arms tensing, Rachel sang more forcefully.

After thirty-three days in the ICU, Shira was breathing room air through the respirator, without added pressure or added oxygen. The doctor extracted the tube from the baby's throat and the machine was shut off. The loud *woosh* of the respirator that had filled every moment of the day and night suddenly was gone. Rachel savored the silence. Her tears slowly collected as Shira comfortably inhaled and exhaled. Rachel had not broken. If a transplant was necessary, she would endure that harrowing treatment as well.

Shira was transferred to a regular hospital ward to await the bone marrow transplant. Rachel felt as if she had stepped through a looking glass into a different world. On the ward, she and Shira were largely left alone through the day. Nurses came on every shift to check vital signs. The dietician helped with liquid feedings, since Shira still was not able to feed by herself; the formula was passed via a tube that went down the esophagus and into the baby's stomach.

With quiet and time to think, Rachel investigated the manifold aspects of SCID, its genetics, diagnosis, and treatment outcomes. And as her knowledge grew, her sense solidified that her child did not have it. She clung to the idea that Shira had a nutritional deficiency, but was at a loss to say what nutrient might be missing. The right choice, Rachel realized, would be known only in retrospect.

Shira gained weight from the tube feedings. Her arms and legs filled out. Over the course of a week, her low-grade fevers abated, and some of the antibiotics were stopped. Rachel observed Shira's every move. There was an alertness to her eyes and, Rachel sensed, a deep hunger to encounter the world. So, to satisfy this imagined need, Rachel sang and talked to Shira about the wonders of God's creation, the sun and moon and stars, the earth with its forests and seas.

Not long after Labor Day, the bone marrow transplant team convened to discuss Shira's case. Three donors were found in the

National Marrow Donor Program Registry, and each was willing to give marrow stem cells for Shira's transplant. The blood of Shira's birth mother in Vietnam, when tested, proved less compatible than that of the unrelated registry donors. Graft-versus-host disease would likely occur even when using the registry donors, the doctors said.

When the resident from the transplant team came on his morning rounds, Rachel decided she had to meet her doubts head-on. "I want Shira's immune testing to be repeated."

The resident looked at her uncertainly. The medical team had come to appreciate the intelligence of Rachel's questions and the efforts she made to research topics. But what more could be learned from repeating the tests?

"Her T-cell numbers have increased," Rachel continued, struggling to maintain a calm, even voice.

"That happens sometimes with SCID, particularly after recovering from a major infection," the resident replied. "It's just expected fluctuation."

"But I don't think she has SCID," Rachel said, her voice rising. "I think . . . I think she has some nutritional deficiency."

The resident looked tiredly at Rachel. He had heard her idea countless times before. Rachel felt her pulse quicken.

"We know you think that, and of course we respect a parent's feelings. But Shira has a variant form of SCID. It's not a typical picture, as you know, but we've discussed it on rounds many times, with all the senior attendings."

Rachel paused and exhaled slowly. "I want . . . her blood . . . retested." She hammered each phrase as if it were a stubborn nail.

Pediatricians are acutely aware of the anguish that mothers and fathers experience when their children are gravely ill. The doctors are trained to respond compassionately even to what they view as misconceived demands born of desperation. In this instance, the resident took pains to explain to Rachel that Shira had already been tested and that retesting would require a laboratory researcher to needlessly put aside other work.

"If Shira is an atypical case," Rachel said, her tone softening, "then an ambitious scientist might be able to publish a paper on her. He could look more closely at her cells, get more data on why they don't function."

The resident considered this, and agreed that an immunologist he was friendly with would be sufficiently intrigued by Shira's case to study her cells. Yes, two sets of data would strengthen a manuscript submitted for publication in a prestigious journal. Rachel stopped her hands from trembling as she watched the resident draw the blood.

Shortly after dawn on the morning of September 11, 2001, the doctor from the transplant team knocked loudly on the door to Shira's room. Rachel quickly fixed her hair and tied the belt on her robe.

"I can't believe it!" the resident exclaimed. "I just can't believe it."

He handed Rachel a printout of the second set of blood tests done on Shira's immune system. One by one he went down the column with her:

> Total T cells: normal
> Helper T cells: normal
> Suppressor T cells: normal
> B cells: normal

"Not only are there normal numbers of all her cells," he continued, "but they're all working perfectly."

When Shira's T cells were exposed to microbes in a test tube, they immediately recognized them and went through the elegant choreography of their biological responses, coordinating scores of enzymes and releasing a repertoire of proteins that, in the body, amounts to a solid wall of immune defense.

"Shira doesn't have anything like SCID," the young doctor said, his face brightening. "She's normal, healthy, fine. I think she should be able to go home by the end of the week."

Rachel closed her eyes. Her heart beat with such force that she felt it would burst through her chest.

God, You answered my prayer.

Shira received her morning feeding through the tube, and then Rachel went to the end of the hospital corridor to a pay phone. She called one of her closest friends from her congregation and told her the news.

"It's so wonderful," her friend exclaimed. But then there was a long silence.

Rachel wondered what was wrong.

"Turn on your TV."

Rachel stood frozen in the room and felt as if her heart, so full of joy, were being torn. At the moment she celebrated Shira's restored life, thousands were likely dead in the attack on the World Trade Center. *How can I rejoice when God's creatures are dying?*

Forty-five days after Rachel and Shira went to the Children's Hospital ER, mother and daughter left for home. It was Friday, just hours before the onset of the Sabbath. When Rachel turned the key and entered her apartment in Brookline, she could smell the meal left by friends. Two candles stood ready to be lit, two fresh challahs ready to be savored. Rachel held Shira after lighting the candles. The soft glow of the flames played off her daughter's face. It was the day of rest and of peace, the day when all woes were meant to cease, the day that Rachel had not truly had for more than six weeks.

At each step, Rachel had not been sure whether she would find the strength she needed to endure, and the courage to question.

Silently, she again thanked God for creating all human beings with such remarkable reservoirs of resilience. She thought how the Sabbath was the time when these reservoirs were refilled. She prayed that during this first Sabbath after 9/11 her country would find the strength and courage to defend itself and to care, with a full heart, for the families who had lost loved ones.

Rachel's reverie was broken by Shira fussing in her arms. It was time for her feeding, time to replenish whatever nutrients must have been missing in the food in the orphanage in Vietnam that caused her immune deficiency. "Enjoy, sweet thing. Enjoy," Rachel said as the formula flowed in.

In May 2002 in Boston, Shira's case was presented at a clinical conference at Children's Hospital. Its purpose was to educate the staff about a diagnosis that had not been seriously considered, and if not made, could have led to a disastrous bone marrow transplant. The young doctor leading the conference, and the ICU and bone marrow transplant teams, of course knew the outcome of Shira's case. But the larger audience did not. So her story was presented from the start, as if each doctor listening had been at the bedside and required to make decisions from the first harrowing moments in the ER.

"What is your differential diagnosis?" the young doctor asked the audience. "List the possible causes for this set of signs and symptoms in our patient." The consensus was SCID.

Then, in a dramatic flourish, a slide was projected on a large screen:

PATIENT DID NOT HAVE SCID.

The doctor presenting the case switched to the next slide, which detailed how malnutrition is a leading cause of immune deficiency worldwide. The most common form of malnutrition and immune deficiency in poor countries is due to the lack of adequate protein, as in severe starvation. This did not seem to be the cause in Shira's case, since her muscles were well formed. But during the intervening months since her discharge, the team of doctors had found scientific articles that reported on how the deficiency of even a single vitamin could impair immune function. Other articles reported on deficiencies of metals like zinc, iron, and magnesium in children that resulted in decreases in T-cell numbers and T-cell function. These were all very rare but well-documented instances. Still, no one could say for sure what accounted for Shira's immune deficiency.

In the stylized speech of the clinical world, the presenter brought the audience up to date: "Patient discussed has been followed since discharge, and her immune function remains normal. The patient is growing well and meeting milestones."

The kind of conference where Shira Stein's case was discussed occurs at every teaching hospital in the country. And in community hospitals that do not have medical students or interns, there are similar forums where intriguing and unusual clinical problems are discussed among the senior staff. These conferences, whether at the academic centers or community institutions, are of great value in educating even the most experienced doctors about arcane and important disorders. But what is generally lacking at the conferences is an in-depth examination of why the diagnosis was missed — specifically, what cognitive errors occurred and how they could have been remedied. There is rarely an explicit dissection of which heuristics were used and where they fell apart.

Understanding the medical context in which Shira Stein was treated is essential to identifying the cognitive biases that almost had her undergo a debilitating, perhaps fatal bone marrow transplant. As Rachel Stein repeatedly told me, and as I well know (because Children's Hospital, by way of full disclosure, saved the life of my oldest child), the institution is among the very best in the world in pediatric care. The physicians there have considerable expertise in SCID and other genetic abnormalities that cause severe immunodeficiency. Laboratories at the hospital study how deranged genes paralyze T cells and other key components of immune defense. Clinicians have refined treatment protocols to administer standard and experimental medications and to maximize success in restoring the body's immunity. Since many cases of SCID are routinely diagnosed and treated at the institution, not only the senior attendings but the interns and residents as well are thoroughly familiar with the disorder.

Because of this expertise and familiarity, a "prototype" SCID child is established in the minds of the staff. And there is a natural cognitive tendency to zero in on certain characteristics of a patient like Shira and match them to the prototype. Familiarity breeds conclusions and sometimes a certain degree of contempt for alternatives. A maxim that I repeatedly heard during my training was "If it looks like a duck, walks like a duck, and quacks like a duck, then guess what? It's a duck." But it isn't always a duck.

Physicians should caution themselves to be not so ready to match a patient's symptoms and clinical findings against their mental templates or clinical prototypes. This is not easy. In medical school, and later during residency training, the emphasis is on learning the typical picture of a certain disorder, whether it is a peptic ulcer or a migraine or a kidney stone. Seemingly unusual or atypical presentations often get short shrift. "Common things are common" is another cliché that was drilled into me during my training. Another echoing maxim on rounds: "When you hear hoofbeats, think about horses, not zebras."

Rachel Stein, trawling through the long list of causes of Pneumocystis pneumonia, found a zebra. A nutritional deficiency can cause impaired immune defense and provide fertile ground for this infection. With his characteristic élan, Pat Croskerry, at Dalhousie University in Halifax, has coined the phrase "zebra retreat" to describe a doctor's shying away from a rare diagnosis. Powerful forces in modern medicine discourage hunting for them. Often the laboratory tests and procedures needed to pin down an arcane diagnosis are hard to perform, highly specialized, and expensive. In an era of cost containment, when insurers and managed care plans scrutinize how much physicians spend on any one patient, doctors have a strong disincentive to pursue ideas that are "out there." In fact, some physicians are called to account for ordering too many tests because they may turn up only one correct diagnosis out of twenty-five, fifty, a hundred, or five hundred, and because the money would be better spent on something else. Unless, of course, that one zebra case turned out to be the bean counter's own child.

To add to that pressure, doctors who hunt zebras are often ridiculed by their peers for being obsessed with the esoteric while ignoring the mainstream. Zebra hunters are said to be showoffs. As an intern on rounds, I often heard senior residents call them "flamers."

There is yet another psychological reason for a physician's "zebra retreat." Because a doctor usually lacks personal experience with the very arcane case, knowing about it only from his reading or a single encounter over years of work, he often lacks the courage of his convictions. He is uncertain of how far to press the hunt.

Participants in the conference on Shira Stein's case at Children's Hospital listed many nutritional inadequacies that result in immune deficiency. I would wager that very few on the staff would know how to identify them. I admit that I don't; I would have to find a specialist or look up the answers, which are not readily available in medical textbooks. Furthermore, aside from relatively common dietary deficiencies — lack of vitamin B_{12} causing pernicious anemia, or insufficient vitamin C giving rise to scurvy — little is known about the effects of nutrition on many bodily functions. This absence of general clinical knowledge prompted physicians to dismiss Rachel Stein's repeated suggestions that her daughter might be lacking some nutrient. Why pursue such a far-out and vague idea? Shira didn't fit the prototype of the malnourished child.

In addition to forming mental prototypes and retreating from zebras, Shira's doctors made a third cognitive mistake, called "diagnosis momentum." Once a particular diagnosis becomes fixed in a physician's mind, despite incomplete evidence — or, in Shira's case, discrepancies in evidence, like the rising T-cell numbers and the rarity of SCID among girls — the first doctor passes on his diagnosis to his peers or subordinates. This, of course, plagued Anne Dodge for fifteen years. Here, the ICU attending became convinced that Shira had SCID. This powerful belief was passed on to his interns and residents and then to the bone marrow transplant team when Shira was moved out of the ICU. Every morning on rounds when Shira's case was reviewed, the opening statement was "Shira Stein, a Vietnamese infant girl with an immune deficiency disorder consistent with SCID . . ." Diagnosis momentum, like a boulder rolling down a mountain, gains enough force to crush anything in its way.

Rachel Stein was not an expert in cognitive psychology and did not study errors in medical decision-making. She was a desperate and frightened mother. But she found the strength to educate herself about her child's plight. And when she found inconsistencies in the many doctors' reasoning, she politely but persistently refused to be deterred. She diverted the boulder.

I have made the same cognitive errors that Shira's doctors did, despite all my training and all my good intentions. When all the pieces of the clinical puzzle did not fit tightly together, I moved some of those that didn't to the side. I made faulty assumptions, seeking to make an undefined condition conform to a well-defined prototype, in order to offer a familiar treatment.

One year after Rachel got word from the adoption agency that an infant awaited her in Vietnam, I took my daughter Emily, then twelve years old, to visit Rachel and Shira. They live on a shaded street in an apartment on a lower floor of an old stone building. I had seen them in synagogue a few times, and commented on how healthy and robust Shira looked. But Rachel and I had not discussed her story in depth. I told Rachel that I was trying to understand how she had been able to think clearly and challenge the many doctors' logic.

She shook her head as she listened. Then she explained how she saw the world: "God is like a best friend for me." A best friend. A friend you can always call upon. A friend who never deserts you. A friend who offers wisdom and resources without question. A friend you can bounce ideas off of with complete trust in his integrity. A friend you can reveal feelings to without fear that he might exploit your vulnerability.

This was the friend who steadied her time and again through the tempest of Shira's illness. This was the friend who held her back from breaking. This was the friend who helped Rachel think clearly, assimilate information, ask questions when she spoke with her sister in Los Angeles and with the many doctors and nurses caring for Shira. Drawing strength and inspiration from this friend, Rachel used all of her intellectual, social, and spiritual resources to press the request that ultimately led to the correct diagnosis.

Typically, my patients look to their faith for solace during a trying time. Some pray for God's intervention, believing as many do that there are moments when His grace enters human lives in a direct and personal way. They pray for a miracle, for God to steer events away from debility or death. Others simply ask for the strength to endure. After hearing Rachel's story, I saw a third way in which faith can function.

Those who read the Bible, cynics say, are merely reading fairy tales. But astute psychologists counter that whatever the reader believes about the literal truth of Scripture, the Bible offers profound insights into human character. No one in its stories, despite his knowledge and power, and despite his good intentions, is perfect, infallible. Everyone is flawed at some time, in thought or in deed, from Abraham to Moses to the Apostles.

In their *Handbook of Religion and Health*, Koenig, Larson, and McCullough review the arguments, pro and con, about how faith influences the ill. One school of thought holds that religion makes people passive, accepting the course of events as God's will. Such patients, these critics assert, relegate their personal responsibility for choices and action to an imagined force outside themselves, thus further infantilizing their part in an already overly paternalistic relationship with their physicians. This view is a corollary of Karl Marx's famous assertion that religion "is the opium of the people," a pacifier of both the individual and the society. For Rachel it was quite the opposite: faith can make a person a productive partner in the uncertain world of medicine. Faith, a well-recognized source of solace, of strength to endure, can also give people the courage to recognize uncertainty, acknowledge not only their own fallibility but also their physicians', and thereby contribute to the search for solutions.

Of course, individuals for whom faith is not a cornerstone can find the resilience to endure and sustain the presence of mind to search for information and parse the logic of their doctors. They often employ strategies that mirror those of religious people. Instead of "praying on" a problem, they shift their mind to quietly contemplate the complexities of an issue. While Rachel Stein looked to God as her best friend, a trusted ally, agnostics and atheists recruit family or colleagues into this role. All of us — people of faith or not — can emulate Rachel Stein when we enter our doctor's mind seeking gaps in his analysis, and pressing for answers that might fill those gaps.

CHAPTER 6

The Uncertainty of the Expert

M OST PEOPLE BELIEVE that a child is rarely born with a malformed heart; in fact, congenital cardiac abnormalities occur at the rate of 8 per 1,000 live births. More than 30,000 such infants are delivered each year in the United States. If the baby can survive beyond twelve months, he or she has an 80 percent chance of entering adulthood. Today, about one million adults in America are living with congenital heart disease. This gratifying statistic is the result of the work of pediatric cardiologists and cardiac surgeons who diagnose and repair malformations of the heart and great vessels, like the aorta. The greatest challenge to these physicians is the extraordinary diversity of abnormalities that they encounter. Even when uncertain, they are often forced to create solutions on the spot, in the ICU or the OR. What kind of doctor is attracted to a specialty that demands repeated innovation, a specialty where the treatment of many cases is an experiment of one?

Dr. James Lock is the chief of cardiology at Boston's Children's Hospital. In his early fifties, Lock is a tall, thin man with thick black hair and aviator glasses. He seems to be in constant motion. As I set up my tape recorder for an interview, he stretched out in his chair, put his feet, shod in cross-trainers, on top of his desk, and then began shifting position, turning his head, crossing and uncrossing his legs, moving his hands up and down the sides of the chair. Lock grew up in a small town in rural Ohio. Nobody in his family had ever gone to college. Because he is a renowned inventor of several cardiac devices, I assumed that he was a tinkerer in his youth. I was wrong. "My brother and father were the ones who fixed cars," Lock said. "I wasn't with them in the garage. I was in my room, reading." Lock explained that for lower-middle-class people, becoming a doctor was the way to get out.

But his escape via a profession was not always certain. He was suspended from school in the second grade and expelled in the sixth. "Both times the principal brought in a psychiatrist from the big city," meaning Akron. The psychiatrist seemed to recognize Lock's potential despite his subpar performance. "The psychiatrist rescued me by suggesting that I be advanced into eighth grade." I commented on the sweep of his head and moving limbs, and suggested that these days the psychiatrist may have diagnosed him with ADHD and prescribed Ritalin. "I surely would have been given something," Lock said and laughed. Lock was a National Merit Scholar, and at the age of fifteen he went to college at Case Western Reserve, then on to medical school at Stanford. "I went to the places where I got a scholarship. It was all about getting a full ride.

"When I was holed up in my room," Lock went on, "I read Arthur Conan Doyle over and over and over again. Sherlock Holmes was all about observation and deduction. So I spent a lot of time thinking about how people make observations and how they make deductions." Arthur Ignatius Conan Doyle was born in 1859 in Edinburgh, Scotland, into a struggling Irish-Catholic family. Wealthy relatives provided for his education at a Jesuit boarding school in England, which he loathed. Looking back on his school days, Doyle wrote, "Perhaps, it was good for me that the times were hard, for I was wild, full-blooded and a trifle reckless. But the situation called for energy and application so that one was bound to try to meet it." Although many members of the family were artists, Conan Doyle chose medicine, and returned from England to Edinburgh for his studies.

In March 1886, Conan Doyle began the novel that would make his fame. Published a year later in *Beeton's Christmas Annual* under the title "A Study in Scarlet," it featured a detective named Sherlock Holmes and his colleague, Dr. Watson. Conan Doyle transposed his fascination with the way physicians observe and make deductions in their search for a clinical diagnosis to another type of sleuthing.

As World War I approached, Conan Doyle, then in his fifties, was frustrated that he could not enlist as a soldier. So he peppered the War Office with ideas and suggestions for inventions that he believed could save British lives. Concerned about a future blockade by enemy submarines, he offered as a solution a tunnel under the English Channel that would connect the southern coast of England with France. The naval experts dismissed this as a Jules Verne fantasy. He also imagined inflatable rubber belts and inflatable lifeboats to save drowning sailors, as well as body armor for the infantry. Again his suggestions were dismissed.

Like his hero Holmes, James Lock ponders the nature and interpretation of available evidence and tries to imagine a better future. "I keep an ongoing tap," he said, "on how I know what I know." Lock stopped talking. His head moved back and forth, like a radar antenna scanning the horizon. After several arcs, he seemed to locate his thoughts and spoke again. "Epistemology, the nature of knowing, is key in my field. What we know is based on only a modest level of understanding. If you carry that truth around with you, you are instantaneously ready to challenge what you think you know the minute you see anything that suggests it might not be right.

"Most of what we do in pediatric cardiology, we make up. In fact, a fraction of what is routinely done today in my specialty, I made up," Lock said with a grin. That is because children often have such unique problems with their hearts that there is little precedent. But, Lock continued, "you simply have to do something. The big problem is that most people assume that once it's made up, it's actually real. Especially the people who make it up themselves. Then they think it came straight from God."

"Couldn't the admission that a certain practice is made up paralyze a clinician?" I asked.

"Not everyone in medicine can be constantly making calculations about the value of the information. You'd go crazy. But if you are in a subspecialty field, as you train, you not only need to know what people know, but how they know it. You have to regularly question everything and everyone."

Ironically, James Lock learned the seminal lesson about the care of children with malformed hearts from the case of a child born with a normal one. Holly Clark was a four-year-old in Minnesota with dark brown eyes and long brown braids. One spring morning she told her mother that she didn't feel good. Mrs. Clark felt her forehead and then reached for a thermometer. Holly's temperature was 100.5° F. A virus was going through the nursery school class. Mrs. Clark gave Holly some liquid Tylenol for her fever and put her to bed. By the next day, she was breathing in short, forced gasps, and her skin had a dusky color. Mrs. Clark drove Holly to the ER at a local hospital affiliated with the University of Minnesota Medical School.

The ER doctor found that when Holly took in a deep breath, her blood pressure fell sharply. A chest x-ray showed that the normal contours of her heart were distorted. Instead of the usual boot shape, the heart had a globular appearance, like a water balloon suspended in the chest. Holly was never seriously ill before, only the occasional runny nose or upset stomach, and as far as Mrs. Clark knew, her daughter's heart and lungs always had been normal. The doctor performed an EKG that showed reduced electrical voltage. "It's a textbook diagnosis," he told Mrs. Clark, "cardiac tamponade." Cardiac tamponade means that fluid had accumulated around the heart and was compressing it. This can occur as a result of swelling of the tissue from a viral infection. The buildup of fluid grips the heart like a fist and prevents much blood from entering the organ or exiting to the body. Holly could go into shock if the fluid was not removed.

An attending pediatric cardiologist was called to the ER. He explained to Holly's mother how he would drain the fluid from around the heart. First he would use a large-bore needle to penetrate the pericardium, the fibrous sac that surrounds the heart; then he would employ a syringe to draw off the liquid. Once the fluid was drained from under the pericardium, the heart would pump unhindered and Holly's circulation would be restored.

"Where do you stick the needle?" Lock asked. We were sitting in his office, and he was telling me about this case from his training some thirty years earlier.

I quickly replied, "Subxiphoid," meaning that the needle was inserted below the xiphoid, the tail of cartilage that extends from the lower end of the breastbone. And, I continued, after inserting the needle below the xiphoid, you angle it up toward the right collarbone and advance until you penetrate the pericardium.

As the young James Lock stood next to the attending cardiologist, learning the procedure, that was exactly what the cardiologist said would be done. The senior doctor first palpated the child's breastbone and then ran his fingertips down to the pliant cartilage that forms the xiphoid. At the lower tip of the xiphoid, he cleaned the skin with an antiseptic and applied a local anesthetic. Then he took the syringe with a large-bore needle attached to an EKG lead. He punctured the skin and a halo of blood formed around the needle's shaft. He moved the needle up under the xiphoid, advancing slowly until he felt the tip meet the firm fibrous sac, the pericardium. The doctor waited a moment and then pushed deeper. The sac gave way.

"Why do you stick the needle under the xiphoid?" Lock asked.

I paused. "Because that was how my teachers taught me in my training."

"And why do you think your teachers taught you the way they did?" Lock asked. "Because that's how *they* were taught."

When the cardiologist pulled back on the plunger of the syringe, he met resistance; straw-colored fluid should have come rushing out, but instead the plunger would not budge. Sometimes, the cardiologist said to Lock, the fluid beneath the pericardium is so thick with protein and inflammatory debris that it is difficult to drain even through a large-bore needle.

The cardiologist cautiously moved the needle a few millimeters deeper, thinking he might reach a less thick collection of fluid. He pulled back on the syringe. Bright red blood gushed in. The cardiologist froze, the needle still in Holly's chest.

"She almost died," Lock recounted. "The needle went right into her heart muscle. It was a catastrophe. She needed emergency surgery." Although the cardiologist had advanced the needle only a short distance, it turned out that there was almost no fluid in that area beneath the pericardium. Nearly all of the fluid had accumulated off to the side.

Lock was shaken by the event. He questioned everyone he could about why the procedure was done this way, and he received the same answer that I had given him, that it was handed down by mentors. "I looked at the medical literature and dug back into the 1920s," Lock told me. "It turned out that one of the earliest reports on how to drain fluid came from a woman physician. Her first attempt was done by sticking the needle through the back, and was a success." At the time, Lock continued, the only way to know whether there was fluid was by percussing the heart, tapping one's fingers over the chest and listening to the dull sound from fluid that contrasted with the high notes from air that filled the lungs.

After the successful report of drainage via the back in the 1920s, the approach was widely adopted. But complications soon ensued. The coronary arteries run over the surface of the heart muscle, and sticking a needle through the back sometimes punctured those vessels. "So cardiologists looked for the part of the heart where you have the smallest chance of meeting a coronary artery," Lock explained, "and that turned out to be under the xiphoid."

Lock returned to the lesson of Holly Clark. "Now I teach my trainees not to go by rote under the xiphoid. We should always go where the fluid is. We follow Sutton's law." Sutton's law is named after the 1930s Brooklyn bank robber Willie Sutton, who robbed bank after bank and accumulated a fortune before he was captured. When Sutton was brought into court, the judge asked him why he robbed banks. "Because that's where the money is," he answered. (The tale is probably apocryphal: the reply attributed to Sutton likely was made up by a reporter at the trial to color his story. But the term "Sutton's law" has stuck.) Lock helped change the way the procedure is done. Now an ultrasound is always performed first, to visualize the fluid around the heart, and a small needle is inserted under ultrasound guidance.

The heart is a pump with four chambers, two on the right and two on the left. Each upper chamber is called an atrium, from the Latin denoting an "entry," and each lower chamber a ventricle, also from Latin, for "belly," since it is somewhat oval in shape. Blood depleted of oxygen returns from the body to the right

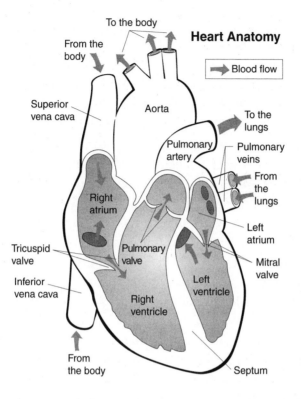

atrium; it moves from this chamber into the right ventricle. The right ventricle pumps the blood out through the pulmonary valve into the pulmonary artery to the lungs. In the lungs, the blood is recharged with fresh oxygen, and waste products like carbon dioxide are released. The refreshed blood returns from the lungs via the pulmonary veins to the left atrium; the valve that separates the left atrium from the left ventricle reminded early anatomists of a bishop's miter, so they named it the mitral valve. Once the blood crosses the mitral valve, it enters the left ventricle. The left ventricle is much thicker than the right ventricle. Its thick muscle contracts and generates high pressure to pump the blood across the aortic valve into the aorta, the large artery that carries it to all parts of the body.

One of the most common congenital abnormalities of the heart is a hole between the two upper chambers, between the right atrium and the left atrium. Since the pressure in the left side of the heart is higher than in the right, blood will flow from the left atrium through the hole into the right atrium. This aberrant blood flow is called a shunt and can overload the right side of the heart, leading to heart failure and other complications. Lock told me that doctors send children for surgery to close these holes if there is a two-to-one shunt, meaning that twice as much blood flows through the right side of the heart than the left.

"Do you know where that two-to-one number came from?" Lock asked. I imagined it was from careful clinical studies of children with the hole. "You would think so. But you'd be wrong. At a medical meeting in the 1960s, a pediatrician presented the question 'When should the hole be closed?' to a group of cardiologists. There was a heated debate about how much shunting required a surgical fix. So the meeting organizers, out of desperation, took a vote. Some voted for a lower number, some for a higher number. The median ended up being two-to-one. This was published in the *American Journal of Cardiology.* So now all textbooks have as the *truth* that you should close a hole when the shunt is two-to-one. But," Lock continued, "children can have a two-to-one shunt and still have a good chance of being healthy and never needing any specific treatment. Many children with two-to-one shunts undergo surgery and probably don't need the operation.

"Why are we still making it up? Because you can't do the clinical study to really find out. You would have to randomize five hundred kids to closure versus nonclosure. It would take forty years to do it." And there are ethical and moral constraints to such a study: "You can't do the kinds of studies in human beings that you can do in cars. You can't crash test a human being," Lock said. So you have to deduce answers from the data on hand, limited though such data may be.

In Lock's specialty a keen spatial sense is essential to deducing those answers. "You need to be able to look at a single-plane image and reconstruct it in three dimensions almost instantaneously." For example, during a cardiac catheterization, the cardiologist manipulates the catheter through the child's blood vessels and into his heart. The catheter appears as a thin white line on a flat monitor screen next to the table. It can be difficult in such a two-dimensional projection to know the catheter's position. "The combination of how your hand moves and what the image looks like will tell you whether the catheter is pointed toward you or away. I can tell where it is even if my hand is off the catheter. Knowing in which direction you are going shouldn't be something you need to think about."

Lock spoke about "physical genius," the kind of genius displayed by stellar athletes who can anticipate exactly where the ball is headed. Growing up, Lock idolized baseball players who could connect with a breaking curve ball and hit it out of the park; he worshiped wide receivers who could run without looking back and place themselves within reach of a spiraling football. "You need to process what you see very quickly and act on the information in a split second," Lock said, "because the heart is beating. It's not like you can stop the child's heart and ponder. Once you are inside of a kid's heart with a catheter, you have an enormous amount you have to accomplish, and there is a great deal of risk if what you do is not done quickly and well."

Recent studies contradict the popular notion that doctors who perform challenging procedures, like Lock, are "born with good hands," that they have innate talent in manual dexterity. Of course, if you are a complete klutz, manipulating instruments in a child's heart would not be your ideal career path. But this research on physician performance of procedures shows that "visual-spatial" ability, meaning the capacity to see in your mind the contours of the blood vessel or the organ, rather than the nimbleness of your fingers, is paramount. Although at the beginning of training there are differences among doctors in their visual-spatial ability, as Geoffrey Norman, a researcher at McMaster University in Ontario, has emphasized, this ability can be enhanced to the expert level by repeated practice and regular feedback about success and error in technique.

Tom and Helen O'Connell had eagerly anticipated the birth of their first child. Tom was a gym teacher in a local Catholic high school, and Helen was an accountant. Every evening they practiced breathing techniques from their birthing class. Tom joked that being a coach was natural for him. They knew from the ultrasound that it was a boy, and decorated the baby's room with Red Sox pennants and a New England Patriots football.

Helen's labor took eight hours and went smoothly until the baby emerged, blue and gasping. The obstetrician and nurse quickly removed a thick brown liquid from his mouth. If there is distress during the birth, the infant defecates this liquid fetal stool, called meconium, and breathes it in during the struggle.

"Even after they aspirated the meconium, the kid was extremely blue," Lock told me. Baby O'Connell was rushed to the cardiac ICU, but despite every measure, the doctors were unable to get enough oxygen into his system. "He had a cardiac arrest within the first thirty minutes of life, so they crashed onto ECMO," Lock recounted. Again, ECMO stands for extracorporeal membrane oxygenation, the special heart-lung machine used only in the most dire circumstances. Shira Stein was headed for ECMO until she rallied. But unlike in Shira's case, there was no surprise turnaround. A large catheter was placed into Baby O'Connell's neck. The venous blood from his body, depleted of oxygen, would ordinarily go to the right side of the heart and be pumped to the lungs where it receives oxygen, but instead the spent blood entered the ECMO machine. Baby O'Connell's depleted blood passed over a broad porous membrane that allows the release of toxic wastes and carbon dioxide and the entry of much-needed oxygen. A pump moved his freshly oxygenated blood into a second catheter in his neck; this entered his aorta, and from his aorta the blood reached the tissues of his body.

ECMO can have dangerous side effects. The large catheters inserted in the baby's neck can provide a fertile field for infection, resulting in fatal sepsis. Friction from the pump and at the membrane surface can destroy fragile blood platelets, predisposing him to life-threatening hemorrhage. It was urgent to decipher his problem and get him off ECMO. But each time the doctors tried to detach Baby O'Connell from ECMO and give him oxygen via a respirator, they failed. Something was seriously wrong. But no one could pinpoint the precise problem.

In normal circulation, as we've seen, spent blood returns from the tissues and enters the right atrium, which pumps it into the right ventricle. The right ventricle then pumps the blood through the pulmonary arteries to the lungs, where fresh oxygen enters and toxic carbon dioxide is released. The newly oxygenated blood returns from the lungs via the pulmonary veins to the left atrium and then the left ventricle. The left ventricle pumps the oxygen-rich blood into the aorta and then through the arteries to the body.

"In a newborn, one cause of being very blue, indicating scant oxygen in the tissues," Lock explained, "is that the pulmonary veins are connected incorrectly — they go somewhere other than the left atrium, or they're blocked for some reason." In such cases, the oxygen-rich blood leaving the lungs can't enter the left heart and be pumped to the body. There is a backup in the system. "You get a blue child. Fluid seeps into his lungs — pulmonary edema."

Baby O'Connell was taken to the cardiac lab for further study. The lab has bright overhead lights, a movable table, a fluoroscope to obtain real-time x-rays. Catheters were threaded into his heart and vessels, and computerized monitors displayed their pressures. Dye was injected into the pulmonary artery. The dye should have passed through the artery into his lungs, then out via the pulmonary veins, and entered the left atrium. "Nothing is going through to the heart," Lock observed. Somewhere, there was an obstruction.

A catheter with a tiny balloon at its end was snaked into the pulmonary artery and inflated. The balloon opened up the artery. Again dye was injected. This time, the dye went through the pulmonary artery into the lungs and entered the pulmonary veins. An image appeared on the fluoroscopic screen that resembled the trunks of a tree with tapering branches. But the tree and its branches seemed suspended in the chest. "The pulmonary veins don't go anywhere," Lock said. "They don't connect to the left heart. They just stop."

For a long moment, there was silence. None of the doctors or nurses could figure out the path of Baby O'Connell's vessels. Lock moved his head back and forth in its radar sweep. Then he stopped. He pointed to a trickle of dye that had somehow made its way into the inferior vena cava, the large vessel that brings blood from the lower part of the body into the right heart. It made no sense: Why would a whiff of dye injected into the arteries of the lungs end up in the belly? "That's what he is trying to live on before he dies," Lock said, referring to the trickle. Again, silence filled the room. It seemed the baby would be lost.

"What doesn't belong here?" Lock asked himself. When he confronts an unknown, he thinks out loud. He manipulated the computer keyboard and called up the stored images onto the screen from the previous injections of dye. He flashed each in succession. No new clues. Then, with a rapid jerk of his arm, he pointed to a thin white line over the right side of the baby's chest. "What's that?" he demanded. No one on the team had any idea.

Lock traced the mysterious line on the screen, moving backward from the baby's chest, down to a tangle of images that represented the tubes and catheters that the doctors had inserted. "It's the umbilical catheter in the umbilical vein!" Lock yelled out. A catheter had been placed in the umbilical vessel that originally connected the mother to the fetus. "But where is that line ending now?" Lock asked. After a few seconds of intense concentration, he announced, "It's in the pulmonary vein!" A vessel in the abdomen was aberrantly connected to a vessel in the chest.

Lock and his colleagues had never encountered a case like this. Using the catheter in the umbilical vessel as a thread, he began to unravel the bizarre connections of Baby O'Connell's anatomy: the umbilical vein connected to the large portal vein in the child's belly, and the portal vein somehow was connected to the pulmonary vein in the chest. "When you have never seen anything before," Lock said to the team, "it becomes an opportunity to do something no one has ever done.

"Let's try to open up the pulmonary veins using the umbilical catheter." Lock took a long guide wire that resembled a straightened coat hanger. He threaded the wire through the umbilical catheter, up through the abdomen, into the chest and the pulmonary vein. Following this wire, Lock inserted a catheter with a balloon on its end. He inflated the balloon and expanded the pulmonary vein; then he injected dye. The dye flowed from the pulmonary vein in the chest into the portal vein in the belly and then began to slowly work its way back up into the baby's chest and into his heart.

"Why is it still only a slow trickle?" Lock asked. There must be a second obstruction. Lock located another vessel branching off the portal vein. He expanded this second vessel with a balloon catheter and threaded two metal stent devices and wedged them into the opening. He paused and moved a catheter into the pulmonary artery of the lungs and injected dye. "Look at the blood blasting out!" he exclaimed. Now blood flowed down from the pulmonary vein in the chest to the portal vein in the abdomen, then up via the stented vessel into the left side of the heart. Lock had created a path to get oxygen-rich blood from the lungs to the left side of the heart and out to the baby's tissues.

Baby O'Connell spent three more days on ECMO as his body gradually adapted to a jury-rigged circulation. Then the doctors placed him on a respirator; his oxygen levels held.

A few days later, I went to visit Baby O'Connell in the cardiac ICU with Jim Lock. The O'Connells warmly greeted him. Lock reviewed with them the procedures he had performed and emphasized they were temporary measures, but effective for now. Soon Baby O'Connell would undergo surgery to fully repair his circulation.

As we walked out of the ICU, I asked Lock how he thinks through these kinds of conundrums.

"When a case first arrives," he told me, "I don't want to hear anyone else's diagnosis. I look at the primary data." He avoids all biases or preconceptions; he tries to identify the key clinical features — pattern recognition — and frame the situation himself. "In this instance, the shadow just didn't belong there," he said, referring to the white line of the umbilical catheter. While everyone was concentrating on what he termed "the main event" — the blocked pulmonary vessels — he said he was able to see the entire picture at once, integrating each component into a coherent whole. And when one piece does not fit, he seizes on it as the key to unlock the mystery. "It's like that game Where's Waldo?" he said.

The surgery was a success. Baby O'Connell's pulmonary vein was attached to the back wall of his left atrium, so there was a robust flow of oxygen-rich blood from the lungs to the left heart, which pumped it out to the aorta. He'll be carefully monitored, and he may need further surgery as he grows, but there was no reason, Lock said, that he couldn't lead a normal life.

A week after we saw Baby O'Connell, I asked Lock about the times when his judgment was off target. "The mistakes that I remember . . . ," he began, and then stopped in midsentence. I was struck by his pause. Studies show that most physicians are unaware of their cognitive errors. Lock's phrasing acknowledged this: there likely were instances when his judgment was wrong but he was yet to learn of them. Then he picked up the thread of his thoughts. "All my mistakes have the same thing in common."

Lock took a blank sheet of paper and began to rapidly sketch the outlines of the heart, its chambers and valves. There was a disorder called "common AV canal," he said, where the wall between the left and right sides of the heart does not fully form. This most often occurs in children with Down syndrome. "The central part of the heart is missing, and this can include the lower wall between the atria, part of the mitral valve and part of the tricuspid valve, and the upper wall between the ventricles — all don't form." Some of these children also have aortic stenosis, Lock explained, meaning partial closure of the aortic valve, or co-arctation of the aorta, meaning that the large vessel is narrowed. "When this happens, the left ventricle can be very small."

The question that faced pediatric cardiologists was whether a baby's left ventricle was large enough for the child to undergo repair of the malformed wall and survive the procedure. When Lock was in his thirties, he reasoned that the decision to operate or not should be based on how much oxygen was in the blood leaving the heart. "I was young and made the argument at a national meeting," he said. "Everyone believed me. It was an exercise in pure logic, an exercise that was, at some level, unassailable." Lock reasoned that if the oxygen level in the blood pumped into the aorta was within normal range, then the left ventricle was sufficiently well formed to receive oxygenated blood from the lungs and pump it out to the body; this showed that enough heart muscle existed to allow recovery after a wall repair. The high oxygen level, Lock also deduced, meant that there was no significant shunting of blood from the right ventricle, meaning the left ventricle was strong enough to keep pressures high on the left side of the heart. "On the face of it, it was intellectually correct. It just happens to be wrong."

It turned out that the oxygen content in the blood leaving the baby's heart could be nearly normal even when a significant amount of blood, some 20 percent, was shunted from the right ventricle. "Impeccable logic," Lock said, "doesn't always suffice. My mistake was that I reasoned from first principles when there was no prior experience. I turned out to be wrong because there are variables that you can't factor in until you actually do it. And you make the wrong recommendation, and the patient doesn't survive.

"I didn't leave enough room for what seems like minor effects," Lock elaborated, "the small fluctuations in oxygen levels, which might amount to one or two or three percent but actually can signal major problems in the heart."

Lock recalled a second example of this type of mistake, of relying on strict logic to answer a clinical question in the absence of empirical data. "I said there were patients with severe narrowing of the mitral valve who would always be better if the hole between the left and right atrium were closed. I reasoned that the body would get more blood if the hole was closed. You would get high enough pressure to fill the left ventricle through the narrowed mitral valve." To translate what Lock was saying: you want to maximize the pressure in the left atrium to force as much blood as possible through a narrowed mitral valve into the left ventricle, so the left ventricle can pump adequate amounts of blood out to the body. "It has to be right, correct?" Lock asked. I nodded in agreement. "It is very sound logic. But it's wrong."

After having surgery to close the hole, some children got sicker. This was ultimately found to result from an unexpected ripple effect: even modest increases in pressure in the left atrium rippled back and caused higher pressure in the vessels of the lungs, or pulmonary hypertension. The right heart, forced to pump against this higher pressure, weakened. "These children developed right-heart failure, and clinically they became worse," Lock said. Again, what seemed to be a rational approach resulted in harm. "There are aspects to human biology and human physiology that you just can't predict. Deductive reasoning doesn't work for every case." Sherlock Holmes is a model detective, but human biology is not a theft or a murder where all the clues can add up neatly. Rather, in medicine, there is uncertainty that can make action against a presumed culprit misguided.

Lock didn't immediately learn that it was a mistake to use logic alone. "Twenty-five years ago, when I asserted that oxygen levels should be sufficient to make the decision to repair or not repair a malformed wall between the left and right heart, and it didn't work out, I thought I should just have been smarter." His second mistake, though, about closing the hole between the left and right atrium, was more troubling to him. Lock averted his gaze and his face fell; to be wrong about a child is a form of suffering unique to his profession. "I learned that I need to be more circumspect about making these predictions. I have to be more clear to myself that even though the reasoning seems extremely tight, I am still making it up. And you absolutely have to recognize that what you think you know can have limitations."

Physicians, like everyone else, display certain psychological characteristics when they act in the face of uncertainty. There is the overconfident mind-set: people convince themselves they are right because they usually are. Also, they tend to focus on positive data rather than negative data. Positive data are emotionally more appealing, because they suggest a successful outcome: apparently normal oxygen levels or higher pressures in the left atrium mean surgery will succeed. Lock's errors pivoted on the power of positive numbers: the near-normal amounts of oxygen in the blood, the high pressure in the left atrium. Each of these positive numbers seemed to predict a good outcome. Such data have a powerful effect on our psyche, particularly in settings of uncertainty; they appear to be safe harbors in a storm, places to firmly dock our minds and point us to the next leg of our journey. But biology, particularly human biology, is inherently variable. Those variations, at times very small and easily ignored, can prove important. They reflect significant differences that our most refined measurements fail to capture. Lock is also concerned that many physicians assume all numbers have equal certitude or validity. "People don't throw in specific gravity," Lock said, meaning that not all results should be given equal weight in making decisions. You learn which numbers to respect and which to discount.

Specialists in particular are known to demonstrate unwarranted clinical certainty. They have trained for so long that they begin too easily to rely on their vast knowledge and overlook the variability in human biology. This is why Lock's epistemological focus is so important. He is constantly trawling his mind, reminding himself that the situation is uncertain and acknowledging that necessary actions and decisions made with the best intentions may not apply to every patient.

It is very difficult to do what Lock does: always to reflect rather than tacitly act on scant precedent. In their book *Professional Judgment: A Reader in Clinical Decision Making,* Jack Dowie and Arthur Elstein assemble articles from experts with contrasting opinions about physician cognition and how to improve it. Many of the contributors are from the Bayesian school of decision-making, invoking "expected utility theory." This theory holds that the utility of a certain outcome is multiplied by its probability, and it determines the expected utility in the face of uncertainty. The calculation, based on axioms, has the doctor choose the path with the highest number emerging from the formula. Of course, much of what doctors like Lock deal with is unique; there is no set of published studies from which decision-analysis researchers can derive a probability.

Some experts contend that it is not only a unique case that makes a Bayesian approach untenable in many clinical settings. Donald A. Schön at MIT has written extensively about how professionals think, and he differs sharply from the decision-analysis camp, which relies on applied mathematics to model diagnosis and treatment — mathematics originally used to optimize submarine searching and bomb tracking, and that has been fostered by the advent of computers. The physician in the trenches, Schön emphasizes, faces "divergent situations where . . . relying on a large database to assign probabilities to a certain diagnosis, or the outcome of a certain treatment, completely breaks down." Lock sees himself as a rational thinker, a physician who looks to logic and makes deductions. But he also understands the limits of that logic, an understanding gained from hard experience.

Schön could be describing Lock when he writes: "Because of some puzzling, troubling, interesting phenomena, a physician expresses uncertainty, takes the time to reflect, and allows himself to be vulnerable. Then he restructures the problem. This is the key to the art of dealing with situations of uncertainty, instability, uniqueness, and value conflict."

Yet it is not only in Lock's world where the specter of uncertainty shadows decisions. David M. Eddy, a professor of health policy at Duke University, says: "Uncertainty creeps into medical practice through every pore. Whether a physician is defining a disease, making a diagnosis, selecting a procedure, observing outcomes, assessing probabilities, assigning preferences, or putting it all together, he is walking on very slippery terrain. It is difficult for non-physicians, and for many physicians, to appreciate how complex these tasks are, how poorly we understand them, and how easy it is for honest people to come to different conclusions."

Jay Katz, a physician who teaches at Yale Law School, has examined the defenses that physicians deploy against awareness of uncertainty. He looks to the earlier work of Renée Fox, who identified three basic types of uncertainty. The first results from incomplete or imperfect mastery of available knowledge. No one can have at his command all skills and all knowledge of the lore of medicine. The second depends on limitations in current medical knowledge. There are innumerable questions to which no physician, however well trained, can provide answers. A third source of uncertainty derives from the first two: this is the difficulty in distinguishing between personal ignorance or ineptitude and the limitations of present medical knowledge. Fox observed physicians on a ward struggling with uncertainty, and their numerous psychological mechanisms to cope with it, including black humor, making bets about who would be right, and engaging in some degree of magical thinking to maintain their poise and an aura of competence in front of the patients while performing uncertain procedures.

Katz lumps Fox's three categories together under the rubric "disregard of uncertainty." He believes that when physicians shift from a theoretical discussion of medicine to its practical application, they do not acknowledge the uncertainty inherent in what they do. Katz argues that while uncertainty itself imposes a significant burden on physicians, the greater burden is "the obligation to keep these uncertainties in mind and acknowledge them to patients." He observes that "the denial of uncertainty, the proclivity to substitute certainty for uncertainty, is one of the most remarkable human psychological traits. It is both adaptive and maladaptive, and therefore both guides and misguides." As a law school professor, Katz knows that witnesses at scenes of accidents "unwittingly fill in their incomplete perceptions and recollections with 'data.'" There is a "pervasive and fateful human need to remain in control of one's internal and external worlds by seemingly understanding them, even at the expense of falsifying the data . . . Physicians' denial of awareness of uncertainty serves similar purposes: it makes matters seem clearer, more understandable, and more certain than they are; it makes action possible. There are limits to living with uncertainty. It can paralyze action." This is a core reality of the practice of medicine, where — in the absence of certitude — decisions must be made.

Another defense against uncertainty is the culture of conformity and orthodoxy that begins in medical school. This is inherent in the apprentice process. For example, in Katz's first year at med school, the faculty of one distinguished university hospital taught his class that thinning the blood with anticoagulants like heparin or Coumadin was the treatment of choice for a threatening pulmonary embolism and that using any other therapy constituted unprofessional conduct. At another equally distinguished hospital, the students were told that the only correct treatment was surgically tying off the inflamed veins. "One could use such an exposure to controversy as training for uncertainty." In neither setting, Katz recounts, was the divergent made a teaching exercise. "Nor were we encouraged to keep an open mind. In both we were educated for dogmatic certainty, for adopting one school of thought or the other, and for playing the game according to the venerable, but contradictory, rules that each institution sought to impose on staff, students, and patients." Katz's observation, made two decades ago, still holds true.

One would think that primary care physicians, such as general practitioners, internists, and pediatricians, grapple most with uncertainty. But Lock opens our eyes to the truth that specialization in medicine confers a false sense of certainty. Recall how Shira Stein was cared for by teams of specialists in one of the world's best pediatric hospitals. Yet a series of cognitive errors went unrecognized. Confirmation bias, the attention to data that support the presumed diagnosis and minimizing data that contradict it, was prominent. Specialists, like Shira's doctors in the previous chapter, are also susceptible to diagnosis momentum: once an authoritative senior physician has fixed a label to the problem, it usually stays firmly attached, because the specialist is usually right.

Specialization can persuade the expert that the treatments his fellow specialists prescribe are superior. For example, in the case of prostate cancer, surgeons, radiation therapists, and chemotherapists often disagree about the respective merits of their treatments, often without sufficiently doubting the effectiveness of their own approach. So a patient's chance first encounter with one specialist may guide that patient to choose the therapy of that discipline — but that is not a true choice. If instead the patient meets with several specialists and is informed of each approach without bias, he might choose another option.

Ideally, as Lock said, we could perform large clinical trials to remedy the differences in opinion among specialists. This seems simple but in fact ignores the complexity of human biology and patients' needs. Says David Eddy:

> In theory, uncertainty could be managed if it were possible to conduct enough experiments under enough conditions, and observe the outcomes. Unfortunately, measuring the outcomes of medical procedures is one of the most difficult problems we face. The goal is to predict the use of a procedure in a particular case and its effects on that patient's health and welfare. Standing in the way are at least a half dozen major obstacles. The central problem is that there is a natural variation in the way people respond to a medical procedure. Take two people who, to the best of our ability to find such things, are identical in all important respects, submit them to the same op-

erative procedure, and one will die on the operating table while the other will not. Because of this natural variation, we can only talk about the probabilities of various outcomes — the probability that a diagnostic test will be positive if the disease is present (sensitivity), the probability that a test would be negative if the disease is absent (specificity), the probability that a treatment will yield a certain result.

An additional problem is that many procedures have multiple outcomes and it is not sufficient to examine just one of them. For example, a coronary artery bypass may change the life expectancy of a 60-year-old man with triple vessel disease, but it will also change his joy of life for several weeks after the operation, the degree and severity of chest pain, his ability to walk and make love, his relationship with his son, the physical appearance of his chest and his pocketbook. Pain, disability, anxiety, family relations, and any number of other outcomes are all important consequences of a procedure that deserve consideration, but the list is too long for practical experiments and many of the items on it are invisible or not measurable at all.

Does acknowledging uncertainty undermine a patient's sense of hope and confidence in his physician and the proposed therapy? Paradoxically, taking uncertainty into account can enhance a physician's therapeutic effectiveness, because it demonstrates his honesty, his willingness to be more engaged with his patients, his commitment to the reality of the situation rather than resorting to evasion, half-truth, and even lies. And it makes it easier for the doctor to change course if the first strategy fails, to keep trying. Uncertainty sometimes is essential for success.

CHAPTER 7

Surgery and Satisfaction

THE HUMAN HAND contains twenty-seven bones and scores of ligaments, muscles, and tendons. Working in concert, these parts give us the ability to thread a needle, bow a cello, deliver a left hook, operate a jackhammer, and caress a lover. Dr. Terry Light of Loyola University is a hand surgeon. When I spoke with him in the autumn of 2005, he had just finished his tenure as president of the American Society for Surgery of the Hand and was about to assume the presidency of the American Orthopedic Association. But at the time, these honors paled next to the fact that Dr. Light had once served as the hand surgeon for the Chicago White Sox. I had no doubt on which side Light stood in the eternal debate about whether a team's pitching or hitting is more important — pitching, of course.

Baseball occupied only part of our conversation, because I took the opportunity to present a complex diagnostic dilemma to Dr. Light, the case of a patient with debilitating pain and swelling in his right hand, the hand he used to write, turn his door key, and perform the innumerable tasks that mark each of our days. Over the course of three years, the patient had consulted six hand surgeons and got four different opinions about what was wrong and what to do about it. I was that patient.

The trouble with my hand can be traced to my never learning to type. My fifth-grade teacher told my parents that I was not college material, and advised that I be tracked to a vocational school to learn a trade. Truth be told, I was not a model child, too eager to engage in mischief, paying little attention in class, looking at the clock and counting the minutes until recess. A psychologist today might fix the label of ADHD to me, but at the time my family concluded that mine was a classic case of *shpilkes,* a Yiddish word meaning, roughly, "ants in your pants." My parents would later reject the teacher's advice, but in fifth grade I spent afternoons in metal shop instead of typing class; there was no expectation that I would ever need to use a typewriter.

Ten years ago, I bought my first laptop and banged clumsily at the keyboard for many hours at a time. I soon developed a roaring case of tendinitis in my wrists. I rested, returned to the computer, and suffered repeated bouts of pain. After a year, I gave up and went back to writing by hand. But I was left with a persistent ache in my right wrist — annoying, but not severe enough to require medical attention. Then, one day in the pool, a swimmer in the neighboring lane happened to fling his arm in a downward arc at the same moment my right arm moved up. He delivered a blow to my right wrist.

I iced the bruised wrist, and after a week the pain went back to its usual dull ache. Some months later at the hospital, an elderly woman was making her way toward the elevator. I was already inside and saw the doors begin to close; reflexively, I extended my right hand, but it was too late for the electric eye to respond. The elevator briefly closed on my wrist. Ice again treated the trauma.

Dr. Light listened closely, not interrupting. I told him I was coming to the key event that caused me to consult the first surgeon. A few weeks after the elevator incident, I struggled to open the lid of a bottle of fruit juice. After much forceful twisting I succeeded, but in a flash, excruciating pain erupted in my right wrist. The hand became hot, beet red, and swollen. I couldn't move it. I took some naproxen, an anti-inflammatory drug, and applied ice. After a few days the swelling subsided. But each time I tried to write more than a few sentences, I developed sharp pain in my wrist below my thumb. I went for x-rays, which revealed cysts, essentially fluid-filled holes, within the scaphoid and lunate, two small bones on the thumb side of the wrist.

The first hand surgeon I consulted I will call Dr. A. In his early forties, A was known in the Boston medical community as the doctor for many professional athletes injured during play. His waiting room was jam-packed. Nearly two hours after my scheduled appointment, his nurse finally ushered me in to an examining room. Five rooms were already occupied by other patients, some with casts, other with pins, still others in slings. Dr. A entered some thirty minutes later, asking me where I worked and what kind of medicine I practiced — a "name, rank, and serial number" bedside manner. As he listened to my story, he jotted a few notes. Dr. A examined my hand, and I winced when he pressed over the bones beneath the thumb. "Let's get some x-rays," he said.

I said that I'd already had x-rays in my own hospital, but he insisted that I repeat them in his clinic. An hour later, he returned. The x-rays were as before. Dr. A told me that many people have cysts in their bones and show no symptoms. Other people have bone cysts and have symptoms from them. Some people have a hereditary disposition to cysts, while others develop cysts that are degenerative, the result of trauma or the wear and tear of work, sports, and daily living. Dr. A suggested that I be splinted for a month, and we would see what happened.

At the end of four weeks, I was back in his clinic, waiting another two hours to be examined. I had used the splint diligently, but when I took it off to shower, I had pain in my wrist. Dr. A briefly examined my hand and then told me to see how my wrist felt when I used it out of the splint over the coming weeks. The appointment ended in minutes.

I gradually started doing things with my right hand. It was painful to hold even light objects, like a mug of coffee, but I persisted. And then one day, while writing a few sentences with a narrow pen, I felt my hand begin to heat up. Within minutes it was swollen and red. I could not bend the wrist, and the smallest shift from a fixed neutral position was excruciating. It was like the episode with the juice bottle.

I called Dr. A's office. His secretary instructed me to come in the next day. Dr. A looked at the hot, swollen hand and shook his head. "Let's get an MRI scan," he said.

I asked what he thought was wrong.

"I really don't know."

In a strange way, I was reassured. Some doctors do not readily admit ignorance.

The next week, Dr. A reviewed the results of the MRI scan with me. The scan was formatted digitally on his computer screen so he could enlarge it and zoom in on various parts. He led me through a tour of my hand. It was fascinating to visualize the connecting bones, ligaments, muscles, and tendons. The MRI showed the cysts in the scaphoid and lunate bones. Against the white background of bone, the cysts resembled craters on the moon. There was considerable swelling, with the rope-like tendons suspended in a sea of fluid. Dr. A still had no diagnosis, and suggested that I be splinted again.

Later, when I reviewed my history with Dr. Terry Light, he agreed with Dr. A's approach. "Better to say you're not sure and take the time to figure it out. Often we don't know what accounts for symptoms of pain in the hand, given that almost everyone has a hole in a bone if you look hard enough."

The splint gave me temporary relief. But over the next few months, with the most minor activity my hand would become swollen, red, and painful. I saw Dr. A at least four times over the course of the year. At each visit I pressed him to try to figure out what was wrong. He wondered whether the hot, swollen wrist might represent some underlying systemic disease, like lupus or rheumatoid arthritis, and whether the history of tendinitis from the computer and the trauma in the swimming pool and the elevator were red herrings. But all of my blood tests for systemic diseases that cause arthritis were negative. A steroid injection into the wrist was no help.

At each follow-up visit, I pressed Dr. A for answers. He would just shrug. Then, a year after I first consulted him, he said, "I think you have developed a hyperreactive synovium." The synovium, the lining of the joints around the wrist and hand, Dr. A explained, had become too sensitive to endure even minor stresses. It overreacted by becoming inflamed. He suggested a surgical procedure to strip away all of it. I asked whether the synovium was essential for the joint to function properly, whether there might be scarring after the procedure. Dr. A allowed that the synovium was necessary, but eventually a new lining would grow back — and yes, there could be residual scar tissue.

I am not a specialist in diseases of the bones and joints, and I'd never heard of a "hyperreactive synovium." Neither had Dr. Light: he said that the diagnosis "didn't register. It doesn't really mean anything to me."

Dr. A had come to the end of his thinking. But instead of returning to the honesty of "I really don't know," he invented something to respond to my plaintive questioning and suggested an operation that could be damaging. It was time to seek another opinion.

I went to a neighboring state to see Dr. B. He was prompt, had a focused, deliberate approach, examined me carefully, and agreed that "hyperreactive synovium" was not a real clinical condition. He said he was determined to find out what was wrong and fix it. Dr. B studied in detail every unusual shadow and shape on my x-rays and MRI scan. In addition to the cysts in the scaphoid and lunate bones, he noted a tiny cyst in another bone, on the pinkie side of the wrist. The tendon that runs toward the pinkie also seemed to have slipped slightly out of position. Dr. B thought there was a hairline fracture in the scaphoid bone, not simply a cyst. He said that I needed three surgeries. The first would pin the fracture, the second would involve draining the three cysts and filling each with bone grafts taken from my hip, and the third would reposition the displaced tendon. "The wrist works like a set of gears," he said. "When one or more of the components is out of alignment or malfunctioning, then you can get stuck all across the hand." My straining to shift the stuck gears caused the swelling and pain.

I asked Dr. B how long the recovery period would be from three sequential operations. "Eighteen to twenty-four months," he said.

Dr. Terry Light said, of course, that to comment properly on Dr. B's opinion, he would have had to examine me and view the MRI; but the idea of three surgeries to address every finding on the scan — this gave Light pause. "That's the problem with MRI. It can show us way too much."

I was increasingly frustrated and desperate for a solution, but leery of the idea of undergoing three operations. My wife, Pam, also a physician, said she was worried that my judgment might be impaired by the long siege of pain and debility, so she came along to my next appointment.

I had to pull strings to see Dr. C, one of the most renowned hand surgeons in the United States. He was the kind of doctor whose name routinely comes to the lips of other physicians and who is listed every year in his city's magazine under "The Best Doctors in . . ." His waiting room was packed, like Dr. A's, but instead of the artwork that typically adorned physicians' offices — photographs of sailboats or paintings of meadows — the walls of Dr. C's clinic were filled with plaques. Hardly a space was left uncovered. I read a few of the plaques; each attested to Dr. C's fame. One was from the International Conference on Abnormalities of the Thumb, held in Rio de Janeiro. Another was on the Repair of the Rheumatoid Finger, held in Saint Moritz, Switzerland (during the height of ski season). Framed conference programs were mounted next to the plaques, and Dr. C was a prominently featured speaker on each.

I was greeted first by a resident in orthopedic surgery. In his mid-twenties, with a boyish smile and Brooks Brothers attire, the resident took my history and looked at my x-rays and MRI as he prepared to present my case to Dr. C.

Dr. C entered the room. He nodded hello to Pam and me. Standing before me, he took my right hand in his and began to examine it while simultaneously listening to the resident recite my clinical history. "Where are the x-rays?" he asked. The resident handed them to him, and without a word Dr. C darted from the room with the resident in tow. He moved so quickly he could have been on roller skates. Not more than five minutes later, Dr. C returned. "We need to do an arthroscopy," he said. This meant inserting an instrument like a flexible telescope into my wrist in order to see the actual bones and ligaments. "I'll have the resident schedule it." Dr. C turned to leave.

"I realize you are in a rush . . . ," I ventured.

"Rush? Why do you think I'm in a rush?" Dr. C shot back.

"Well, I wonder if you could tell me what you expect to find with the arthroscopy."

"I'll figure it out when I get in there," he said, and left the room.

The resident sat down and took out the sheet of paper that I was to sign to authorize the arthroscopy.

Pam had been quiet, communicating through glances with me. As I read the paper, she began to question the resident, politely but pointedly. She wanted to know how long the procedure took, what the likelihood of each complication was — not just a list of possible complications — and how long it took to recover. Pam tells her patients that no intervention in medicine is completely innocuous or without risk. The resident answered her in a tense voice, unaccustomed to being the primary interlocutor in place of Dr. C. The procedure would take about twenty minutes, not counting the preparation with anesthesia that involved numbing the nerves to the arm; pain and swelling were the main complications, infection being rare; a full recovery would take about two to three weeks.

I did not sign the paper. I felt dazed. I had called in numerous favors to get to Dr. C, and he had flown by without pausing to share any of his reputed brilliance. Pam continued to query the resident. If Dr. C decided the cysts in the bones accounted for the pain and swelling, what kind of grafts would he insert?

"No, we don't do bone grafts here," the resident said. "Here, we fuse the bones."

Pam and I looked at each other knowingly. We had both trained at the Massachusetts General Hospital, where at times in a complex situation the rationale given trainees for choosing one therapy over another was that an eminent MGH physician "did it that way." It was received wisdom, handed down as if from the heavens. When we left Boston and went to the University of California at Los Angeles, we found another kind of received wisdom. Again, a distinguished physician on the UCLA staff had his personal approach to the same complex clinical problem, but to our surprise it could be very different from the one at the MGH. Nevertheless, the UCLA strategy was spoken of just as reverently, as if it too had descended from celestial heights.

"I really would like to hear what Dr. C thinks is going on," I said to the resident. "I don't know if he realizes that we are both doctors."

The resident said that he would try to bring Dr. C back to the room. Twenty minutes later, Dr. C returned. "Nice to meet you," he said, not exactly calmly, but not at the Gatling-gun pace of the earlier visit. Dr. C began to list the names of doctors he knew who might have crossed paths with me during my career in Boston and Los Angeles. It turned out, not unexpectedly, that we knew several in common.

Pam asked what he thought was the leading diagnosis. "Chondrocalcinosis," Dr. C replied. Chondrocalcinosis is also called pseudogout. Calcium crystals form deposits in the cartilage, making the normally pliable tissue stiff and inflamed. The crystals also float in the fluid of the joint space.

"Wouldn't you see the calcium deposits on the x-rays?" Pam asked.

"There are cases where the x-rays are negative," Dr. C replied.

"And the bone cysts?"

Dr. C said again that he would "figure them out" during the arthroscopy.

Dr. C started to fidget in his chair and then took my left hand and grasped it as a sign of concluding the contact. "My resident will set up the procedure. Don't worry."

But I was worried. Pam was worried. And both of us were disheartened. We had come with great expectations, and everything about Dr. C deflated them. Many years before, when I had serious back pain from a sports injury, the surgeons said they would explore my spine and "figure it out." Out of frustration, I had impulsively opted for the procedure. They ended up fusing the vertebrae. It left me debilitated. In hindsight, I blamed myself more than the surgeons: I had pressed them for a solution when, in fact, none was apparent because the cause of the pain was obscure. That catastrophe had chastened me. It felt like déjà vu with Dr. C.

But Dr. C was world-renowned, the featured speaker at international conferences. So I went to a standard medical textbook and reviewed the chapter on chondrocalcinosis. Nothing in any of my prior tests suggested chondrocalcinosis. If the x-rays don't show the calcium deposits, the easiest way to find the crystals is to withdraw some fluid from the joint with a small needle — not by performing an arthroscopy. And treatment of chondrocalcinosis involved anti-inflammatory drugs like naproxen or steroid injections into the joint — both of which I had already tried, to no effect. Dr. Light echoed these thoughts. Chondrocalcinosis made no sense. "If you think someone has chondrocalcinosis, they don't need arthroscopy. They need a strong anti-inflammatory medication like indomethacin." Dr. C had offered a diagnosis that, while not invented, like Dr. A's hyperreactive synovium, was nevertheless inventive. I decided to do nothing.

Nearly a year passed. I did not use my right hand much. Instead of writing, I switched to using a dictating machine. I avoided the computer entirely. Occasionally, something trivial, like swimming a few extra laps, followed by writing three or four checks to pay bills, would cause a flare-up. My hand would turn red, swell, and become excruciatingly painful. I would apply ice, support it with a splint, and after a few days the inflammation would subside.

A new young hand surgeon whom I will call Dr. D came to Boston, and the word among the senior staff was that he was a hotshot. I was curious and scheduled an appointment with him. Dr. D had a warm, affable manner and listened intently as I recounted the sequence of traumatic events to the hand and the episodic flare-ups. He surprised me by examining not only my right hand but also my left, and then he said that he wanted x-rays of both hands, not only when they were stationary, but when I flexed them as if gripping something tightly. This was the first time any-one had ever paid attention to the left wrist or tried to picture the bones of my hands during a maneuver.

"As I suspected," Dr. D said without a whiff of arrogance in his tone. He put the x-rays on a light box and showed me how the space between the scaphoid and lunate bones widened when my right hand was in a gripping position; the left hand showed no widening of the joint.

"I think the ligament between the scaphoid and lunate is par-tially torn, or at least not functioning well," he said. The reason I had pain with even minor stress on my right hand was that the lax or torn ligament caused friction between the bones. He went on to explain that there also could be channels from the cysts into the joint, so that they functioned like lakes with thin canals: as the fluid in the cysts came under pressure, the liquid would be squeezed out through the canals into the joint. This set off the in-flammation.

Dr. D's scenario made sense to me, but the MRI had shown neither problems with the ligament nor channels from the cysts. Dr. D replied that despite the MRI, he would bet the ligament was abnormal and that connections existed between the cysts and the joints. Doctors relied too much on such sophisticated scans, he continued, so sometimes you had to discount their findings if they were out of sync with the clinical picture. Filling the cysts with bone grafts would probably not do much good in the long run without repairing the ligament, because the loose joint would continue to generate friction, causing pain. Dr. D proposed tak-ing bone grafts from my hip, filling in the cysts, and repairing the ligament. As to the other abnormalities on the MRI scan that Dr. B wanted to fix — the tendon to the pinkie and the tiny cyst in the other bone — Dr. D was reluctant to operate on them. He said the wear and tear on the hands of a man in his fifties who banged on a computer and played sports and was something of a klutz in elevators could cause such findings on an MRI, but trying to fix them might do more harm than good.

Dr. D seemed sober and independent in his thinking, not bowing to technology when it clashed with a patient's history and physical exam. But was he right? I decided to assume for a moment that he was, and asked him how many times he had performed the kind of operation he was proposing. He paused and said, "Once." Then he elaborated, saying that he had done it several times with supervision, but only a single time by himself. He was just at the beginning of his career.

"That's the struggle when patients are having pain," Dr. Light said after hearing Dr. D's thoughts and contrasting them with Dr. B's. "You can see many things on an MRI, but nothing that's clearly responsible for the symptoms. So you begin to go around and around. The hateful part of MRIs — I mean they can be a wonderful technology — but they find abnormalities in everybody. More often than not, I am stuck trying to figure out whether the MRI abnormality is responsible for the pain. That is the really hard part."

The key, Dr. Light continued, is for "everything to add up — the patient's symptoms, the findings on physical examination, what appears meaningful on the MRI or other x-rays. It has to come together and form a coherent picture." In effect he was describing pattern recognition, and saying that if a clear pattern is not apparent, the surgeon is in a quandary. "Picking up a scalpel and cutting can be just the wrong thing." This, though, was what Drs. A, B, and C, without recognizing a coherent and consistent pattern, were set to do.

"I have made the diagnosis Dr. D made, of dynamic scaphoid-lunate instability," Light told me, affixing the technical term to the problem of a lax ligament that causes the bones to shift out of alignment. "The patient usually comes in with a stack of x-rays, like you did. And then I tell him that I want to get a grip view, an x-ray when he is crunching his hand, and he says, 'But you guys have taken every possible x-ray already.' Then you look at the joint space between the scaphoid and lunate bones, and you can drive a truck through it. The point is, you have to think of it."

Why did it take three years to "think of it"?

Light said that no one had ever really taught him how to "think of it." Instead, he learned to observe senior surgeons closely, often one-on-one in the OR, and then began to imitate those who worked with "clarity and effectiveness." He also observed surgeons who did not seem especially clear in their judgments or effective in the OR. He tried to figure out what made the difference. "It is still very much an art, a guild, where you are an apprentice and work with a master craftsman," he said.

Light added that although the conventional wisdom states that surgeons must have "great hands," that successful surgery requires manual dexterity, in fact it is more about deft decision-making. "Of course, if you are a total klutz, you have a problem in the OR," Light allowed. And having good eye-hand coordination is helpful. But Light referred to an article titled "Less Than Ten" by Dr. Paul Brown, an ex–military surgeon practicing in Hartford, Connecticut. Brown reported on surgeons who themselves suffered injuries to their hands, like losing part of or an entire finger. "Of course, there are certain very technically demanding procedures, like sewing together a small blood vessel, that require exquisite dexterity," Light said, but short of this, as Brown's article showed, there is a surprising degree of latitude. Most surgeons learn dexterity through repeated practice. Where they differ most, Light said, is not in technique, the kind of stitch they prefer, or the particular instrument they like to use in a particular setting, but in how they conceptualize a patient's problem and understand what surgery can and cannot do to remedy it. The surgeon's brain is more important than his hands.

Terry Light trained at Yale–New Haven Hospital, and during his internship worked closely with Dr. Richard Selzer, renowned not only as a surgeon but also as a writer. Selzer showed the young Terry Light that a surgeon has to have a high level of confidence to operate, or, as Selzer had written, the "audacity to take a knife to another human being." A certain bravado goes with being a surgeon, Light admitted.

I told Light that I had begun to learn about the types of cognitive shortcuts we use as doctors, and how at times that "certain bravado" affects cognition. Together, Light and I assessed the pitfalls in the thinking of the hand surgeons I had consulted. Dr. A showed what is called "commission bias." This is the tendency toward action rather than inaction. Such an error is more likely to happen with a doctor who is overconfident, whose ego is inflated, but it can also occur when a physician is desperate and gives in to the urge to "do something." The error, not infrequently, is sparked by pressure from a patient, and it takes considerable effort for a doctor to resist. "Don't just do something, stand there," Dr. Linda Lewis, one of my mentors, once said when I was unsure of a diagnosis. This was one of the rare instances, I told Terry Light, when a senior physician had explicitly cautioned me about what can be categorized as a cognitive mistake. It was a firm, no-nonsense injunction from Dr. Lewis, culled from her decades of clinical experience, handed down as master craftswoman to apprentice. Lewis explained that inaction is not at all what is expected from a physician, nor what a physician expects from himself. But sometimes it is the best course.

Dr. B made a different cognitive error, called "satisfaction of search" by some and "search satisficing" by others. This is the tendency to stop searching for a diagnosis once you find something. It has an analogy in everyday life. Say you are getting ready to

leave the house for work and time is short to catch your train. Perhaps you were out late the night before, or had a little too much
wine at dinner, or had an argument with your teenager, and all of
this is on your mind. You look for your wallet, and it's not on your
desk where you usually leave it. You look some more and find it
on the night table. You feel relieved that you found your wallet,
and put it in your pocket. Now you'll make the train.

Back to a doctor trying to solve a patient's problem. The patient has a symptom that the doctor needs to explain. As he
searches for the explanation, the doctor finds something wrong in
the physical examination or a lab test or an x-ray. That is what
happened when Dr. B jumped on the bone cysts in the MRI scan
— the equivalent of locating the wallet on the night table. The
problem is that there may be more than one thing to be found.
Dr. Pat Croskerry put it this way: "Finding something may be satisfactory, but not finding everything is suboptimal." After putting
your wallet in your pocket, walking out of your house, closing the
door, and approaching your car to drive to the train, you realize
that you're missing your key chain. Now you not only lack the car
key, you have closed the front door and can't get back in without
your house key. You were so pleased about finding your wallet
that your mind shut down and you didn't consider what else was
missing. Suboptimal indeed.

Dr. D was able to avoid this type of error by asking himself
whether there was more to be found beyond what was seen on the
plain x-rays and MRI scans. He kept searching because he was not
satisfied that what he had before him was enough to account for
all of my symptoms. To get me to where I needed to go, he had to
find not only the wallet, but the keys.

Dr. D avoided another error in thinking, called "vertical line
failure," more commonly known as thinking inside the box. Although "thinking outside the box" has become a hackneyed phrase,
it still embodies the truth that sometimes "lateral thinking" that

breaks out of the ordinary is vital. That "box" is the MRI scan, a revered technology that strongly constrains a doctor's thinking. Creativity and imagination, rather than adherence to the obvious, are needed in situations where the data and clinical findings do not all fit neatly together.

Dr. Karen Delgado, the specialist in endocrinology and metabolism, is well recognized in her city for her lateral thinking, making diagnoses that require such creativity and imagination. When I asked her how she learned to think this way, she said she wasn't sure, but that when she was an intern she liked to play a mind game. When she admitted a patient with what seemed to be a clear and obvious diagnosis, she would stop and ask herself, What else could this be? Sometimes she was unable to come up with any other diagnosis. The obvious was almost certainly the answer. But on occasion she could rearrange the data in her mind to form another plausible picture, a different pattern that could also account for the patient's symptoms. If this proved to be the case, then she searched further. She was careful never to be satisfied from the outset. Often the search was fruitless, and the initial and obvious diagnosis was correct. But once in a while her deviation from vertical thinking, her breakout from the box where everything seemed to fit neatly, was critical in disproving that initial diagnosis — or in finding that lightning had struck more than once, that the patient had multiple problems requiring multiple diagnoses. This goes against the time-honored principle of Ockham's razor: go with a single cause if it appears to explain all the data.

Dr. Light said that during an exploratory arthroscopy in the OR, before the actual surgery, one of the other surgeons might have discovered what Dr. D found in his office, that the ligament was not functioning, that the joint between the scaphoid and lunate bones was distorted.

But, I pointed out, it doesn't inspire confidence when a doctor tells you, "I'll figure it out in the OR."

He agreed. Paradoxically, such confidence is bolstered, Light said, when a physician opens his mind to a patient and explains what he knows and what he doesn't know, what is firm about his findings and what is still unclear, which symptoms he can account for and which still demand explanation. Suppose Dr. C had stated things this way and explained that in the OR he would be able to assess the dynamic function of my wrist, be able to evaluate which joints might be deranged, instead of saying, "Leave it up to me." He would at least have shown me he was open to solving the puzzle rather than just throwing out a diagnosis, chondrocalcinosis, that didn't fit. Similarly, if Dr. B had explained, as Dr. Light did, that an MRI scan can overread a problem, showing changes in the hand that deviate from the normal but nonetheless should not be taken at face value, he would have inspired greater confidence and perhaps tacked away from deciding that three operations were necessary.

After several weeks of considering Dr. D's advice, and after getting a similar diagnosis from a hand surgeon who is a friend and member of my synagogue, I learned that a major orthopedic center in another city was beta-testing a new MRI that provided greater resolution of the bones, tendons, and ligaments in the hand. I was curious about the reach of the new technology and whether it might shed light on Dr. D's analysis. I went for the experimental scan. As Dr. D had predicted, the ligament between the scaphoid and lunate bones was frayed and lax. Moreover, tiny channels extended from the cysts. I inquired of friends at the orthopedic center and learned that a Dr. E, some thirty years the senior of Dr. D, had performed repairs of this type scores of times.

I met with Dr. E. He was formal and focused in his speech, saying that the arthroscopy and the surgery would be performed at one sitting. In addition, he used a new form of synthetic bone material for grafts, making it unnecessary to cut into my hip to harvest bone chips. Overall, the surgery was a success. After five months of rehabilitation, my wrist was about 80 percent of normal — not 100 percent. Struggling with a can opener set off swelling and a deep ache. "You have arthritis in the joint," Dr. E said in his no-nonsense manner. "Just be careful. There are limits."

This was another message that Dr. Light believes surgeons should communicate to their patients, especially in advance of an operation. "The perfect is the enemy of the good," Light said. "Nothing that you do in surgery is perfect. Everything is a compromise. Eighty percent of normal after surgery — well, that's pretty good," he said. Frankly, I had hoped for 100 percent, and like most patients I expected to be restored to pristine condition. More often than not, that is unrealistic. While you cannot predict a specific outcome for any particular patient, Light emphasized, you need to be candid and not paint too rosy a scenario.

This requires an uncommon degree of honesty — uncommon because it demands a certain deflation of the physician's ego. Here we have the contrast between what Selzer wrote about, the healthy ego necessary to putting a knife to another human being's flesh — a belief in one's own ability to make the right judgments in the OR and to work with dispatch — and the ego that imagines the scalpel as a magic wand that can restore a diseased body part perfectly. Such honesty is not rewarded in today's society. Patients shop for doctors; some doctors are keen to market themselves, knowing that it's easier to make the sale if they present their work as top-of-the-line, like a luxury automobile that flawlessly navigates the toughest curves and shifts gears seamlessly. But my banged-up hand was a 1952 Studebaker, and only so much could be done in the shop. It would never emerge as a brand-new Lexus.

"One of the intriguing things about hand surgery," Dr. Light said, is that "every patient comes in with his story, and you decode that story and then figure out not only what you can do for him, but what you can't.

"Early on in the life of a surgeon, the technical component is very important. When you are a resident in training, you say to yourself, 'I just did my first total hip replacement, skin to skin, and I feel great.' Oh, my gosh, what a sense of accomplishment! I remember the first time I reattached a finger, and I saw it pink up, and it was wondrous. As you get older, the sense of accomplishment becomes the patient who returns and tells you how much better he can function now. It's not the surgery per se but the person who is happy and pleased. So you don't want to leave people disappointed. To do that, you have to clarify the expectations up front. And then you have some people come in and demand a certain procedure, and you know in your heart that they are not going to be satisfied. Although it might be fine for someone else."

Dr. Light was revealing the kind of thinking that the most seasoned and expert doctors display: they think in sync with the patient. The patient should be helped to think in sync with the doctors, too.

In the case of my problem hand, did it all turn out pretty well because I am a doctor? Of course, I am at a great advantage being a physician and being married to one. But much of this three-year odyssey was guided by my having suffered earlier from a failed operation on my spine. Yes, my technical knowledge helped, but common sense was key. "There is nothing in biology or medicine that is so complicated that, if explained in clear and simple language, cannot be understood by any layperson. It's not quantum physics," Dr. Linda Lewis, my mentor at Columbia, once said on rounds.

There was an easily understood set of explanations for what was wrong with my hand. The cysts developed because of trauma, the wear and tear on the scaphoid and lunate bones from the banging on the computer, the karate chop in the swimming pool, the slamming elevator door. All this resulted in a breakdown of the matrix in these bones, and they filled with viscous fluid. The ligament probably was further damaged along the way by the extreme force I exerted while struggling with the juice bottle. Invented answers like "hyperreactive synovium" sound scientific and might initially impress a layman. Latin and Greek terms make up much of medical jargon and can take on unwarranted authority. But a layman speaking with another specialist, or checking in a medical textbook or on one of the better Internet sites, would soon discover that hyperreactive synovium is a unicorn, a mythical beast.

Dr. B was well intentioned, but not conservative enough. Sometimes less is more, and more can be too much. The compulsion to do everything, to address every abnormality even when those abnormalities are not particularly bothersome, reveals an irrationally idealized approach to practicing medicine. As Terry Light said, the perfect can be the enemy of the good.

Patients can help the doctor think by asking questions. If he mentions a possible complication from surgery, they can ask how often it happens. If he talks about pain and lingering discomfort from a procedure, they can ask how the pain compares with having a tooth pulled under Novocain, or some other unpleasant event. If he recommends a procedure, patients can ask why, what might be found, with what probability, and, importantly, how much difference it will make to find it. Some physicians will be uneasy, some even angry, when queried this way, because they may not have all the answers. Others will take the time and clearly respond to these simple, direct, reasonable questions. The kind of response illuminates how much the doctor really knows about your case, and how much still needs to be discovered.

Dr. D is a hero here. Not only did he think, and think independently, figuring out the genesis of my unusual problem, but he challenged today's high-tech god, the MRI scan. He was totally honest about his track record. He could have brushed aside my question and said something like, "I've done the operation successfully," which would have been true — in a single case. Terry Light had no doubt that with each passing year Dr. D will only get better, because a searching mind guides his hands.

CHAPTER 8

The Eye of the Beholder

PRIMARY CARE PHYSICIANS regularly look to doctors like Dennis Orwig to confirm the health of certain patients and identify disease in others. But despite his importance in the diagnosis and treatment of patients, very few ever meet him. In fact, Dr. Orwig spends most of his day alone, sitting in the dark. If there were a window in his office, he would look out on some of the most stunning landscape in the United States. Marin General Hospital, north of San Francisco, where Orwig works, has a commanding view of Mount Tamalpais, the undulating rise named by the Miwok Indians for its resemblance to a sleeping maiden. Eucalyptus trees surround the hospital, and soft breezes filter through their branches. But Orwig is purposely cloistered from these surroundings because he is a radiologist. Nothing should distract him from the three monitors at his workstation. On a typical day, he reads the digital images projected on the monitors: chest x-rays that show the heart, lungs, ribs, and clavicles; mammograms that unmask growths, some benign, others malignant; CT and MRI scans that reveal the architecture of organs, blood vessels, and bones.

"Radiology is a discipline broken down into two processes: the process of perception and the process of cognition," he said. This means that first a radiologist must make an observation; second, he needs to analyze what he perceived, what it means, the possible explanations for the finding. This dual process is repeated second by second, minute by minute, hour after hour during his working day. Like primary care physicians, he risks missing something significant in the blur: a change in contour of a tissue or a variation in density of an organ that he needs to notice. And as with Dr. Victoria McEvoy and others, the sheer volume has become daunting. A decade ago, a radiologist like Orwig in private practice might evaluate from twelve to fifteen thousand cases a year. By one estimate, the workload currently reaches from sixteen to twenty-five thousand cases. Some cases generate only a few images, but others involve hundreds or thousands. For example, a patient in the emergency room with fever and a cough may have a chest x-ray. This study is done with the individual in two positions: one with the chest pressed against the plate and the second with the chest pressed at the side. Thus, there are two images that a radiologist examines in this case. But a CT scan of the abdomen, which is often ordered in the ER when there is a suspicion of appendicitis, generates many hundreds of images, and the radiologist has to select the key ones to analyze from this multitude.

For that reason, radiologists are expected to look at and analyze images very quickly. In fact, conclusions from first impressions, or "gestalt," are supposed to be the mark of good training, much as "shooting from the hip" is prized among ER doctors. But Orwig takes issue with this celebrated form of thinking. "I was trained at the University of California, San Francisco," Orwig told me. "It is ranked as one of the top programs in the country. But I believe there was a deficiency in the training, and I know from colleagues that the flaw was not only there, but at many other centers." As novices, they were taught to systematically inspect each anatomic component on the x-ray. But the aim was to develop sufficient expertise so that they could abandon the deliberate deconstruction of pictures and see at a glance what is abnormal. "Somehow, over time, you were supposed to 'get it' when looking at an image." The stated reason for fostering this mode of perception and cognition was that it fit with the large number of images that a radiologist would view each working day. And, indeed, many doctors in this specialty rely heavily on first impression — gestalt — rapidly distinguishing normal from abnormal, drawing conclusions within seconds of viewing an image. But Orwig soon realized that while this often succeeded, many radiologists, including seasoned ones, missed important findings. His concern about gestalt comes not only from his own experience in practice but from studies in the medical literature.

Dr. E. James Potchen at Michigan State University in East Lansing has studied performance in reading chest x-rays. More than one hundred certified radiologists were assessed. These studies at Michigan State used a series of sixty chest x-rays that included duplicates of some of the films. When the radiologists were asked, "Is the film normal?" they disagreed among themselves an average of 20 percent of the time. This is called "interobserver variability." When a single radiologist reread on a later day the same sixty films, he contradicted his earlier analysis from 5 to 10 percent of the time. This is called "intraobserver variability."

One film of the sixty was of a patient who was missing his left clavicle. Presenting such a chest x-ray was meant to assess performance in noticing what was *not* on the film rather than merely searching for a positive finding — an exercise that points out our natural preference for focusing on positive data and ignoring the negative, as James Lock emphasized. Remarkably, 60 percent of the radiologists failed to identify the missing clavicle. When clinical data were added to the exercise, informing the radiologist that the sixty chest x-rays were obtained as part of an "annual physical examination," which primary care doctors perform in order to screen for serious diseases like lung cancer, 58 percent of the radiologists still missed it and scored the film as normal. However, when they were told that the chest x-rays were obtained as part of a series of studies to find a cancer, then 83 percent of the radiologists identified the missing bone. This highlighted that a specific clinical cue can substantially improve performance, because the radiologist is systematically searching with attention to a particular condition, rather than relying on a flash impression.

One of the most interesting outcomes of Potchen's study using the sixty films was to compare the top twenty radiologists, who had a diagnostic accuracy of nearly 95 percent, with the bottom twenty, who had a diagnostic accuracy of 75 percent. Most worrisome was the level of confidence each group had in its analysis. The radiologists who performed poorly were not only inaccurate; they were also very confident that they were right when they were in fact wrong. "Observers' lack of ability to discriminate normal from abnormal films does not necessarily diminish their confidence," Potchen wrote. His study also measured the time it took to read a set of films as an indication of the observer's decisiveness. "All observers have characteristic ways in which they manage the threshold of uncertainty in making decisions. Some people are risk takers, and they are likely to have more false-positive errors." This means that they "overread" the images, calling a normal finding abnormal — a false positive. "Others are risk averse, and they are more likely to have high false-negative rates." This means that their excess caution causes them to classify as normal what is actually diseased — a false negative. "Still others cannot make up their minds, and they will have high ambiguity numbers and more frequently require additional films before reaching conclusions."

Ironically, Potchen pointed out, based on his studies of radiologists, "if you look at a film too long, you increase the risk of hurting the patient." After about thirty-eight seconds, he found, many radiologists begin to "see things that are not there." In essence, they generate false positives and begin to designate normal structures as abnormal. Potchen believes that this reflects their level of insecurity about what they are observing. As we have seen in the studies of Roter and Hall, and the writings of Croskerry, temperament can have a significant impact on diagnostic accuracy, even among doctors like radiologists, who are not in direct contact with the patient.

There is ample precedent for both significant intraobserver and interobserver variability beyond the diagnosis of lung cancer. For example, interpretation of chest x-rays used for screening for tuberculosis showed interobserver variability of about 33 percent and intraobserver variability of about 20 percent. In screening mammography, a sample of 110 radiologists who interpreted the mammograms of 148 women, the fraction of patients actually having cancer who were correctly diagnosed varied from 59 to 100 percent, and the fraction of patients without disease who were correctly diagnosed as normal ranged from 35 to 98 percent. Overall, the accuracy rate varied from 73 to 97 percent.

Ehsan Samei of the Advanced Imaging Laboratories at Duke University Medical Center recently summarized results from a variety of radiological procedures: "Currently, the average diagnostic error in interpreting medical images is in the twenty percent to thirty percent range. These errors, being either of the false-negative or false-positive type, have significant impact on patient care." The question then is, how can radiologists improve their performance?

It is not only in radiology that observation and analysis can vary widely among doctors. David Eddy, the health policy professor at Duke, writes about the physical examination, specifically for cyanosis, the bluing of the face and fingers, that indicates a low level of oxygen in the blood: "A study of 22 doctors was performed to assess their ability to diagnose cyanosis in 20 patients, with the true diagnosis confirmed by direct measurement of oxygen levels. Only 53 percent of the physicians were definite in diagnosing cyanosis in subjects with extremely low blood oxygen, and 26 percent of the physicians said cyanosis existed in subjects who had normal blood oxygen."

Similarly, EKGs can be variously interpreted by physicians. One group of experts compiled 100 EKG readings, 50 of which showed myocardial infarction (heart attack), 25 of which were normal, and 25 of which showed some other abnormality. These EKGs were then given to ten other cardiologists to test their diagnostic skills. The proportion of EKGs judged by the ten fellow cardiologists to show a myocardial infarct varied by a factor of two. If you had an infarct and went to Physician A, there would be a 20 percent chance he would miss it. If you did not have an infarct and went to Physician B, there would be a 26 percent chance that he would say you had one. Even among specialists examining a routine test, like an EKG, there can be widely divergent conclusions.

Medical instruments do not necessarily yield definitive answers. Using a microscope, thirteen pathologists read 1,001 specimens obtained from biopsies of the cervix, and repeated the readings later. On average, each pathologist agreed with himself only 89 percent of the time, and with a panel of senior pathologists only 87 percent of the time. With the patients who actually had an abnormal cervix, the doctors who reconsidered their own earlier conclusions agreed with their first readings only 68 percent of the time; the senior pathologists concurred with their juniors in only 51 percent of the cases. While the pathologists generally did well on distinguishing clearly cancerous tissue from clearly normal tissue, they did less well in identifying precancerous lesions.

Orwig has sought ways to avoid making errors by slowing his perception and analysis. He uses his dictated report as a mechanism to be systematic. The format of his dictation follows a highly structured checklist. For example, in reading a chest x-ray, he will explicitly comment not only on the lungs and heart, but also on the bones, the soft tissues of the chest, and the mediastinum (the central structure of the thorax), as well as the pleura, the lining of the lungs; only when he comes to the summary will he home in on the explicit clinical question that was posed by the internist or surgeon who requested the x-ray. "Once I got a call from a clinician who said: 'I ordered this x-ray to see if this man had pneumonia. Why did you put all the stuff in about his ribs?'" Indeed, there was a large patch of white within the black image of the man's right lung, indicating a pneumonia. But Orwig had made special note in his dictated report of several healed rib fractures. "Some radiologists would not take the breath to report these old fractures because they do not seem to be an active issue or relevant to the primary diagnosis, which is an infection," Orwig told me. Part of his rationale is just to be complete, but part is because any observation could prove to have clinical import. For example, old fractures might suggest that the patient had fallen in the past, because he is an alcoholic, or might have passed out due to a seizure disorder that was not recognized. People who are drunk or have a seizure sometimes aspirate their mucus, setting up a fertile field for bacteria to enter the lungs and trigger pneumonia. As it happened, the clinician went back and interviewed the man, who confessed that he was a binge drinker.

The morning I spoke with Orwig, he had just returned home after a night on call. He had been asked to read a CT scan of a middle-aged man in the ICU. The patient was an alcoholic with liver disease and had been admitted to Marin General Hospital confused and delirious. It turned out that he was bleeding internally, and like many patients with cirrhosis, was tipped into his delirious state because his liver was unable to detoxify the products of digested blood from his gut. The CT scan was ordered because after initially improving, the patient had become delirious again. The ICU physician assumed that the man was once more bleeding internally.

Orwig looked at the CT scan and then went through his methodical checklist. He traced every loop of bowel on an abdominal CT scan; his colleagues often joke when he lingers over the study, "There goes Dennis again, tracing every loop from the stomach to the anus." As he followed the turns of the intestines, he noticed what appeared to be small air bubbles in the abdomen. These bubbles did not look like the kind of gas we all have in our bowels. "I finally decided that the air bubbles couldn't be in the bowel," Orwig told me, "so they had to be in the superior mesenteric vein." Somehow, gas had accumulated in the vessels that drain blood from the intestines. "Then I noticed that the loops of bowel near the gas bubbles were thickened." Orwig reasoned that the blood supply to the intestines must somehow be impaired, so there had been a breakdown in tissue, with gas from inside the bowel moving into the surrounding blood vessels. This condition is called ischemic bowel, meaning the bowel is starved of its nourishing blood supply and begins to decompose.

When Orwig spoke with the clinician in the ICU, he was met with skepticism. "You guys aren't very good in diagnosing ischemic bowel," the physician said. Orwig agreed that it was a difficult diagnosis based on a CT scan, but explained that he had thoroughly traced every loop of intestine in the man's abdomen, and the gas didn't belong where he found it. It was imperative that a surgeon be called to assess the patient; if Orwig's presumption was correct, there was an urgency to operate and restore the blood supply to the bowel. Orwig was right, and the patient's life was saved.

"Sometimes, going with your gut just doesn't work in my field," Orwig quipped. "There is so much gas in the abdomen that just seeing a few little bubbles doesn't mean anything in the picture as a whole. It only has significance when you segregate out each structure, and then you can see that the gas doesn't belong there."

As he systematically reviews every aspect of the film, Orwig explained, "My brain is forced to work in a similar stepwise way. It is easier — certainly quicker — to simply look at the pneumonia in the right lower lobe of the lung," he said, "and not take the time to detail all of the other information. But this protects me." Orwig is "protected" from the most common mistake that radiologists make, the error of search satisfaction. As we saw earlier, it is a natural cognitive tendency to stop searching, and therefore stop thinking, when one makes a major finding. This is all the more true in radiology, where a busy internist informs the radiologist that the patient has typical findings of fever, cough, and yellow sputum, and so directs the radiologist's attention on the lungs in his search for the expected pneumonia; but if he focuses solely on the lungs, Orwig said, and snaps to the correct diagnosis of pneumonia, he risks missing a dense area in an upper rib that suggests there may be an underlying cancer, or a widening in the mediastinum that could be an aneurysm of the aorta.

Orwig is part of a large private radiology practice that consists of eleven doctors. They are conscious of the risk of making errors if overloaded, so recently they added two new members to the practice in order to limit the number of x-rays each one is required to read on a shift. Like primary care physicians, they are seeking new ways to secure enough time to think about each case. They also instituted a quality assurance program. Every day, each radiologist in Orwig's group reads four or five x-rays that are independently read by a colleague. Then the two readings are compared for discrepancies. Sometimes a discrepancy is insignificant; other times it may be of major import. The results of this daily exercise are entered into a database for the entire group, so that there is ongoing monitoring of each radiologist as well as the whole team. "This way, we learn from each other's mistakes as well as our own," Orwig said.

Orwig was chastened some time ago when one of his fellow radiologists came into the dark reading room with an MRI scan of a knee. "What do you think of this case?" his colleague asked. Orwig looked at the scan and said, "Torn ACL" — anterior cruciate ligament, a common sports injury. The colleague put Orwig's report down in front of him. It read: "normal anterior cruciate ligament." "I was mystified," Orwig told me. "It's incredible that at one time I could look at a film and only later see what I had missed." The only explanation that came to Orwig's mind was that he had relied too much on "gestalt" and not methodically traced every anatomic component in the knee.

"This is also a problem of high volume," Orwig said. "A hematologist like you, Jerry, cares for patients over the course of months to years. You see them in follow-up visits, so when something goes wrong, you can deconstruct the steps in the diagnosis and treatment and figure out where you made mistakes. I am literally reading hundreds of x-rays, day after day after day, on different patients. Most of the x-rays are not follow-ups. So it is difficult for me to go back and figure out why I erred in my observation. I have no ability to put myself back in the seat when that knee case was in front of me." Because of this, Orwig said, "I have to keep reminding myself to be systematic. The more experience you have, the more seasoned you are, the greater the temptation to rely on gestalt."

E. James Potchen of Michigan State commented on Orwig's strategy of sticking to a methodical checklist. He agreed that Orwig would have some "marginal gain" by forcing himself to look at each of the anatomic structures on the film. But the "real added value," Potchen said, was what Orwig did in drawing the clinician's attention to the rib fractures or gas bubbles. Potchen has studied decision-making under uncertainty, not only in medicine but also in law and in business. He recalled how Dr. Merrill Sosman, who was chief of radiology at the Brigham Hospital in Boston, would be given a chest x-ray and then declare to the residents in training, "This patient has kidney failure." This was a deduction worthy of Arthur Conan Doyle, and the residents would wonder: How can you diagnose a problem with the kidneys by looking at the chest? Sosman explained that he saw a thickening of the ribs, which led to the insight that there had been remodeling of the bones because the kidneys had failed, changing the metabolism of calcium and phosphate. "That's how you add value as a radiologist," Potchen said. "You discover what is not known about the patient at the time that the x-ray was taken. And that's how you develop your cachet. You add something beyond what other people do." This, of course, is why primary care physicians are sending so many patients for radiological studies.

Mammography is routinely ordered by primary care physicians as a screening test to detect early cancer in women entering middle age. "Mammograms are the most monotonous type of work that we do," Orwig said. "And mammograms are the most anxiety provoking of all x-rays," he added. To miss a cancer is devastating, because the tumors that are found early are readily removed, and missing the cancer can result in metastases that are hard to control and rarely, if ever, cured. On the other hand, overreading a mammogram will subject a healthy woman to the emotional roller coaster of further imaging, a biopsy, and then the lingering doubt about whether there actually was a cancer that was missed despite the biopsy result.

Not surprisingly, mammography is a fertile field for medical-legal conflict, and radiologists are acutely aware that errors can result in a malpractice lawsuit. Even the best radiologists will inaccurately read a mammogram in 2 to 3 percent of the cases, while some series show that other doctors incorrectly read the images in

20 percent or more. The aim is to recommend a biopsy on the women who will prove to have a tumor, and not to recommend a biopsy for women with benign changes on the mammogram. The women who undergo a biopsy are said to be "called back." "In theory, it would be best to have a four or five percent callback rate," Orwig said. This is considered to be the optimal rate. "But the norm," Orwig said, "is about ten to eleven percent." This higher callback rate results in a larger number of women with benign changes who undergo further evaluation and biopsy.

There is a tradeoff here: causing emotional distress in women with benign changes versus the need to "capture" a number of breast cancers that otherwise would be missed. In Orwig's group of eleven radiologists, he falls in the callback rate of 10 to 11 percent, the norm, but one colleague has a 15 to 16 percent callback rate. Many of the women he calls back end up having benign biopsies. "He was sued," Orwig told me. "Years ago, he missed a breast cancer." This experience caused him to become more "aggressive," as Orwig put it, in assessing mammograms and calling more women back for further studies and biopsy. While his colleague's callback rate is still within "reasonable bounds," Orwig said, there is no doubt that the consequences of missing a malignant lesion and being sued caused him to think in a different way.

Dr. Potchen published a paper analyzing medical decision-making and concluded that what most influenced clinical choices was "the last bad experience." Potchen's conclusion mirrors the availability error, which Croskerry and Redelmeier highlighted earlier: what is most available in your mind strongly colors your thinking about a new case that has some similarities, but it can cause you to ignore important differences and come to an incorrect diagnosis.

Imaging the body using x-rays began at the end of the nineteenth century. Over the ensuing years, advances in technology such as the CT scan and the MRI scan have greatly enhanced a radiologist's ability to visualize our anatomy, but they pose new cognitive challenges. As we saw earlier, a chest x-ray shows a single, static view of the thorax along with the heart, lungs, bones, soft tissues, and mediastinum, the area of the chest that includes the aorta. The chest x-ray, again, is performed with a patient in two positions, so that two images are generated, one with a view of the front of the chest, another of the side. When CT scans were first developed, they contained dozens of images; the first MRI scans produced hundreds. When the images from these scans were presented on a film, they averaged twelve per film; this was termed a "tile display." Another way to view the images from these scans was one after another on a monitor, called a "cine" mode, referring to the experience of viewing a movie.

A landmark study compared tile with cine viewing of CT images of the chest, specifically the detection of lung nodules. These nodules are small, solid masses in the lungs that can be benign, such as after an infection, or malignant, indicating a lung cancer or a metastasis to the lungs. Radiologists were much more successful in detecting lung nodules using the cine mode than the tile display; they were also more accurate in identifying artifacts, such as blood vessels in the lungs that can sometimes resemble a nodule if viewed in a certain plane. The researchers noted that moving images created a novel cognitive cue, particularly with smaller nodules: they seemed to "pop out" on the cine display, and thus more frequently caught the eye of the radiologist. Throughout the 1990s, cine viewing became the preferred image display mode, allowing more efficient evaluation of scans that contained hundreds of images.

But as refinements were made in CT scanning, particularly rapid imaging over large parts of the body that allowed for the visualization of multiple organs and vessels simultaneously, radiologists were presented with a dilemma. There could be a thousand or more images with many tissues moving at once before the radiologist's gaze. As Dr. Herbert Kressel, the Stoneman Professor of Radiology at Harvard and a specialist in abdominal imaging, recently told me, "Over an average weekend in a busy emergency department, a radiologist may have to read a hundred fifty CT scans. It's impossible for him to look at a hundred fifty thousand or more images."

It is not only in the ER that scans have become routine. Between 1998 and 2002, the number of CT studies in the United States increased by 59 percent, MRI by 51 percent, and ultrasound by 30 percent, during traditional work hours, and each increased by 15 percent during on-call off-hours. Survey studies show that with this increased workload, radiologists reported more symptoms of blurred vision, eyestrain, difficulty focusing, and headache. Elizabeth Krupinski of the University of Arizona pointed out in a recent publication that the huge amount of imaging data generated has the high potential for fatigue, discontent, and possibly increased error rates.

Kressel extends this concern to the naïve reliance on high-tech imaging by busy clinicians. Patients are sometimes sent for studies without a detailed clinical history. Some doctors scribble "rule out pathology" on the referral slip. Others can be too directive, or show a poor understanding of how the newer CT and MRI scans work. For example, Kressel told me, recently a woman had been sent for an imaging study with the request "rule out pulmonary embolus." Pulmonary embolus is a life-threatening condition when a clot, often from the legs, breaks off and lodges in the pulmonary artery. "We performed the study and timed the images when the contrast material would be filling the pulmonary vessels," Kressel told me. The study showed nothing to suggest a pulmonary embolus, since there was no blunting or obstruction of the contrast material in the pulmonary arteries. A few days later, the reason for the woman's chest pain and difficulty breathing became apparent: she had a tear in her aorta. "We could have detected this tear by timing the images on the scan to follow the contrast material through the aorta," Kressel said. The shape of the aorta was not distorted, so the tear was not visualized in the absence of contrast material that would enter the torn part of the wall.

"The old idea based on a static study — that an image is an image is an image — is obsolete now with technology that is dynamic, that can show us active changes in blood flow and other aspects of physiology," Kressel said. "How you use the machine translates into what you get to see."

The problem with applying a methodical and rigorous approach to every image, Kressel said, is that with a CT scan or an MRI, "there is just so much data." There may be more than a thousand images per CT scan or per MRI, so that a single radiologist's entire day could well be occupied with looking at just one of these studies. The solution, in part, Kressel said, is to go organ by organ. In his field, abdominal radiology, he will rigorously view the liver, then the kidneys, then the spleen, and so on. Kressel's strategy, like other radiologists who specialize in MRI, is to analyze primarily the "data-rich sequences," those segments of the study that can provide the most information, then arrive at a tentative list of possible diagnoses and selectively look at other images to find data that support or contradict the possibilities.

Sometimes the technology itself sabotages this careful approach. The tracker ball, equivalent to a mouse on a computer, can accelerate rapidly the speed of the images flashing before the radiologist's eyes with small increases in pressure from his fingers. This means that the images may speed up without the radiologist's being aware of it. "You may not get each image coming at three per second," Kressel said. "You go to an emergency room, where a radiologist is working under an incredible load, and you watch him go through a CT scan case, and you will see he is flying through it." Kressel has seen how radiologists press on the tracker ball, consciously or subconsciously, in an effort to get through the thousand or so images. "With your hand on a tracker ball, you can literally skip three or four images and not even realize it." This is because while you are looking at images in two dimensions, "your mind is working to integrate the three-dimensional space that you are moving through." When Kressel supervises residents, "I drive them nuts. I force them to slow down so they have to see each image." There should be no shortcuts, either intended or subliminal. After decades of looking at images, Kressel's eye has become so acute that he can pick up "subtle differences in contour of a structure in the abdomen, even with a rapid look," he said, which a resident cannot do. For example, there may be a lymph node near the pancreas that is observable in a single image on a scan, "and the resident doesn't see it." Identifying this lymph node could be clinically meaningful in assessing whether a cancer of the pancreas had spread beyond the organ, a critical piece of information in its treatment and prognosis. "So I will go through the case and force him to go back and show him how he missed it."

"In some ways, we are victims of our own success," Dennis Orwig said. "We have so many excellent imaging techniques. Some doctors hardly examine patients or take histories anymore. They just order scans and say to the radiologist, 'Give me the diagnosis.'" In fact, the week we spoke, there was an article in the *New England Journal of Medicine* about whether the stethoscope had become a vestige of a bygone era, since cardiac imaging techniques were so advanced that the findings cardiologists traditionally make by listening had been rendered moot. "And when clinicians order sophisticated scans," Orwig continued, "they expect a definitive answer back. They don't want to hear a radiologist's description of a constellation of observations — they want one diagnosis. There is tremendous pressure on us to come to a conclusion," Orwig said, "and we have to resist that, because sometimes you can't make an exact diagnosis. The best you can do is to describe what you see."

A seasoned radiologist also learns not to give in when a clinician demands a discrete diagnosis. "Sometimes," Orwig allowed, "you can say, 'This is diverticulitis.' It's ninety-nine percent certain, and the clinician then can feel comfortable and go ahead and treat the patient with antibiotics. And that one percent may be a perforated colon cancer. But then there are patients who undergo CT scans and the best you can say is that there is 'a complex inflammatory process in the pelvis of this gentleman.' Many clinicians don't like to hear that. They think that the radiologist is waffling. But what the radiologist is doing is showing the doctor his thinking, sharing with him the most that can be said based on his expert observations."

Just as a clinician needs to choose his words carefully in communicating with patients, he must tailor the language of his request to a radiologist. "There is this notion that the clinician wants to keep the radiologist honest, so he doesn't tell him anything specific," Kressel noted. "In my field, you will get a referral that says 'patient with abdominal pain.' But without more specific history, you reduce the kind of clinical cues that are so important and actually make it much more difficult to assess the images.

"I always thought this was maximally stupid," Kressel said. "Why would you want to tie someone's arm behind his back?" Not only can this hamper perception and cognition, as Potchen's studies show, but, as Kressel elaborated, it can also affect technique and lead to errors. With the new multidetector CT scans, very large volumes of tissue are scanned in a short time, so for the best results the settings on the machine have to be adjusted to take into account the patient's clinical history. "If the clinician doesn't give us a full history, just the one question in his mind, then we will technically tailor the exam to that one question —

like, Is there pulmonary embolus? — and risk missing something else that is important."

It is not only the clinician's language that can be misleading. Different radiologists use different terms to describe what they see. "People usually don't think about radiologists in terms of nuances of communication," Kressel said. "When you think of a doctor speaking, you imagine a clinician at the bedside explaining something to a patient. But radiologists become very impassioned about the words they use in their reports. And, of course, the language used reflects your type of thinking. Moreover, there is no agreement about different terms, no uniform structured approach to communicating findings." This is especially true with the more advanced CT and MRI scanners. "Even if different radiologists see the same thing on an image, just from the way they describe it, there are nuances and ambiguities communicated by the terms." Kressel referred again to the woman who was evaluated for a possible pulmonary embolus. "The radiologist reported that the aorta was 'not enlarged.' That term 'not enlarged' can be taken in many different ways. First, it doesn't mean that the radiologist saw the interior of the vessel. He is just making a descriptive statement. And 'not enlarged' is not the same as saying that the vessel is normal, although many clinicians would take that as the meaning of the radiologist's phrase. Because different terms mean different things to different doctors, a single term can guide thinking in different directions."

My hospital recently created a Web site called "Patient Site" in response to patients' desire for access to their own medical records. All the lab tests and radiology reports are ready for viewing as soon as they are generated. This provides an opportunity for patient and doctor to sit together and go over the results. Reading the language in these reports can be trying — mostly, of course, for patients — so the clinician should point out the radiologist's words that signal a level of uncertainty. The radiologist may have said the area behind the uterus was not well visualized by the scan, or the thickening of the wall of the bowel was not diagnostic for a tumor and could also represent inflammation. This should prompt the clinician to explain to his patient why he needs to revisit the history, perform a more comprehensive physical examination, or order further tests to define the problem.

Communicating this uncertainty poses a challenge. Recently, Orwig viewed a mammogram with a pattern of calcium deposits that are classically diagnosed as benign. But the woman's previous mammogram showed no calcium deposits. He debated with his colleagues about whether to biopsy the breast and came down on the side of biopsy. Orwig went out to speak with the woman whose mammogram showed the new calcium deposits. "I want to apologize in advance," he said. "I think that what we found is benign, but I am going to recommend that it be biopsied." He paused. "I know this will cause you great anxiety. So let me explain my reasoning. What we found on your mammogram reaches the threshold to make this recommendation because it's new. It wasn't present on your prior study. Nonetheless, I am fairly certain that it will turn out to be fine, but we should go ahead, to be complete." It turned out there was a high-grade invasive cancer in the woman's breast, which would be removed by lumpectomy followed by radiation treatment.

Orwig suggested that the case be shown at the quality assurance conferences where the radiologists review their choices and try to refine their skills to avoid future errors. "One colleague said to me: 'If we show this case, given this pattern of calcium deposits, then we are going to have women lining up to the end of the block for biopsies. What good is it going to do? We show this case, people are going to freak out, because then they feel they have to biopsy every patient who has this kind of calcification. We should show cases that will help us because they have very specific findings.'" Orwig agreed with his colleague that, based only on the pattern of calcium deposits, there was no teaching lesson per se, but he believed the key point was changing one's mind based on a previous mammogram. More broadly, he felt that sometimes a teaching point is made by showing the exception to the rule, and emphasizing that there is this gray zone in radiology, particularly in mammography, where judgment comes into play and specific aspects of a case, like the new appearance of calcium deposits, that would otherwise be ignored as benign should be a cause for concern.

Orwig's colleague was afraid that discussing the case would spark an outbreak of "availability errors," the same kinds of errors we saw in the emergency room earlier: a sharp bias in thinking based on a striking, unusual event that recently occurred and becomes prominent in the doctor's mind. Yet, as Orwig argued, not sharing the case could cause colleagues to miss what might be a lethal malignancy. The struggle is to find a middle ground, to be aware of the availability fallacy while recognizing that certain patterns may not conform to the prototype; it is a matter of juggling seemingly contradictory bits of data simultaneously in one's mind and then seeking other information to make a decision, one way or another. This juggling, and this kind of decision-making, marks the expert physician — at the bedside or in a darkened radiology suite.

Orwig thinks about this woman's case often when he is reading mammograms. When he sees a similar pattern of clustered calcium deposits, not only does he check the prior mammogram to see if they were present then, he also checks studies from earlier years to see when the deposits were first noted. Orwig realizes that he could begin to overread mammograms, lowering his threshold to such an extent that he begins recommending unnecessary biopsies. He still is trying to find that middle ground.

Dr. Harold Kundel of the University of Pennsylvania has studied the physiology of image perception by tracking the eye movements of his fellow radiologists. The doctor sits with an apparatus on his head that resembles a bicycle rider's helmet. The apparatus has several parts, including a visor and a miniature video camera. As a doctor examines a series of images, a beam of invisible infrared light is trained on his eye. The camera, trained on his pupil, determines where he is directing his gaze by tracking the infrared beam's reflection. In some of Kundel's studies, a radiologist looked at chest x-rays where there were small lung nodules, each measuring between a half centimeter and one centimeter, or about a quarter to half an inch long. Such nodules are important to detect, since they can represent an early cancer or a serious infection like tuberculosis or fungus. In about 20 percent of the cases, the eyes did not focus at all on the nodules. In the remaining 80 percent, the gaze was directed toward the nodule, but in half of these cases, the nodule simply was not perceived.

"The brain makes a covert decision," Kundel explained. Below the level of consciousness, the mind decides that the image is not important, not worth bringing up to the level of conscious recognition. The radiologists whose eyes dwelled on the nodule for some two to three seconds were more likely to consciously recognize it. Recognition would be enhanced if there was sharp contrast between the nodule and the surrounding lung, the contrast between white for a solid mass and black for air. Recognition was also enhanced if the nodule had a clear border rather than a blurry edge.

Earlier studies tracking eye gaze, done at the University of Iowa, showed that search satisfaction was a common error among radiologists. In follow-up studies, Kundel's team showed that in some cases the gaze did fix on a second abnormality, but it was not recognized. For example, a patient with pneumonia might have a small cancer in the scapula, the wing bone, but the radiologist reported only the pneumonia in the lung, even though the apparatus revealed that his eyes had passed over the tumor in the bone. His mind had already snapped closed after identifying the pneumonia and would not consciously accept other findings. "It comes down to what your preconceived notions of the image are, which I classify as bias," Kundel explained. Echoing a maxim of Merrill Sosman of Brigham Hospital, Kundel said, "You see what you want to see." The expert, though, having learned about bias and search satisfaction, consciously tries to keep his mind open so that he sees beyond his preconceptions. He is helped in this effort by how the clinical history is framed, by the cues provided in the language of the clinician, and by adhering to the kind of systematic deconstruction of the image that Dennis Orwig follows in his dictated reports.

Given the difficulties in perception and cognition that Kundel and other researchers have reported, could computers replace radiologists, or at least lower their error rates? One computer-aided diagnostic system was approved in 2006 by the Food and Drug Administration for identifying lung nodules on chest x-rays. Other systems are being studied, including those for mammograms. The pivotal clinical trial on malignant lung nodules that led to the FDA approval involved fifteen radiologists who were asked to note their level of suspicion that a chest x-ray contained cancer. They used a scoring system of 1 to 100, and they were to mark the location that caused their suspicion. Eighty cancer cases and 160 cancer-free cases were in the study. Each radiologist interpreted these 240 cases three times: two times separated by one to four months without computer assistance and then, immediately after the second interpretation, with computer assistance. Computer assistance improved detection of the cancer between 14 and 24 percent, depending on its size. But the computer system also caused radiologists to change almost 10 percent of their correct decisions (identifying the cancer) to incorrect diagnoses (stating that it was unimportant or benign). Of the fifteen radiologists in the clinical trial, no two had identical results in evaluating the 80 cancer cases and 160 cancer-free cases. All but 25 percent of the cancers were identified by all fifteen radiologists. But the difficult-to-diagnose cancers were found by only four of the radiologists. No radiologist identified all 80 of the cancers correctly.

One unwelcome effect of computer-assisted detection was that after being prompted by the computer, more radiologists suspected cancer in chest x-rays that came from patients without a malignancy — a false-positive reading. This demonstrates the power of technology, particularly computer-based, in shaking the confidence of a specialist in his initial diagnosis. It also demonstrates that machines do not provide perfect solutions to the imperfection of perception and thinking. Perhaps, as radiologists become more accustomed to computer-assisted detection and receive clinical feedback about the risk of becoming overly suspicious about benign findings on a chest x-ray, they will accommodate their thinking to the new technology. In the meantime, as they search for another new middle ground, there will be a trade-off, with more accurate cancer detection but greater patient anxiety, as more people without cancer are subjected to the emotional upheaval and invasive procedures that follow on false positives.

A short drive south from Marin County, across the Golden Gate Bridge, brings you to San Francisco. Perched on Parnassus Heights is the University of California Medical Center and the nearby Moffitt Hospital. Vickie Feldstein is a professor of radiology at UCSF specializing in ultrasonography. (Dr. Dennis Orwig happens to be her husband.) Most people are familiar with ultra-sound examinations from a pregnancy. The developing baby is imaged, appearing in a two-dimensional representation inside the uterus, a swirl of black and white and gray. "Some people consider an ultrasound image to look like a weather map," Feldstein said with a chuckle. It certainly looks like a weather map to me, spe-cifically a snowstorm. The flux of white specks across a black background makes the discrete outlines of organs difficult, if not impossible, for me to make out. Of course, for Feldstein and radi-ologists who use this technology daily, the images are as familiar as the palms of their hands, and the contrasts of black, white, and gray full of meaning.

Given the complexity of the images in ultrasonography, one might think that in this case computers would better assist diag-nosis. The computer would provide a quantitative assessment of each structure in the developing fetus. For example, at twenty weeks' gestation, an ultrasound is used to measure the ventricles of the fetus, which are the fluid-filled cisterns in the brain. If the length of the ventricle is greater than ten millimeters, then the fe-tus is carefully monitored for hydrocephaly, commonly called wa-ter on the brain, a disorder of ballooning ventricles that can result in brain damage as well as other developmental abnormalities. But it turns out that the numbers a computer would supply may not reveal what the radiologist wishes to consider. "The numbers will help you and raise your level of attention," Feldstein said, "but you have to take the whole picture. You have to look at the shape of the ventricles and the associated surrounding tissue. It's not just based on reading the numbers."

A normal cerebral ventricle is shaped like a teardrop. The ven-tricle on an ultrasound is defined by a black central core, which is the fluid, and a white lining, the choroid plexus that produces the fluid. Feldstein recently saw a woman close to her due date. "She was near term," she recalled, "and the size of the fetus's ventricles was within the numerical limits of normal. But when I looked at it, the shape didn't seem right." The changes in the contour of the teardrop were subtle, but to Feldstein's trained eye, potentially significant: the borders were not smooth but slightly irregular, and the teardrop was not finely tapered at its apex. Both of these observations could be easily ignored or discounted, particularly since the dimensions were not beyond the accepted limits of health. Feldstein decided that she needed to pursue this, although the clinical consequences of her findings were not immediately clear. At thirty-five weeks, the question in her mind was, What would the mother do with the information? It was too late to consider terminating the pregnancy, but Feldstein concluded that it was important to know whether her impression — that there was some underlying abnormality in the baby's brain — was correct or not. In part, determining this would help the parents anticipate problems after birth, preparing them emotionally and logistically for raising a child that might be retarded or need special neonatal care.

Another dimension that influenced Feldstein's decision-making: the medical-legal ramifications. If indeed there was an abnormality in the brain that was not visualized on the ultrasound but had caused the fetus's ventricles to change their contour, then it would be best to know that before delivery so no one would suggest that an inept obstetrician had caused trauma that led to brain damage. Feldstein explained to the mother that although her baby's ventricles were within the limits of normal, there also were subtle changes in shape that might bespeak something abnormal in the brain. Feldstein didn't want to unduly frighten the mother, but on the other hand, she felt it was her responsibility to communicate her analysis. The mother decided to undergo MRI scanning, and a cerebral hemorrhage was detected. Bleeding in the fetus's brain had caused the ragged borders of the ventricles and the distortion of the apex of the teardrop. Feldstein's sharp eye had been proven true. The mother delivered her baby with the necessary pediatric neurologists in attendance.

Every radiologist I spoke to could immediately recount not only successes like Feldstein's but also unnerving errors. Herbert Kressel, the imaging specialist at Harvard, told me that recently he had missed seeing an abnormality on an MRI scan: a small but discernible cancer of the liver that was present on several of the images. "It was a definite miss. I just didn't see it. And to this day, I really don't know why." He wondered whether he had moved too quickly through the cine presentation, put too much pressure on the tracker ball. "But that's a speculation. I just don't know," he said, his voice heavy. "People have to understand that there always will be a certain amount of imprecision in imaging and interpretation."

Machines cannot replace the doctor's mind, his thinking about what he sees and what he does not see. Attention to language — the words of a referring clinician and the report of the radiologist — can make perception and analysis better. Laymen should understand the inherent limits and potential biases in the beholder's eye, so that when there are important decisions to make, they can ask for another set of expert eyes.

CHAPTER 9

Marketing, Money, and Medical Decisions

I FIRST ENCOUNTERED Karen Delgado in the early 1980s and have followed her career ever since. She carries great sway in her specialty of internal medicine and endocrinology. She sits on national committees that review practice guidelines and set out curricula in physician education. Colleagues look to her for counsel on complicated cases.

She is a typically busy clinician with a typically heavy load of patients. One day not long ago, she had ten minutes to grab lunch before her clinic began, with three new patients and six follow-ups. Two residents would be working with her, but, if anything, these trainees would extend her hours.

As Delgado gathered a sheaf of lab reports to take to the clinic, she saw a face out of the corner of her eye and froze. Rick Duggan filled the doorway of her office. There was no escaping him.

"I don't know what more I can do, Dr. Delgado," Duggan said. He was a sales representative for a pharmaceutical company that made a testosterone product. "You haven't written a single prescription for my drug. Not one." He was dressed in a bright blue shirt, gold tie, and sharply cut suit. "Dr. Delgado," he said, his

voice taking on a forceful tone. "I want you to write three prescriptions a week for the next month."

She was dumbstruck. Duggan had been shadowing her for
nearly a year, trying to promote his product. He brought boxes of
candy to her office three times, and when this ploy failed (the
candy wasn't very good, Delgado noted), he left invitations to "educational dinners" at the most expensive restaurants in town.
Delgado ignored the invitations, telling herself that if she wanted
a good meal, she would have it with her husband on her own tab.
What astonished her was that the salesman knew which prescriptions she was writing.

"I need you to do this," Duggan pressed. "Three a week for the
next month."

She stared icily at him, said "No," put the lab reports in the
pocket of her white coat, and walked out of her office.

The first patient Delgado saw in clinic was Nick Mancini.
Mancini was a solidly built handyman in his early fifties whom
she'd first met in the ICU. He had come to the ER complaining of
blurred vision and the worst headache of his life. He had hemor-
rhaged into his brain. Brain scans failed to reveal why he bled, but
showed that his pituitary gland was enlarged, so Delgado, an endocrinologist, was one of the specialists called to the ICU on his
case. She approached the bedside. She couldn't see his face clearly;
the lights had been dimmed because of his blistering headache.
But as she shook Mancini's hand and pressed his palm, she made
the diagnosis that had eluded all the other doctors. Each had pre-
sumably shaken his hand as well, but the thick, doughy flesh sig-
nified to Delgado more than the mitt of a handyman.

Mancini had acromegaly. This disorder occurs when a tumor
causes the pituitary gland to produce too much growth hormone,
so the hands and feet grow larger and the facial features become
coarser. Located at the base of the brain, the pituitary is called the
master gland because it signals other glands in the body, like the

thyroid and the adrenal, to make essential hormones. As a pituitary tumor grows, it can rupture its feeding blood vessels, resulting in a cerebral hemorrhage. This is called pituitary apoplexy. The nerves to the eyes run near the pituitary, which accounted for Mancini's blurry vision. If the hemorrhage destroys the pituitary gland, it no longer sends signals to the body, so production of essential hormones stops. The adrenal glands make cortisol, one of the most critical of these hormones. Without it, people are prone to shock, especially under stress — as in surgery, for example.

Delgado gave Mancini protective doses of corticosteroids, and he was taken to the OR. The surgery to drain the blood succeeded. He no longer had a functioning pituitary gland, so Delgado prescribed replacement therapy for the missing hormones; in addition to daily doses of thyroxine and corticosteroids, she gave him testosterone, which the pituitary also controls.

"Everything okay at home with the kids?" Delgado asked.

"Great. My daughter is starting high school next week." Mancini smiled.

Delgado nodded. The testosterone preparation she wrote on the prescription pad was not the one made by Duggan's company.

The next afternoon, Delgado attended the weekly clinical conference where trainees present cases and the senior endocrinologists comment on them. At the end of the hour, Dr. Bert Foyer approached Delgado. Foyer was in his late sixties, also a prominent member of the staff, active in both clinical care and research. His specialty was testosterone replacement for men with various endocrine disorders.

"Good cases today," Foyer said.

Delgado agreed.

"I ran into Rick Duggan yesterday," Foyer said. "Couldn't you take a few moments with him?"

"Bert, I'm really busy." The silence that hung between them finished Delgado's reply.

That night at home, over dinner, Delgado's husband, a surgeon at her hospital, surprised her by bringing up Duggan's name. "I don't know if he was looking for me," Delgado's husband said, "but he was in the corridor when I was leaving the OR." She raised her eyebrow. "He introduced himself and said, 'Why doesn't your wife like me?'" Delgado's husband grinned. "I had a few one-liners, but I just shrugged. What's this about?"

The answer to his question is that some pharmaceutical companies are striving to change the way doctors think about health and disease. In this case, they are medicalizing normal change in aging men. These companies make testosterone products; they want not only to have their drug prescribed instead of the competition's, but to expand the market beyond what medical science dictates. When I spoke with Delgado, she acknowledged that Duggan had targeted her because she was, in marketing parlance, an "opinion leader." Working at a prominent teaching hospital, widely recognized as one of the top clinicians in her specialty, supervising the education of the next generation of doctors, readily given the floor at conferences, and having a steady flow of patients, she influenced clinical decision-making in her city and beyond.

Duggan had used several classic marketing strategies to get her, in essence, to endorse his brand. The first was gift-giving. Besides the candy and the dinner invitations, he had brought other small gifts, including a calculator, a desk clock, and pens. Delgado left these unopened on her secretary's desk. Duggan — well dressed, and with a practiced seductive manner — then chatted up Delgado's secretary. He knew that without her assent he stood no chance of pitching Delgado face to face. Delgado politely ignored her secretary's enthusiasm for the sales representative. Once Delgado rejected these approaches, Duggan switched from honey to vinegar.

"I was really offended by him," Delgado told me. "He was trying to bully me. It may work with some doctors, but not with me."

At dinner, Delgado told her husband how surprised she was that Duggan knew which products she prescribed. Her husband recently had read in a business magazine that pharmaceutical companies contract with drugstores to learn physicians' prescribing patterns. Of course, the companies did not know whom she prescribed the drugs for, but they could obtain a complete list of how many prescriptions she wrote for which products over a designated time period. "It's perfectly legal," Delgado's husband said.

"But I don't like it," she replied.

She noted that Duggan's company seemed to be using a strategy of escalation, from gifts to confrontation and then the intervention of her colleague Dr. Foyer.

"I don't really think it's about money for Bert," she said, although Duggan's company had given him grants for some of his clinical trials of testosterone products. "I think it's simply that he's a believer."

For many years, the market for testosterone replacement therapy was relatively small. Doctors treated patients like Nick Mancini, who lacked a functioning pituitary gland, or men born with an extra X chromosome, who have what is called Klinefelter syndrome; their shrunken testicles don't produce enough of the hormone. Androgen pills were originally used in replacement therapy, but they often caused liver damage. Then intramuscular injections were tried; these produced a sharp spike of testosterone and a sharp fall, often accompanied by parallel swings in mood, sex drive, and energy. In the late 1980s, a transdermal patch was developed. This allowed safer and steadier dosing, but sometimes the skin became irritated or the patch fell off during exercise. Finally the hormone was prepared in a form almost any man could conveniently use: a colorless gel that could easily be rubbed on a part of the body, like the shoulders, once a day. This would simplify treatment and expand the potential market — if a group of men could be shown to benefit.

A few months before Rick Duggan confronted Dr. Delgado, a two-page ad in *Time* magazine showed a car's gas gauge and beside it the words "Fatigued? Depressed mood? Low sex drive? Could be your testosterone is running on empty." The ad went on to explain that "as some men grow old, their testosterone levels decline," and recommended that they consult their doctors about testosterone replacement therapy. At the bottom of the ad, the gas gauge pointed to "Full."

Delgado had seen the ad in *Time;* it was just one of many. There had been a flurry of similar advertisements in medical journals over the preceding year. One of them called on doctors to "identify the men in your practice with low testosterone who may benefit from clinical performance in a packet." The ad featured photographs of robust and happy men placed beside the words "improved sexual function," "improved mood," and "increased bone mineral density." Doctors were told to "screen for symptoms of low testosterone" and "restore normal testosterone levels."

One pharmaceutical company, a competitor of Rick Duggan's employer, developed a questionnaire physicians could use to identify aging patients with testosterone levels below "normal." These men were said to be experiencing the equivalent of female menopause. "Male menopause" may be the popular term, but physicians call it andropause or PADAM, for partial androgen deficiency in aging men. Some of the questions were quite specific: an experience of decreased libido, for example, could be related to a decline in the male hormone. Other questions were more vague. A sense of lowered energy or endurance might also indicate a testosterone deficiency, but could also result from many other disorders. And some questions cast an even wider net. Was the man enjoying life less? Was he irritable, less efficient at work, falling asleep after the evening meal? I discussed the ad with Delgado. "Who doesn't sometimes doze off after dinner?" she pointed out. The question, she felt, was simply a way to get doctors to measure an aging man's testosterone levels. With that result in hand, the physician would be obliged to tell the patient, who might then expect the doctor to prescribe the hormone. But was this medicine or marketing?

As men age, the response of their testes to signals from the pituitary gland becomes muted. After the age of forty, testosterone levels in a man's bloodstream decline, on average, about 1.2 percent a year. "Normal" testosterone levels refer to what is normal for men in their twenties. But even the definition of "normal" for younger men can mislead a doctor who is not expert in endocrinology. Among younger men, testosterone levels can vary markedly over the course of a day. Dr. William Crowley, chief of the reproductive endocrinology unit at the Massachusetts General Hospital, and his associate, Dr. Frances Hayes, are studying the consequences of testosterone deficiency in men. To do so, Crowley told me, they needed a clear definition of normal testosterone levels. So he sampled the blood of healthy men in their twenties every ten minutes for twenty-four hours. He also evaluated testicle size, body hair, erectile function, sperm count, muscle mass, bone density, and pituitary function. The men were completely normal by every measure, yet at some time during the day, 15 percent of them had testosterone levels well below the presumed lower limit of normal — more than 50 percent below it, in fact.

Many men sixty and older often test below this normal range. Does this decline impair their health and functioning to the extent that they need testosterone replacement therapy? In short, does male menopause exist?

Karen Delgado and many other internists and endocrinologists worry about what they see as a concerted effort to change how doctors think — to create a clinical disorder by medicalizing normal changes and challenges in life. In this instance, some drug companies were meaning to turn the natural aging process into such a disorder. In other settings, aspects of personality and temperament that deviate from a narrow norm are being labeled as psychological illnesses requiring medication. Of course, there are children and adults with disabling anxiety that cripples their ability to form friendships, but some people who are simply very shy are labeled with social affective disorder and given powerful psychotropic drugs. Others, who work with extraordinary intensity and precision, reluctant to unhinge from a task and worried that they are overlooking an error, are too quickly given the diagnosis of obsessive-compulsive disorder and medicated.

In Delgado's field, testosterone is only the latest hormonal elixir in the medicalizing of aging. The growth in prescriptions of estrogen for postmenopausal women can be traced to a bestseller published in the 1960s, *Feminine Forever,* by Dr. Robert A. Wilson. It turned out that a drug company that made estrogen had paid Dr. Wilson to write the book. Some came to see a supposedly well-reasoned analysis of the biology of female menopause, and how its consequences could be remedied with hormone replacement therapy, as a marketing manifesto, not an objective clinical treatise.

In the past decade or so, marketing directly to the public prompts people like aging men or postmenopausal women to ask their doctor for a drug even if the drug has not been proven to work for their problem. In the United States, once a drug is approved for sale for a particular purpose, a physician can prescribe it for any clinical condition. The Food and Drug Administration has approved testosterone replacement therapy, using products such as the one Rick Duggan promotes, for patients like Nick Mancini, whose pituitary gland no longer can signal his testes to produce the hormone, or for men with inherited conditions like an extra X chromosome. These are uncommon disorders; the market would number only tens of thousands of patients. But there are nearly forty million men in the United States over the age of fifty. If physicians were to prescribe testosterone to those whose levels are declining, the market could reach billions of dollars. While the FDA forbids drug companies to advertise their products for uses other than those it has approved, they can use other strategies. The ads in *Time* magazine and medical journals were designed to "raise awareness" of the "condition" of testosterone deficiency without naming a specific drug. And, to complement the advertising approach, the drug companies enlisted "opinion leaders" like Bert Foyer who may influence their peers or trainees.

The freedom to prescribe that the FDA grants doctors can have clinical benefits. In my own field of oncology, drugs approved for a specific cancer — cisplatin for testicular carcinoma, or gemcitabine for pancreatic cancer — turned out to have wider application. Many women with ovarian cancer have received a successful platinum-based treatment like cisplatin, and patients with lung cancer or breast cancer have benefited from gemcitabine. A pharmaceutical company may legally carry out clinical trials of a product for conditions beyond those covered by the initial FDA approval. If the data demonstrate benefit, it can then ask the FDA to widen the approved scope of treatment. The problem arises when the marketing is ahead of the medicine — when the data to support treatment are thin, contradictory, or even negative. Then sales depend on opinion leaders who assert benefit despite the absence of proof.

The existence of andropause is unproved. Studies to date on testosterone replacement therapy show no convincing benefits for older men with modestly reduced hormone levels who exhibit the vague symptoms on the questionnaire. Treatment does not significantly increase strength in most muscle groups; compared to a placebo, it neither boosts libido nor increases energy. A panel convened by the National Institutes of Health concluded that the andropause hypothesis had no scientific basis. Nonetheless, the number of prescriptions for testosterone replacement products continues to rise sharply, reaching far beyond patients with well-defined deficiencies like Nick Mancini. Drug companies, whose primary goal is profit, can drive doctors' thinking about what constitutes a malady and how to remedy it.

In 1998, I became enamored with a family of new medications because of my own clinical condition. I had suffered a failed spine surgery and was left with chronic arthritic symptoms that made it impossible for me to pursue my favorite sport, distance running. Every time I began to run, I developed muscle spasms in my lumbar region, with shooting pains into my buttocks. Reluctantly, I gave up running, and although I swam and cycled, I never relinquished a sense of loss. Then a colleague who is a rheumatologist told me about novel anti-inflammatory medications then under development: the COX-2 inhibitors, which eventually were marketed as Celebrex and Vioxx. I began to investigate these inhibitors and was gripped by the idea that they might restore me to my favorite sport. My enthusiasm was such that I eventually wrote an article for *The New Yorker* entitled "Superaspirin." The article drew on data that had been recently released from a six-month-long trial of Celebrex in patients with chronic arthritis. And while my *New Yorker* piece included some caveats, overall it heralded a paradigm change in the therapy of arthritis. I ended the article with a fantasy that after taking the COX-2 inhibitor, I could lace up my sneakers and run again.

So Dr. Foyer's enthusiasm for testosterone was familiar to me, mirrored in my desire to believe that there would be a way to temper, if not reverse, the degenerative changes in my spine. Of course, the story of the COX-2 inhibitors did not end that way. Although some patients clearly benefited from the drugs, their impact, compared with other anti-inflammatory agents, like naproxen and ibuprofen, was not dramatically different; the patients who would most benefit were those who had a history of gastrointestinal bleeding, since the cox-2 inhibitors reduced, but did not eliminate, the side effect of stomach irritation seen with other anti-inflammatory drugs. But the notion that they would have no significant toxicity and would usher in a new era in treatment proved wrong. More rigorous studies showed that there was a small but definite incidence of heart attack and stroke, likely due to changes in blood vessels brought about by the inhibition of the cox-2 enzyme.

Another of my dreams about Celebrex and Vioxx was that they might help prevent Alzheimer's disease. One hypothesis was that the damage to the brain was caused by inflammation, so that anti-inflammatory drugs could be useful. My maternal grandfather, Max Sherman, had played an important role in my life when I was growing up. He had worked in the post office, but told us tall tales about his exploits with Teddy Roosevelt and the Rough Riders. Only years later did I realize that he was much too young to have been a Rough Rider, but at the time it caught my imagination and made him into a living part of history and family glory.

Not long after the death of my grandmother, my grandfather Max's behavior changed. He became sullen and withdrawn, and at first we thought he was depressed. But then his flat affect gave way to periods of aggression, both verbal and physical. My grandfather was one of the sweetest and gentlest men I have ever met, and this kind of behavior was completely foreign to him and to his family. It turned out that he had Alzheimer's disease and ultimately had to be institutionalized. He died unable to recognize any of us. This specter of Alzheimer's, which haunts so many families, certainly haunts mine, so the notion that a safe drug like a cox-2 inhibitor could be taken daily for decades and not only restore me to my running but also protect me from the disease that took my grandfather held profound appeal — so profound that it blinded me to critical thinking. As Karen Delgado points out time and again to her patients, it is a common illusion that a drug will arrive that has no toxicity and can, in a near-miraculous way, reverse the consequences of aging. As we now know, certain data on COX-2 inhibitors were not initially made public, and while it is understandable to make recommendations based on available information, it is also important to sustain a sense of sobriety and wait for more extensive and long-range assessment before being swept toward a conclusion influenced, in part, by one's personal desires or the seduction of pharmaceutical marketing.

For decades, the bulk of the data concerning estrogen therapy for premenopausal women came from the Nurses' Health Study, begun in 1976 and sponsored by Harvard. This was a so-called observational study, meaning that large numbers of nurses reported what drugs they took, what they ate, and what they did during the day. From those reports, researchers drew inferences about what constituted healthy activity and what did not. Although observational studies can yield useful information, they can be misleading. Hidden biases may prevent subjects from reporting certain factors that affect health or disease. A prospective trial including both treatment and a placebo almost always results in more reliable data than an observational study. The Women's Health Initiative, established in 1991, sponsored by the NIH, and involving more than fifteen thousand women, was a prospective study of hormone replacement therapy and its benefits and risks. The study was to last for fifteen years but was stopped early when an independent board of experts concluded that the hormones estrogen and progestin increased the risk of breast cancer in healthy menopausal women. An increased incidence of coronary heart disease, stroke, and pulmonary embolism also was observed among the women taking hormones, compared with those receiving placebo pills. These results cast serious doubt on what had become conventional wisdom since the Nurses' Health Study.

But even before the Women's Health Initiative results were released in 2002, other data contradicted the idea that aging women should be given estrogen to prevent heart disease, stroke, and Alzheimer's. "It always bothered me that the Framingham Study did not show that estrogen protected women against heart disease," Delgado said. The Framingham Heart Study, a large, long-term study of risk factors for atherosclerosis and heart disease, was an "outlier," since it seemed to contradict the Nurses' Health Study. "It was hanging in my head all those years," Delgado said. But unlike many of her colleagues, she chose not to ignore it. Then the Heart and Estrogen/Progestin Replacement Study (HERS) appeared. A drug company sponsored this placebo-controlled trial of estrogen hoping to show that the hormone helped prevent a second heart attack in older women. The results, however, showed the opposite. Yet that negative outcome gave most clinicians no pause in prescribing estrogen. The powerful marketing juggernaut seemed to sweep aside any obstacle in its way.

In early 2006, a *Wall Street Journal* headline declared: "In Study of Women's Health, Design Flaws Raise Questions." A *New York Times* headline read, "Rethinking Hormones, Again." Headlines are meant to catch the eye, but they risk imprinting misinformation in the mind. The *Journal of Women's Health* also published an article using data from the Nurses' Health Study. Although one should not necessarily judge an article by where it appears, there is a pecking order in clinical medicine. The *New England Journal of Medicine* and the *Journal of the American Medical Association* (*JAMA*) are the alpha roosters. In my own specialties, the *Annals of Internal Medicine, Blood,* and the *Journal of Clinical Oncology* are the most prestigious. When researchers have rigorous, groundbreaking data to announce, they try to publish in one of the top-tier journals; by the same token, these journals seek out epochal reports to add to their luster.

The Women's Health Initiative and the HERS study were published, respectively, in the *New England Journal of Medicine* and *JAMA*. The earlier papers from the observational Nurses' Health Study appeared in these journals as well, but as it became clear that self-reporting and other biases seriously limited the Nurses' Study, its credibility declined. The media are hungry to pursue topics that are not only controversial but draw in readers with desirable demographics; hormone replacement therapy is sure to find an eager audience with disposable income. Journalists accurately reported the information in the news articles: women who started hormone therapy right after menopause reduced their risk of coronary heart disease by about 30 percent. This observation led to the hypothesis that estrogen might best be used in women in their early fifties, at the onset of menopause, and that the average age of the participants in the Women's Health Initiative — sixty-four — could account for the failure of estrogen to protect their hearts.

The articles revealed a subtle insight into the culture of medicine. Where you stand depends on where you sit: your specialty can affect, even determine, your position. In this case, gynecologists and cardiologists came out on different sides. Some gynecologists, who are often the primary care physicians for women, and who had prescribed estrogen as a mainstay of their practice for decades, rushed to embrace the new data from the Nurses' Health Study, even while acknowledging that they were not definitive. Dr. Mary Jane Minkin, a clinical professor of obstetrics and gynecology at Yale, told the *New York Times,* "Personally, in my heart of hearts, I think there is a benefit." Dr. Minkin disclosed that she was a consultant and paid speaker for drug companies that make estrogen, and she took the hormone herself.

Delgado likened Minkin's remarks to Dr. Foyer's. "She is a believer, too." Delgado thought it unlikely that Minkin's "belief" was based on money. But was it based on science? For a patient to hear that a professor at a prestigious medical school like Yale believes "in my heart of hearts" in a treatment so strongly that she takes it herself — that has a powerful impact. "I didn't think these doctors are prostituting themselves for the drug companies," Delgado said. Rather, they are speaking not objectively, but from faith. It is not uncommon to find such believers among physicians.

Many readers do not go beyond an article's headline or its opening paragraph; it is also difficult for laymen to critically assess statements coming from apparent voices of authority. For example, toward the end of the *Times* article, Dr. Frederick Naftolin, the retired chairman of the Department of Obstetrics, Gynecology, and Reproductive Sciences at Yale, disputed the data from the Women's Health Initiative study as counterintuitive. "The relationship between the fall in estrogen and the rise in cardiovascular disease in women is incontrovertible," Dr. Naftolin said. "So why in the world would you not try to find out whether simply maintaining estrogen at the levels of reproductive life could be cardio-protective?"

In response, cardiologists argue that this theory has been discredited. "Atherosclerosis starts well before the age of menopause," said Dr. Deborah Grady, a principal investigator in the HERS trial. "On top of that, why would you want a preventive intervention that has a lot of other side effects like blood clots? These people have a theory they don't want to give up on, no matter what." Dr. Richard M. Fuchs, a cardiologist and clinical professor of medicine at Weill Medical College in New York, echoed this view. "There is no good evidence that hormone therapy reduces the risk of heart disease, and there is reasonable evidence to say it increases heart disease and stroke, pulmonary embolism and breast cancer," Dr. Fuchs said. "My advice is all women should try to get off it."

"It didn't make sense that nature could be so wrong," Delgado said, talking about the steady decline in hormone levels in women after menopause. "It didn't make sense that every woman should be on the same medication. You have to look at each patient as an individual and assess what is best as a preventive." A one-size-fits-all approach to prescriptions was flawed. Although Delgado felt vindicated by the Women's Health Initiative, the NIH-sponsored trial of hormones versus placebo in postmenopausal women, it seemed like common sense to her that a single hormone could not return a woman to biological youth.

Delgado does not consider the Women's Health Initiative an absolute condemnation of estrogen. She still treats women who she believes might benefit from hormonal treatment. "You have to weigh the information," she told me. "You assess the risks and then make a tradeoff." For example, she had recently seen a woman, entering menopause with incapacitating hot flashes, whose mother had had breast cancer. Estrogens are known to promote cancer of the breast, and such a family history is cause for concern. But the woman had such severe symptoms that she could not work or socialize. "I recommended she take estrogen to tide her through this period," Delgado said. She explained in detail to the patient the tradeoffs involved before recommending the hormone treatment, emphasizing that breast cancer could develop even with close monitoring. Furthermore, she hoped that the hormone could soon be discontinued. It wasn't an easy decision, not a simple tradeoff, but such choices rarely are simple.

So for women like this with severe, acute symptoms of menopause, Delgado prescribes estrogen for short periods until the change of life passes. Then, unless there is a clear need for continued treatment and no alternative, she stops. "Hormones are not the fountain of youth," Delgado said, no matter how they are depicted by the media and some physicians. To believe that a hormone like estrogen can prevent most of the consequences of aging, such as heart disease and memory loss, "simply makes no sense," she told me. The biology of aging involves many physiological systems, changes in many molecules. Fixating on a single molecule like estrogen as a remedy is naïve and, as the Women's Health Initiative study showed, potentially dangerous. "There is a powerful temptation felt by patients and doctors alike to have a simple answer to complicated problems," Delgado concluded.

Douglas Watson was an executive in the pharmaceutical industry for thirty-three years, rising to be the president and CEO of Novartis Corporation, the U.S. subsidiary of Swiss-based Novartis AG. I spoke with Watson to gain the perspective of an experienced pharmaceutical executive whom I knew to be ethical and data-driven. Watson hails from Scotland and has the straight-talking, direct manner that characterizes so many of his countrymen. He studied pure mathematics at Cambridge University in the United Kingdom and then rose through the ranks of large pharmaceutical companies until his early retirement from Novartis in 1999. Watson had once made a statement that caught my attention: if a new drug signals a significant improvement, either in its efficacy against a clinical condition or in its safety profile, with fewer side effects, then statistical gymnastics should not be needed to persuade a doctor to try it. "My goal in terms of marketing is to have a physician try a new therapy in one or two of his patients — and I mean one or two, not in hundreds," he told me. "We would want the physician to have a positive experience with the drug, to see its benefits for these one or two patients. That way, he would become comfortable in learning how to use it appropriately, and incorporate it into his standard of care."

Watson said marketing studies show that most physicians routinely prescribe only around two dozen drugs, and that the majority of these drugs were adopted during their medical training or shortly thereafter, even if that training occurred decades earlier. Most practicing doctors like to feel in control of their treatments, and that sense of control is derived from long-term experience with a particular drug. In fact, there often is no need to prescribe the latest drug for hypertension or arthritis, for example, because most new therapies for these maladies are either "me too" agents that are substantially similar to their predecessors or they represent only a small increment in benefit rather than a marked advance. "There may be one or two generations of products that offer 'marginal improvement' — my words for these kinds of new drugs — but the experienced clinician rightly relies on his golden oldies and still delivers appropriate care." Watson laughed. "I can see two perspectives on this. As a businessman, it can drive you nuts, because I want to sell you a product. But as a patient myself, it makes perfect sense, because usually I don't need the latest and greatest drug to improve my health.

"Patients' satisfaction with the relief they get from arthritic pain with anti-inflammatory agents is very low," Watson continued, "a subject, Jerry, that I know is close to your heart." He was familiar with my long-standing difficulties with low back pain. "When a new arthritis drug is developed, there is a very rapid penetration of the market, because people say, 'What I'm on now isn't doing a very good job, so I may as well give this new drug a try.'" Usually within six months, Watson said, nearly the entire market share that this new anti-arthritic agent will capture has been captured. "Everyone and their sister run down the road to their doctor and say, 'I saw this ad on the TV for Celebrex or Vioxx.' And," Watson continued, "the doctor, aware that the patient's arthritis was not being meaningfully ameliorated, is ready to prescribe the new drug." If the advertisement were for a blood pressure medication, then, Watson said, "today's drugs, not to mention yesterday's drugs, control blood pressure quite well for the vast majority of people," so a doctor is less willing to try a new agent, even if a patient requests it.

Watson sees testosterone replacement therapy as an example, like Viagra, where the pharmaceutical industry is capitalizing on a cultural shift. "Sexual function was not a dinner table conversation when I was growing up," he said. "Even twenty years ago, I am not sure that you would have seen the social expectations around sex being what they are today. Testosterone, Viagra, and other drugs being prescribed are driven by the change in society, and men's usage overall has very little association with the word 'need.'" Watson admits with a laugh that when Viagra was in development, he didn't realize its full potential. He had in mind the relatively small number of men who'd had damage to the nerves of their penis or had pelvic radiation or surgery. He did not anticipate the large numbers of men who would take the drug, not for such a clear medical indication, but recreationally. "Who would have predicted that Bob Dole gets on the TV and talks about it?" The ads featuring Dole, in Watson's view, caused a dramatic change in the public and a ripple effect among physicians, resulting in Viagra's multibillion-dollar revenues. If a respected war hero from Kansas, whose politics were generally conservative, with a dynamic, glamorous wife, could advocate such a drug, then anyone could feel comfortable using it to improve his own sex life. The major difference between testosterone and drugs like Viagra is that Viagra produces a clear physical result, a sustained erection, while the studies on testosterone often show no enhanced libido compared with a placebo.

When I asked Watson for his definition of "ethical marketing" of drugs, he replied that the primary aim of marketing should be the accurate education of a physician in the side effects and potential benefits of a particular agent. Most doctors, he said, learn about new products from the pharmaceutical industry. "The physician who takes the time and effort to go read in depth about a new drug is the exception to the rule," he allowed, and studies support this contention. For that reason, he believed that busy doctors with scant time to dig into the data on their own should be given educational materials that position the treatment in its correct clinical niche. "A good sales rep will focus the physician's attention on what are the critical issues around the drug, and then the doctor, hopefully, will take the time to read the package insert and other materials that the drug rep leaves behind, again focusing on what's key." As opposed to simply selling, the industry should help in physicians' education.

"I'm not trying to pretend that we are not selling, because we are," Watson said. "But the ethical company with a good product should be primarily trying to teach the physician how to use it." There is financial self-interest in this approach, of course. With a better understanding of the drug, a physician is more likely to "give it a try," Watson said. And try it correctly. "We want a good product to be given to the right patient. Because if it's not prescribed properly, then either it doesn't work or it has unexpected side effects, and that's the last thing we want, for the patient's sake and because it will turn off the doctor.

"Some doctors, frankly, are weak-willed wimps, so when a guy comes in and says he has a pain in his knee, and the doctor is scared that the guy is going to go down the road to another doctor if they don't give something, they write a prescription — and you can fill in the blank for whatever is the latest drug that's been advertised," Watson told me. Other doctors, in response to advertisements directed to the public, Watson continued, "say to themselves, 'Well, he wants this drug, I might have prescribed something else, but it really doesn't make much difference, so I will give him what he wants.'" It is in this "public-driven" arena, Watson said, that you see "real marketing," the effort by certain pharmaceutical companies to create demand for products that don't merit it based on a medical need. Watson's words brought to mind the expensive pills advertised for indigestion when common antacids are equally effective for most people at a fraction of the cost. Contrary to the branding of many pharmaceuticals, Watson asserts that most generic drugs are equally safe and effective and offer great cost savings. But companies market aggressively against generics and try to mold a doctor's behavior with gifts and perks. "I can tell you, if a doctor prescribes an overly expensive brand drug for me because some salesman gave him a Mont Blanc pen, that is not the kind of doctor I would want."

Shortly after my conversation with Watson, I spoke with a surgeon I know. As it happened, he was leaving the next day for a skiing trip in Colorado to attend a medical conference. The entire cost of the trip — air fare, hotel, food, and registration for the meeting — was paid for by a company that makes a surgical device he frequently uses in the OR. This was not a Mont Blanc pen. The trip was worth thousands of dollars.

"I don't think this will influence me to use their product any more than I do," the surgeon insisted. I told him I was skeptical. "In fact," he replied, "I split my work right down the middle. Half the time I use this company's instruments, and half the time I use their competitor's." He laughed, saying that by keeping each one at bay, he would get more perks.

What he didn't mention was whether some of the surgeries he performed with either product were necessary in the first place. Sometimes high fees for a particular operation, combined with the largesse of a device company, appear to drive up the number of unnecessary surgeries. Spinal fusion is a prime example.

A historical perspective helps in understanding the controversial subject of surgery for chronic back pain. Surgeons have touted a long list of procedures that ultimately proved disappointing, if not ineffective. In the 1950s, many patients with angina and coronary artery disease underwent an operation that involved tying off an artery that runs under the breastbone. At the time, physicians believed that the procedure would increase blood flow to a heart starved of its normal supply by blockages in the coronary arteries. Then, at the end of the decade, a clinical trial showed that patients who had a sham operation did just as well as those who had the real one. Apparently, the placebo effect accounted for the fact that many patients felt better after the surgery.

Other once popular procedures resulted from a misunderstanding of the biology of a particular condition. William Halstead pioneered the radical mastectomy in 1895 at the Johns Hopkins Hospital; it became routine therapy for breast cancer. When I was a medical student at Columbia in the early 1970s, no one questioned it. Surgeons throughout the country believed that breast cancer spread in a contiguous, stepwise fashion from the primary tumor and that the only cure was to remove the entire breast and underlying muscles. By the 1980s, it had become clear that tumor cells can spread throughout the body early in the disease through the lymph channels and blood vessels. A lumpectomy, which involved excising the tumor and preserving the breast, followed by radiation to the affected area, proved as effective as a radical mastectomy in treating the cancer and was much less mutilating and traumatic for the patient.

Spinal fusion may be the radical mastectomy of our time. In 2006, more than 150,000 lower lumbar spine fusions were performed in the United States. The operation involves removing discs from the lower spine and mechanically bracing the vertebrae with metal rods and screws. The procedure is of tremendous benefit to patients with fractured spines or spinal cancer, but these make up a minuscule number of the total cases. More frequently, spinal fusion is performed to alleviate chronic low back pain. There are serious questions about whether the operation is effective and why some doctors perform it.

CT and MRI scans are often used to make the case for surgery, but the correlation between damaged or degenerated discs and low back pain is poor. For example, studies have shown that 27 percent of healthy people over the age of forty had a herniated disc, 10 percent had an abnormality of the vertebral facet joints, and 50 percent had other anatomical changes that appeared significant on CT scans. Yet none of these people had back pain. Similar results were found in a study using MRI scanning: 36 percent of people over sixty had herniated discs, and some 80 to 90 percent of them had significant disc degeneration in the form of narrowing or bulging. Again, despite significant anatomical changes in the lumbar spine, these healthy people had no nagging back pain. For some people, of course, the rupture of a disc coincides with the acute onset of pain. But even then, studies show that surgery is often unnecessary. More than 80 percent of people will recover with conservative measures, like anti-inflammatory medication, a short period of rest, and then progressive mobilization and physical therapy. A simple operation called a discectomy — shaving off the lip of the disc that has herniated and that presses on the nerve root — can relieve pain more rapidly; those who wish to avoid an operation can do so, but they may be uncomfortable for a longer time.

Each of the various muscles, tendons, bones, joints, and ligaments in the lower back contains sensory nerves that can transmit messages of pain through the spinal cord to the brain. There are also organs in the abdomen and pelvis that, when they become inflamed or diseased, can signal pain in the back. Given all of these structures, the source of the chronic low back pain is often a mystery. Doctors can be hard-pressed to identify why a patient is uncomfortable.

How doctors think about a problem like chronic low back pain is heavily influenced by the specialty that they trained in. A research study published in 1994 entitled "Who You See Is What You Get" showed that each group of specialists favored the diagnostic tools of their discipline in evaluating patients. Neurologists called for electromyograms (EMGs) that assess the integrity of the conduction system of nerves. An EMG involves inserting needles into muscles and nerves and then applying a small jolt of electricity. Rheumatologists, who are experts in arthritis and other joint disorders, ordered blood tests called serologies that can identify relatively rare autoimmune disorders that affect the spine. Surgeons requested MRI scans, which reveal the anatomy of the vertebral bones and discs and may suggest a surgical solution.

One doctor who sees many patients with chronic low back pain and is an expert in anesthesiology and pain management told me that each approach to diagnosis and treatment is essentially a "franchise," and that too many franchises are battling for control. I recognized that he was using a business term as more than a mere metaphor. He pointed out that in medicine, when you do a procedure on a patient, even if it is just sticking a needle into him, the insurance company reimburses you at a much better rate than if you perform a physical examination. So, he said, there is a powerful drive to perform invasive procedures.

On the other hand, Dr. Richard Deyo, a primary care physician at the University of Washington who has studied the results of treating thousands of patients with low back pain, emphasized that in most cases these diagnostic tests are neither informative nor useful in guiding treatment. Research showed that 85 percent of patients who suffer from low back pain cannot be given a precise diagnosis; the pain is usually vaguely ascribed to "strain" or "sprain" in the lumbar region. It turns out that the diagnosis is not critical, because the outcomes tend to be similar anyway. With acute low back pain, 90 percent improve within two to seven weeks without specific therapy. Even with an acute ruptured disc the prognosis is good, although recovery is usually slower; 80 percent feel significantly better within six weeks without surgery. Over time, the disc retracts, so it no longer presses on the nerves and the inflammation subsides. As noted before, a simple discectomy will make you feel better faster if you have acute sciatica, so some people opt for this procedure. But the rationale for surgery for chronic, as opposed to acute, low back pain is much less clear;

how physicians guide patients with chronic pain, alas, may be significantly influenced by economics.

The spine surgeons I spoke with were reluctant to be identified by name out of concern that candid answers would damage their standing in the medical community and reduce patient referrals. So let me call one of these surgeons Dr. Wheeler. He performs two or three spinal fusions a week. For many years, Wheeler recommended that his patients with back trouble avoid fusion surgery unless it was absolutely necessary — when the vertebral bones have been dislocated or damaged by diseases that endanger the spinal cord or the nerves. But such conditions are unusual, accounting for less than 2 percent of all cases of chronic low back pain. "'Spinal instability' is routinely given as a diagnosis to these patients with chronic lower back pain," Wheeler said. "It is a term used to justify an operation. And it is a great diagnosis, because it cannot be directly disproved."

Like Dr. Foyer, who is a believer in testosterone replacement therapy for older men, several spine surgeons I spoke with were believers in both spinal instability and the need for fusion surgery. They routinely ordered x-rays of the spine and interpreted minor movements in the vertebral bones when flexed or extended as evidence for this diagnosis. But experts in spine surgery, like Wheeler, and in rehabilitation medicine, like Dr. James Rainville at the New England Spine Center, expressed profound skepticism that these minor changes on x-rays could account for chronic pain.

Although Wheeler advised patients with long-standing back pain to avoid fusion surgery, he found that considerable forces weighed against his conservative recommendations, particularly when patients had a job-related accident or injury and thus could benefit financially from persistent disability. He told me that one group of four neurologists in his community works directly with lawyers. The lawyers refer the patients to these neurologists after an accident or work-related injury associated with back trouble. The neurologists charge up to $1,500 for an EMG and then get another $500 from the attorney for their report. (Wheeler averred that in more than twenty years of practice, he had never seen these neurologists read an EMG as negative in accident cases.) The neurologists then tell the patients that they have severe disc disease, which can enhance their perception of pain. Moreover, if they do have the surgery, they are told that they don't necessarily have to go back to work afterward.

Wheeler said that he is put in a difficult position whenever one of these referring neurologists tells a patient that the EMG or MRI indicates something seriously wrong with the spine. In the past, when Wheeler challenged one of these neurologists, the doctor would counter, "I'm a pro-patient advocate."

Of course, most doctors do not behave so egregiously, and most of them believe they advise their patients correctly with the information available from tests and scans. Nonetheless, the current culture of medicine fosters lucrative networks of referrals and procedures but discourages critical examination of their value. Insurance benefits also favor surgery: patients usually get greater disability payments if they undergo back surgery. Eventually Wheeler discovered that nearly all of the patients he turned away were operated on by other surgeons in his area. He decided that if his patients were to have surgery, he might as well be the one to do it. At least he would know that the operation had been competently done.

Insurance nearly always reimburses a surgeon at a much higher rate for a fusion operation than for a discectomy. For example, where Wheeler practices, the surgeon's full fee for a simple discectomy is around $5,000, as opposed to some $20,000 for a fusion procedure. The financial incentive tips heavily toward fusion.

For the majority of patients with chronic lumbar pain, fusion surgery has no dramatic impact on either their pain or their mobility. Yet many surgeons pay scant attention to the poor results. A prospective trial in Scandinavia compared patients who underwent fusion surgery for chronic low back pain with those who did not. After two years, an independent observer rated only one out of every six patients in the surgical group as having an "excellent" result — only marginally better than patients who had intensive physical therapy. Despite such a disappointing outcome, some spine surgeons cite the study to support the legitimacy of the operation.

In 1993, the federal Agency for Health Care Policy and Research convened a panel of twenty-three experts in back pain from a wide spectrum of disciplines — neurology, orthopedics, internal medicine, radiology, chiropractic, rheumatology, psychology, and nursing. The University of Washington's Richard Deyo was on the panel. He had recently published a statistical analysis of existing research which suggested that spinal fusion lacked a scientific rationale and that it had a significantly higher rate of complications than simple discectomy. The federal panel was to formulate guidelines for the clinical management of acute low back pain by assessing the scientific evidence concerning its diagnosis and treatment. Although the panel did not discuss insurance coverage, it seemed likely that Medicare and private insurers would consider these guidelines when determining reimbursements.

The federal group came under attack almost as soon as it met. The North American Spine Society criticized the panel for not having open deliberations and claimed that the panelists were biased against surgery. The society lobbied Congress to cut off funding for panels of the Agency for Health Care Policy and Research. Deyo told me that the line taken by the opponents was "These guys are antisurgery, antifusion." But, he insisted, "we really had no ax to grind. Our aim was to critically examine the evidence and outcomes of these common medical practices."

After the November 1994 congressional elections, which featured a dramatic shift from a Democratic to a Republican majority, the newly configured House of Representatives was receptive to the accusations against the panel. Although the American Medical Association, the American College of Physicians, and the American Hospital Association all tried to save the healthcare policy agency, the House zeroed out its budget. Then the battle moved to the Senate. Although the agency ultimately survived, Congress cut its funds drastically. A company that manufactures devices used in fusion surgery sought a court injunction to block publication of the panel's findings. The guidelines that were eventually published emphasized conservative measures like physical therapy, but the controversy surrounding the panel tainted its credibility, and its recommendations have had little impact on surgical practice.

While one spine surgeon I spoke with still defends his actions against the panel, even he admitted that fusion operations have proliferated in the United States. He pointed out that when he began his training more than two decades ago, only a handful of fellowships in spine surgery existed; now there are more than eighty. Each year, more and more specialists are being trained, and those specialists naturally look for opportunities to use their training. The technology has also developed rapidly. New sorts of screws, rods, and cages, as well as other devices, can be inserted into the spine. These instruments are aggressively marketed and generate high profit margins for both the manufacturers and the hospitals that use them.

I spoke with a surgeon after his return from a meeting on spine surgery held at a luxurious resort. As with my surgeon friend mentioned earlier, the entire trip was paid for by a company that manufactures the hardware he uses in performing fusions. He claimed that the perk would not alter his practice, but also affirmed that he was a "believer" in fusion surgery. "My outcomes are better than anything in the published literature," he said. But when pressed, he admitted that long-term follow-ups are rare and that he has not participated in any randomized prospective controlled trials comparing fusion surgery with conservative measures such as physical therapy.

When the government won't stop unnecessary procedures, when corporate interests push for them, and when doctors come to believe in them, the only institutions that might stem the tide of needless surgery are the medical schools and their affiliated hospitals. And, indeed, many hospitals do try to disentangle medicine from corporate influence. The *Journal of the American Medical Association* published a paper in January 2006 that got considerable attention. In it, academic physicians from Columbia and Harvard recommended that doctors begin to police themselves against untoward influence by the pharmaceutical industry. No medical advance can be made without a partnership with the private sector, whether it be the development of a drug or a new implantable device. A free-enterprise economy presupposes that a business will try to gain as large a share of the market as possible and maximize profits. On the other hand, the decisions a doctor makes about his patients should be free from any thought of personal financial gain. The authors of the *JAMA* article went so far as to assert that even apparently trivial gifts could subtly influence a physician. They argued that in the psychology of gift-giving, consciously or subconsciously one feels obligated to give back.

Sometimes, though hardly always, the giving back may be at the patient's expense. Many hospitals and universities, as well as medical journals, now require that physicians disclose their financial relationships with businesses. Some of these relationships involve consulting; others, funding for research or educational activities. The purpose of disclosure is to make public the relationship and alert the patient or the reader of the journal to potential prejudice or bias.

But the authors of the *JAMA* article argued that such disclosure is not enough. They pointed to Wall Street, where stock analysts have inappropriately promoted the shares of certain companies despite financial links between the analysts' employers and the companies concerned. Indeed, such disclosure may work against its purpose: patients or readers may believe that disclosure frees the physician or scientist from potential bias associated with personal gain when in fact disclosure does no such thing. Dr. Thomas Stossell, an eminent hematologist at the Brigham and Women's Hospital in Boston, wrote a rebuttal in *Forbes* arguing that relationships with industry are essential to medical progress, and to sever or severely strain these relationships would, in the end, hurt patients in need of new drugs.

In appraising potential conflicts of interest, the hospital where I work distinguishes between clinical care and laboratory research. Laboratory researchers are encouraged to have relationships with industry, since these relationships are essential to developing cures for currently incurable diseases. On the other hand, the risk that personal financial gain could color clinical thinking is considered too great to allow doctors to test drugs in experimental protocols if they are consultants to a pharmaceutical company or device manufacturer. The restrictions do not extend as far as the *JAMA* article proposed, so personal perks like dinners at expensive restaurants or honoraria for speaking at conferences (given to doctors in the form of "educational grants" by the conference's sponsor) are still permitted. Most hospitals and medical schools today find themselves in this gray zone.

It is unlikely that in the near future personal financial gain will be extracted from certain clinical decisions. Several spine surgeons told me they would not participate in a trial comparing simple discectomy with fusion surgery, because fusion surgery is a main source of their income and because they are convinced of its value. These were the obstacles that Dr. James Weinstein, at Dartmouth Medical School, faced in trying to launch a national study. Weinstein, an orthopedic surgeon and a leading expert in back pain, told me that the way doctors approach treatment of chronic lumbar complaints needs radical improvement. Patients, he said, must be given unbiased information about what is known and not known about back pain and the various ways of treating it. Instead of informed consent, Weinstein advocates what is called informed choice — a comprehensive understanding of all the options and their possible risks and benefits.

Informed choice means, in part, learning how different doctors think about a particular medical problem and how science, tradition, financial incentives, and personal bias mold that thinking. There is no single source for all of this information about each disorder, so a patient and family should ask the doctor whether a proposed treatment is standard or whether different specialists recommend different approaches, and why. Laypeople also should inquire about how time-tested a new treatment is. Karen Delgado is a model in this regard. She infuses common sense into the scientific results from clinical trials; she is unafraid to question custom and tradition; she sees medicine as a calling and not a business; and she avoids financial temptations that could subtly guide her practice. Patients often come to her after reading newspaper articles or watching TV reports that feature physicians' testimonials about results from a research study or an alleged breakthrough. "That may be what they believe," Delgado tells her patients, "but now let's talk about what we know and what we don't know."

CHAPTER 10

In Service of the Soul

M EMORIAL HOSPITAL is a brown brick building that rises twenty-one stories and occupies the entire block between 67th and 68th streets on York Avenue, on the east side of Manhattan. Connected to the hospital is the Sloan-Kettering Institute, a warren of steel-and-glass structures that house research laboratories. In 2005, more than 21,000 patients were admitted to the hospital, and there were 445,000 outpatient visits; nearly 16,000 surgeries were performed and 110,000 radiation treatments administered. Each day, some 9,000 physicians, nurses, psychologists, social workers, laboratory technologists, and support personnel arrive to care for people with cancer.

This massive enterprise can be traced back to the plight of a single young woman, Elizabeth Dashiell, who fell ill during the summer of 1890. In his wonderful book *A Commotion in the Blood,* Stephen S. Hall recounts her case. Her problem began when she took a train trip across the United States. During the journey, her hand was caught between two seats of a Pullman car. It soon became swollen and painful; she assumed it was infected. The pain persisted after she returned home to New Jersey. In September, she consulted William Coley, a twenty-eight-year-old surgeon in private practice in New York City.

Dr. Coley was uncertain about the diagnosis. Still hoping it was an infection, he made a small incision below the joint that connects the little finger to the back of the hand. But only a few drops of pus fell from the lanced area. Over the next three months, Coley saw Dashiell regularly, determined to diagnose her underlying problem and relieve her growing pain. After consulting with several senior surgeons at New York Hospital, he decided that he needed to probe the swollen tissues more deeply.

In October 1890, Dashiell underwent surgery. Coley scraped firm, gristle-like material off her tendons and bones. But the procedure failed to yield an answer and gave her only temporary respite from the pain. In early November, Coley performed a biopsy and finally made a diagnosis: sarcoma. A sarcoma is a cancer of the connective tissue, developing from bone, tendon, or muscle. Coley desperately wanted to save Dashiell and attempted to do so by amputating the young woman's arm just below the elbow. But it was too late. Over the ensuing months, the sarcoma spread to her face, breasts, and abdomen. Her pain became so severe that only high doses of morphine could control it. Elizabeth Dashiell died at home at 7 A.M. on January 23, 1891. Dr. Coley was at her bedside.

Several months later, he presented Dashiell's case to his surgical colleagues at the New York Academy of Medicine. He concluded his presentation with these remarks: "A disease that . . . can attack a person in perfect health, in the full vigor of early maturity, and in some insidious, mysterious way, within a few months, destroy life, is surely a subject important enough to demand our best thought and continued study."

Dashiell would have been just another young woman tragically dying with an incurable cancer, except that one of her closest friends was John D. Rockefeller, Jr., the only son of the founder of Standard Oil. Rockefeller had met Dashiell through her older brother, and he grew so fond of her that he came to think of Elizabeth as his adopted sister. Rockefeller was shocked by Dashiell's death. Several years later, he continued a program of philanthropy that his family has sustained for generations and that resulted in the founding of Memorial Hospital.

Dr. Stephen Nimer is a physician at Memorial who cares for his patients in the tradition of William Coley, devoting to them his "best thought and continued study." On a recent spring morning, Dr. Nimer walked down the corridor of the eleventh floor of the hospital and entered a conference room to begin his teaching rounds. He is a hematologist who specializes in leukemia, lymphoma, and other malignant disorders of the bone marrow. Nimer stands just shy of six feet and has a prominent widow's peak and an oval face that frames his rimless glasses. He likes to joke that he is one of the few MIT graduates who went there to play hockey.

That day, Nimer was dressed in a spotless white coat, starched blue shirt, and perfectly knotted silk tie. He noted with satisfaction that he was precisely on time. The hematology fellow and the senior resident on the clinical service were waiting. There was a new case for the fellow to present, and after exchanging pleasantries, he began: "Max Bornstein is a fifty-nine-year-old gentleman who had a large-cell lymphoma successfully treated two years ago and now has MDS." MDS stands for myelodysplastic syndrome — a conglomerate term of Greek roots that signifies injury to the primitive cells of the bone marrow, the stem cells; the injured stem cells grow in a stunted, disorderly way and fail to produce enough blood. In Bornstein's case, it was the chemotherapy that cured his lymphoma two years before that had injured the marrow stem cells. "His white blood cell count is 1,900, his platelets 74,000, and his hemoglobin 9.8," the fellow said. "I calculated all of his parameters, including his marrow findings. His calculated score puts him at intermediate-II risk on the IPSS. Based on his score, I would just transfuse him and not do anything beyond such supportive measures."

Nimer's face tightened. "I'm not interested in where he scores on the International Prognostic Scoring System," he said to the fellow.

"Well, we could use a different scoring system, based on the World Health Organization classification —"

"You are missing the point," Nimer interrupted. It was a point that was all too often missed, and one that Nimer sees as essential in training the next generation of hematologists.

"But he has IPSS intermediate-risk-II disease," the fellow said.

"Wait a minute," Nimer said. He turned to the resident and asked, "Did the fellow just say that this man had IPSS intermediate-risk-II disease?" The resident looked confused. "Yes," he answered.

"But what's wrong with that?" Nimer shot back, then turned to the fellow. "Did you really mean to say that?"

"Well, why not?" the fellow replied.

"Do you agree that the patient has MDS due to prior chemotherapy?" Nimer asked, beginning to lead the fellow down a different path.

"Yes."

"Then you should know that the IPSS classification excludes patients who have had prior therapy as a cause of their MDS." Nimer paused. "Okay. That's my first point. But more importantly, do you need to know the IPSS classification in order to take care of *any* patient?"

"Well, we calculate the IPSS all the time," the fellow said.

"Yes, that's true. But last week this man's white blood cell count was 3,200, and in seven days it fell to 1,900. His platelets fell from 105,000 to 74,000. So I don't really care about the IPSS at this point. I know this is a man who is headed for big trouble, a man who's rapidly deteriorating and needs treatment right away. Not simple supportive measures like transfusion. Treatment *right away*."

As Nimer later explained to me, he routinely encounters young physicians who relinquish their own thinking and instead look to classification schemes and algorithms to think for them. In this instance, the fellow was fitting Mr. Bornstein onto a grid based on his blood counts and bone marrow picture. When Nimer challenged him, the fellow's response was to invoke another classification scheme. "It's a static way of looking at people," Nimer said. "Strictly speaking, it's correct. But clinically speaking, it's wrong." The proliferation of these boilerplate schemes, Nimer believes, has caused doctors to become so wedded to generic profiles that they ignore the individual characteristics of the patient. "This man doesn't come out looking bad on this classification system," Nimer continued, which is why the fellow suggested supportive measures rather than aggressive treatment. But, in fact, viewing Bornstein's case in this way was an illusion, an artifact of the schema, because the classification system fails to take into account the course of the person's disease, the rate of fall in his blood counts. Based on his trajectory, Bornstein's blood counts soon would plummet to perilous levels; he likely would die from an infection or hemorrhage before any treatment could take effect.

Scoring schemes are proliferating in all branches of medicine. They can be useful ways of organizing clinical data, providing a structure to assess complex and heterogeneous disorders. But they are also very seductive. It is not always clear when to treat a person with highly toxic and potentially lethal chemotherapy; in this instance, Nimer recommended a bone marrow transplant, arguably the most drastic therapy available in hematology and oncology, a therapy that can cure or kill. Deciding whether a patient needs a marrow transplant, and when to perform it, is a profound responsibility. Fitting a patient into a spot on a grid that doesn't dictate a harsh therapy, like a marrow transplant, comes as a relief for the physician as well as the patient. But it would be a grave mistake. Relying on schemas also suits the hectic pace of today's clinical care. Bornstein was just one of dozens of patients the fellow would see in the course of a week. Algorithms and grids gave him short-cuts around the onerous process of assessing each of these dozens of complex cases. Nimer wanted to push him toward a difficult but necessary type of thinking about every patient.

In addition to his work with patients, Nimer oversees a large research program studying malignant blood diseases like lymphoma and leukemia. "I believe that my thinking in the clinic is helped by having a laboratory. If you do an experiment two times and you don't get results, then it doesn't make sense to do it the same way a third time. You have to ask yourself: What am I missing? How should I do it differently the next time? It is the same iterative process in the clinic. If you are taking care of someone and he is not getting better, then you have to think of a new way to treat him, not just keep giving him the same therapy. You also have to wonder whether you are missing something."

This seemingly obvious set of statements is actually a profound realization, because it is much easier both psychologically and logistically for a doctor to keep treating a serious disease with a familiar therapy even when the disease is not responding. In hematology and oncology, diseases often are difficult to cure. Specialists sometimes say privately, "It's a bad disease," meaning that it is complex and often resistant to textbook therapies. But repeatedly affirming how severe a certain type of lymphoma usually is, how aggressive a certain leukemia can be, has a subtle psychological effect. The mantra "It's a bad disease" can shift the burden of thinking off the specialist. Instead of struggling to come at the malady from a different angle, seeking its vulnerable point by adding other drugs or customizing a regimen, the physician, in essence, surrenders. This surrender is not conscious, but an astute patient can pick up on the fact that his doctor is sticking with the same treatment, not taking the risk of devising a novel, individual approach when the condition is not improving, because "it's a bad disease."

When I was a fellow in training at UCLA, some of the senior attending physicians invoked this mantra, and I found myself repeating it with a guilty sense of relief. It acted as a buffer against the fear of failure, a fear that even an accomplished physician, which I was not, carries within himself. It is healthy and beneficial to invest your ego in healing your patient's disease. But when your ego overshadows that goal, there lies danger.

"I tell patients that I am going to do everything possible to help them," Nimer said, "and that means that I am also setting myself up to fail." Failure is something that physicians deeply dislike. This became apparent to me when I researched outcomes of surgery for prostate cancer. Different surgeons reported a wide range of postoperative impotence and incontinence. Although the individual skill of the surgeon may account for some of this variation, as I probed some more it appeared to be largely a function of which patients the surgeon chose to operate on. Some surgeons turned down difficult cases involving large, aggressive cancers. Others refused to operate on patients with serious medical problems like diabetes, even though surgery was their best option to eradicate the cancer. Such patients are more prone to nerve damage, and thus to impotence.

"I tell my patients that the more aggressive the disease, the more aggressive the treatment," Nimer said. And because it is a "bad disease," the doctor should increase his efforts rather than retreat. Sometimes even very bad diseases can be cured.

George Franklin was a successful independent investor with a cavernous apartment on Park Avenue and a weekend house in the

Hudson River Valley. He had traveled to remote corners of the world, hunting and fishing and enjoying the richness of nature. I was a friend of his sister-in-law, and she told me he had the energetic spirit of a Theodore Roosevelt. About fifteen years ago, Franklin was languishing in a Manhattan hospital with a high fever and low blood cell counts. His internist was a man from his social set, advanced in years and, by his own admission, perplexed as to the cause of Franklin's problem. The hematologist who consulted on his case failed to make a diagnosis; she thought he might have aplastic anemia, a disorder where the marrow blood cells are scant. I prevailed upon George Franklin to see a specialist I knew at Memorial Sloan-Kettering, and in short order the correct diagnosis was made: T-cell lymphoma.

Lymphoma is a cancer of the lymphocytes, a type of blood cell. There are two major types of lymphocytes: B and T. Most lymphomas originate in the B cells. A smaller fraction affect T cells and are notoriously aggressive. T-cell lymphomas are, in the parlance of the corridor, bad diseases.

George Franklin was initially treated using a combination chemotherapy regimen called ICE, for ifosfamide, carboplatin, and etoposide. It is a difficult treatment. Franklin suffered the expected complications: mouth blisters and diarrhea. He stoically allowed that he didn't like the treatment, but he was even more unhappy when informed that it had hardly made a dent in his disease. He wanted another approach and another doctor. I suggested Stephen Nimer.

Some hematologists would have given Franklin more cycles of ICE, hoping that the cumulative effect would send the T-cell lymphoma into remission. But Nimer believed that the lack of any improvement, despite full doses of the regimen, demanded an immediate and radical change in therapy.

Nimer outlined a strategy with Franklin. They would try different drugs in the hope that one or more would reduce the

amount of lymphoma in his body to the point where he could undergo a bone marrow transplant. Because Franklin did not have a
matched donor, Nimer would harvest the stem cells from Franklin's own bone marrow, treat him with what would be lethal
amounts of chemotherapy, and then "rescue" him with his own
stem cells. "It scares me," Franklin said to Nimer, "but I really
don't have a choice, do I?" Nimer replied that everyone always has
a choice, but that this was the most rational way to proceed, and
the only chance of a cure.

The way a physician phrases his recommendations can power-
fully sway a patient's choices. For example, by phrasing results in
the positive, patients are more likely to accept the recommendation. "We have a thirty percent chance of improvement with this
approach" triggers a different reaction than "There is a seventy
percent chance of failure and death," although the two statements
are clinically equivalent. Also, some patients may interpret the
word "improvement" to mean "cure," when in fact it can indicate
only a temporary shrinkage of a cancer.

Patients also respond differently when data are presented in
percentages rather than absolute numbers. For example, an elderly man in my community called to ask my opinion about
treatment for a recently diagnosed colon cancer. The cancer was
relatively limited and hadn't spread to any vital organs. He had
multiple medical problems, and had recently undergone cardiac
bypass surgery as well as a hip replacement. He was acutely aware
of the quality of his life and worried more about debility from
chemotherapy. One oncologist had told him that there was a 30
percent reduction in mortality if he took the chemotherapy. This
sounded impressive to him, but I explained that his prognosis
overall was very good, so that in five years, a 30 percent reduction
in mortality might mean that out of a hundred people, ten who
did not take chemotherapy would die, while seven, or 30 percent
fewer, who took the chemotherapy would die. Presenting the data

this way, in absolute numbers — seven versus ten out of a hundred after five years — made it clear to him which course to take: no chemotherapy.

Nimer treated George Franklin with high doses of cyclophosphamide. The T-cell lymphoma in his lymph nodes, spleen, and bone marrow melted away. Once the cancer was in remission, Nimer proceeded with bone marrow transplantation of Franklin's own stem cells. The disease disappeared for six years. During this time, Franklin continued his extensive travels, undertook some new business deals in Africa and Asia, and drew closer to his children. Then one day, drying himself off after a long swim, Franklin noticed a lump under his left armpit. The T-cell lymphoma had returned, but an extensive evaluation showed that it was confined to this area of his body. "There is no protocol, no road map about what to do at this point," Nimer explained. Of the scores of patients with Franklin's type of lymphoma who had not responded to ICE treatment, he was the only one who had survived more than a year. "Each person's biology is different, both the biology of his tumor and his own innate biology," Nimer told Franklin. Nimer recommended radiation to the mass under his arm, followed by a short course of chemotherapy. The disease would probably return, he allowed, but this was the least toxic form of treatment, would eradicate the local recurrence, and, he hoped, remove a tumor that could seed other parts of Franklin's body. And indeed that was the result. It was nearly two years before the lymphoma returned, this time in the marrow. "I have so much to live for," Franklin told Nimer. "Keep me alive."

At moments like this, a patient grabs hold of a doctor's heart and twists it with his plea. "I try to respect a person's wishes as best I can," Nimer later told me. Given the severity of Franklin's situation and his desperate desire to live, Nimer recommended a second bone marrow transplant. Some doctors might argue that this was too extreme, the likelihood of success too remote, the chance of failure overwhelming. All of that is true, except that without risking failure there was zero chance of success.

Franklin's second transplant was much more difficult than the first, and he was in and out of Memorial Hospital with infections over several months. But eventually he recovered, and for nearly a year returned to his normal activities. Then the cancer seemed to explode in his body, growing in large masses in his abdomen. "I am not ready to die, Jerry," Franklin told me in a quavering voice. "And I think I am going to die. I don't want to die."

It took nearly a month for Stephen Nimer to bring George Franklin to accept that everything that was humanly possible had been done, and now their joint effort should be devoted to giving him as much time as remained to be with his family and friends in comfort. "Just because you can't treat someone any longer for his cancer doesn't mean that you stop treating him," Nimer told me. In fact, it is at this stage that treatment can be most challenging: how to balance therapy with medications to control pain without so narcotizing a person that he is unaware of his surroundings and unable to communicate with loved ones; how to give words of comfort while speaking the truth, acknowledging that while the end is approaching, the person can still make a difference in the lives of others.

Many of the patients Nimer cares for face very small odds of remission and an even more remote chance of a cure. For example, he consults on the cases of many elderly people with acute leukemia, who usually fare poorly. "The question is always whether to treat or not," Nimer told me, "and I usually favor treatment." He elaborated: "What I tell people, and what I believe, is that if you don't treat a person with acute leukemia, his white blood cell count goes down and he becomes infected, or his platelet count falls and he hemorrhages. If you don't treat, then there is no chance at all that the person can get better. He will be in the hospital anyway, so in my opinion it's worth giving it a try. If you do treat them, then after chemotherapy they have low white blood cell counts, and are prone to infection, and low platelets, and prone to bleeding. But at least if you treat, then after a few weeks there is a chance they could get better and leave the hospital. If it works, then the person can have a nice year or more when he feels good. Even if it's fifteen percent, or in better cases twenty-five percent. And if it doesn't work, if the chemotherapy has no impact against the leukemia, then we can stop."

Nimer uses more than numbers to explain his advice. He cited another issue: patients and their families frequently become preoccupied with side effects when they are reluctant to undergo treatment. Oncologists have made considerable progress recently using antiemetics to control nausea and vomiting, so patients now generally do not suffer these side effects. That, in his mind, removes much of the toxicity that people might associate with chemotherapy. Nimer believes that doctors also overestimate side effects. He illustrated this point not with a dire disease like leukemia but with osteoporosis. A family member of his, a woman in her seventies, whose bone density was at the lower limit of normal and who faced a high risk of getting fractures, had consulted an internist about treatment. The physician did not want to prescribe a bisphosphonate because of recent reports, featured on the front pages of newspapers, that the drug causes the jawbone to break down. Instead, he advised a vitamin D supplement, although she had a normal diet and good intake of both this vitamin and calcium. Nimer discussed the doctor's recommendations with the family member, and favored a bisphosphonate. To validate his thinking, since bone metabolism is not his area, he spoke with Dr. John Bilezikian, a world expert in the field at New York–Presbyterian Hospital. When the family member returned to her internist, the doctor said, "But you can get jaw problems. I told you, some people who received the drug have had breakdown of the bone in the jaw."

"This frightened the woman," Nimer recounted. "I told her that is a very low risk, maybe a percent, and usually after dental work. It is something to worry about in the far future. The urgent problem was to stabilize her bones and prevent a fracture from osteoporosis. She had been focused on a side effect by her doctor, and I understand why people do focus on side effects. But that distorts the risk-to-benefit ratio." The same, he said, holds true for chemotherapy. People worry a great deal about the risks of chemotherapy, but those risks, he asserts, are minor in comparison to the potential benefits against an aggressive malignancy. "You have to deal with the problem at hand," he tells his patients.

"Most of the patients I have encountered who refused treatment do so because they are so focused on the downside," Nimer elaborated. "They are only thinking about what's happening to them that day." This is an acute insight into certain patients' psychology, and also into the psychology of certain physicians. Nimer wants his patients to adopt a broad perspective, the long view, not a vision narrowed by fear. The real concern should be the underlying disease, but that is often displaced in the patient's mind by fear of the treatment. "If you have multiple myeloma, and I suggest thalidomide, and you say you are worried about nerve damage, I reply, 'Okay, if it occurs, then we'll stop the drug. But we need to combat the cancer.'"

Paradoxically, people are more likely to worry about the well-defined side effects of a therapy than about the uncertain and seemingly boundless suffering from an illness. All of us, as James Lock, the cardiologist at Children's Hospital, pointed out earlier, instinctively latch on to certainty when faced with uncertainty. "People come to me and say, 'Dr. Nimer, I've read all about this chemotherapy, and I don't think I could ever tolerate it.' And I say, 'Maybe, but maybe you *will* tolerate it. So try it. And if it turns out you can't tolerate it, then we'll stop it.'" He continues, "If you do tolerate it, then we will continue it so long as it is tolerable, and so long as it's working." This approach, he says, "takes care of most of the ethics of decision-making."

"It's a huge responsibility," Nimer said of the ability to guide a patient and family to make a certain treatment choice. "But you begin by finding out what the patient wants, and in order to do that, you have to know how to talk to the patient." Nimer said his role is actually to help the patient figure out what he really wants and then to use the power of persuasion to show the patient the way there. Dr. Karen Delgado agreed. "This is what it really means for a person to be empowered when he is sick," she said.

Most patients don't know what they really want when confronted with a crushing diagnosis and a confusing array of treatments. "You have to show them a path that doesn't violate any principles of their life or their obligations to their family," Nimer said. "Then you help them make decisions that are medically correct and have them feel good about the decisions."

Nimer is acutely aware of how he talks with a patient, how he tries to draw out from the person the principles of his life and his family obligations. This kind of information cannot be captured in an algorithm, nor is it to be found in the alphabet soup of chemotherapy acronyms or in a quantified classification scheme. It transcends statistics and the latest research paper in the medical literature. As Nimer put it, "Their choice has to be consistent with their philosophy of living."

He reminded me of a patient we both cared for years ago who asserted that quality of life had no significance to him; only life itself mattered, however painful or difficult staying alive might be. He would not recoil from the most debilitating chemotherapy and radiation treatments. He had only one goal, he said: to be cured. Another patient we also shared in care with the same type of blood cancer ultimately decided that the cost was too great, the odds too long, and the suffering too extreme. He chose not to continue his treatment. In each case, Nimer worked with the patient to find the choice that made sense to him. While their diseases were biologically similar, their philosophies of life diverged.

To further illustrate this point, Nimer told me about Vincent Rivera, a man in his seventies from Long Island whose wife had advanced multiple sclerosis and was in a wheelchair. Rivera was diagnosed by his hematologist with myelodysplasia, or MDS. Again, this is an abnormality of the bone marrow that hinders production of white blood cells, red blood cells, and platelets, causing anemia, susceptibility to infection, and bleeding. When Nimer saw Rivera, his white blood cell count was under 500 and his platelet count was 3,000, both severely low. His hematologist was transfusing him every week. Nimer reviewed the bone marrow biopsy and saw that Rivera was on the verge of transforming from MDS to florid acute leukemia. "I talked to him about different intensive treatments, and he kept returning to the fact that he enjoyed going duck hunting on Long Island and that he was the one who cared for his wife at home." Rivera's implicit message was that Nimer should find a therapy that would keep him as an outpatient and allow him to continue to look after his wife.

"I told him about 5-azacytidine," Nimer recalled — a chemotherapy drug being tested for MDS that required a special release from the National Cancer Institute. "If you think that's best, then let's go ahead with that," Rivera said. But after several treatments with 5-azacytidine, there was no improvement in his blood cell counts, and his marrow still showed the brewing leukemia. Next Nimer suggested antithymocyte globulin, or ATG, an antibody preparation that works in part by altering the immune system. ATG also proved ineffective. "He kept telling me stories about his wife, what they talked about in the evenings, the movies they rented," Nimer said. When Nimer again raised the possibility of combination chemotherapy for the brewing leukemia, he could see the reluctance in Rivera's eyes.

"I kept thinking about what to do for him," he said, "and I decided to try cyclosporine, even though the medical literature is lousy with respect to its effects in MDS." Cyclosporine could be administered to an outpatient. Within several weeks of treatment, Rivera's blood cell counts started to improve. His platelets rose to 30,000 and reached a peak of 80,000; his white blood cell count rose to over 1,000, and his anemia improved so much that he no longer needed transfusions. "Mr. Rivera decided to sell his house on Long Island," Nimer told me, "so he had enough money to move with his wife into an assisted-living facility."

For nearly nine months, on a drug that had scant possibility of working in the long run, Vincent Rivera did not require admission to the hospital and felt good. During those nine months, Nimer got repeated phone calls from his children. "They kept pressing me to bring him into the hospital, to give him chemotherapy, knowing that his disease was transforming into acute leukemia. I explained that I had arrived at this path with their father and that we were doing the best we could in terms of what made sense to him." Ultimately the leukemia proliferated, and Rivera's platelets sharply fell. He died of an internal hemorrhage. "I received the most beautiful letter from his children," Nimer told me. "They finally understood why I didn't give intensive treatment in the hospital, that those nine months meant so much to their parents."

Dr. Jeffrey Tepler is a hematologist and oncologist in private practice at New York–Presbyterian Hospital, his office a few blocks north of Dr. Nimer's. Tepler is a thin, compact man with a fringe of hair and a soft voice. After more than two decades of practicing hematology/oncology, he has seen hundreds, if not thousands, of people with maladies like breast cancer, lymphoma, and prostate cancer. As years pass, physicians derive gratification not only from the challenge of solving difficult cases, but also from trying to decipher the character of their patients. Tepler's interest in fully understanding his patients grew from his love of literature. Tepler counts among his favorite authors John Updike and John Cheever, Philip Roth and Saul Bellow, all of whom probe the conflicts and needs of modern-day men and women.

"Primarily, what I love doing is doctoring and talking to patients," Tepler told me. "I think the reason a doctor goes into oncology — or *should* go into oncology — is because he or she can form a special relationship with patients, a kind of relationship that is unique and not that common in other specialties, because of the nature of the diseases that we deal with.

"I don't want to sound corny," he said, "but I feel this desperate urge to always do the right thing. People's lives are at stake." This did not strike me as trite, because I had referred Naomi Freylich, a retired scholar, to him. Years before, a hematologist had fixed the label of "chronic lymphocytic leukemia" onto Freylich's case, and this diagnosis was passed from specialist to specialist; no doctor looked critically at the clinical behavior of her blood disease or repeated the analysis of the abnormal cells in her circulation.

Her family had called me when a hematologist in the city told them that Naomi would soon die, because all appropriate therapies for chronic lymphocytic leukemia had been exhausted. I suggested that she seek other opinions, with a specialist at Memorial Hospital and with Tepler. Both doctors discovered that the initial diagnosis was wrong. It was not this form of leukemia but rather an unusual type of lymphoma that was readily improved with Rituxan, an antibody treatment that targets the malignant lymphocytes. Naomi told me she appreciated the consultation at Memorial Hospital but felt more comfortable with Tepler's understated demeanor. "He's very calm, not rushed in his work," she observed. She received Rituxan, lived for two years, and completed several major literary research projects. She then developed acute leukemia from the chemotherapy for the misdiagnosis years before, and died.

People with a sharp, aggressive side to their character gravitate to doctors who come on strong, believing that aggressive traits result in success. Tepler, as Naomi Freylich found, is soft-spoken and deliberate, so that kind of person is most likely to feel connected with him. "For sure, surgeons and internists and others who commonly refer patients to me will send people who fit with my style and personality," Tepler said. "I am referred people when a doctor thinks we will be simpatico." I had never thought much about the consequences of this aspect of medicine. A physician's demeanor and personality often mirror his type of thinking, so there is the potential for a self-fulfilling prophecy: particular character types among patients will be channeled to similar character types among doctors, so certain modes of clinical thinking and clinical action will be applied to patients based on their character.

As a general hematologist and oncologist, Jeffrey Tepler sees a broad mix of cases in the course of a day. This means that he must work hard to stay abreast of the trends and discoveries in a variety of different diseases. "I really enjoy being that kind of doctor," Tepler said. "At this stage of my career, I've seen so many different disorders. And I love to think broadly." Last summer, Tepler saw a patient who had been on vacation in Nantucket. She had fever, anemia, and an enlarged spleen. Many different diseases can cause this constellation of findings. The evaluation by the infectious disease specialist had included a search for babesiosis, a parasitic disease that comes from deer ticks and is clustered in coastal areas and offshore islands like Nantucket. "The report from the laboratory said that thick and thin smears were done and they were negative for babesia," Tepler told me. But he takes nothing for granted. So he made his own smears in his office and looked at them under his own microscope. "And there it was — one single babesia form on the smear. It was easy to see why it had been missed. I was so excited to find it." The patient was successfully treated and recovered fully.

"I always go back and read the recent literature with almost every patient who has a nuanced clinical case, a variation of a diagnosis," Tepler said. "I try hard to stay on top of my game. So much of the joy is reading the medical literature and then judging what in a paper informs how you care for an individual." This "joy" often leads Tepler to linger in his office reading medical journals and textbooks well into the evening. "It's hard to think deeply about patients at the moment when you are seeing them. You need some quiet time to reflect and formulate a cogent opinion." For that reason, he often tells patients that he wants to think more about their cases rather than immediately offering a treatment plan. He routinely leaves his office around eight-thirty or nine at night, devoting the end of the day to thinking.

"While I really love seeing people with these different types of problems," Tepler said, "if I believe that the patient would be better served elsewhere, then I will send him to another doctor." This is another mark of a caring physician who, despite his expertise, knows his limits and wants to do what is best for his patients.

Many of the patients referred to Tepler have very advanced cancer. "Sometimes I think that one of the most important things I do for patients is to spare them the misery of futile treatment," he said. Occasionally people with advanced cancers are "flogged," a distasteful term used in clinical medicine to describe continued toxic therapy with no real point. There are some oncologists who seem to believe that it's wrong for someone to die without receiving every possible drug. Tepler is not one of them. "People really wouldn't want to be treated this way if they truly understood what the likelihood of benefit was," he said. Patients do not always understand that, even when a caring doctor tries to explain it clearly.

"When patients want something that I feel is wrong, I am insistent," Tepler told me. "I tell them that it's wrong." He refuses to humor someone if he thinks the request can cause serious harm. This issue often comes up in the context of a cancer that can be controlled reasonably well but cannot be eradicated — cannot be truly cured. Here Tepler's interest in character comes into play. "Patients want to be cured, and that's understandable," he said, "but then some people demand extreme therapy, or combinations of chemotherapy, when a single agent is just as good and less toxic." He recalled Alex Woo, a designer who had stable metastases from colon cancer. The tumors hadn't grown for three years with the treatment Tepler was giving. "But Alex just couldn't live with the knowledge that he was coexisting with his cancer. He wanted it gone, just gone from his life. But I could not *not* tell him what I was really thinking — that pursuing more extreme therapy would likely hurt him." Woo left Tepler for another doctor.

Another of Tepler's patients, Diane Waters, had breast cancer and a single metastasis to her liver. He had cared for her for more than eight years. Diane's cancer exhibited the HER2 protein on its surface, so he was able to effectively control it using Herceptin, an antibody that targets the surface protein, in conjunction with various chemotherapy agents. "She consulted many, many doctors in New York," he said. "And then she found a radiologist at another center who told her that he could treat the metastasis in her liver through chemoembolization." The radiologist recommended delivering chemotherapy directly via a catheter into the tumor in her liver and said he would then try to choke off the blood supply — chemoembolization. Tepler had advised against this, explaining that metastatic breast cancer is a systemic disease, that there were microscopic deposits beyond the single tumor in her liver; moreover, she had no symptoms from her solitary metastasis — it was being well controlled by the treatment she was receiving. "She almost died from the chemoembolization," Tepler told me. "The left lobe of her liver completely broke down, and she accumulated liters of fluid in her chest. She was in the ICU for weeks."

As he predicted, the disease returned in the liver. "I am usually successful in convincing people, but in this instance I wasn't." But, unlike Alex Woo, Diane Waters returned to him for care. "I didn't make her feel bad about her decision," he said. To her, he said, "You did what you thought you had to do, and you are lucky that you survived." Tepler worked with her on whatever new treatment was then most appropriate; currently her breast cancer is being well controlled with chemotherapy.

Sometimes catastrophic complications of desperate treatments, like the one Diane Waters received, lead to lawsuits. Looming behind every high-risk decision in today's medicine is the specter of litigation. Tepler has found himself in the uncomfortable position of disagreeing with a doctor who recommended an intervention because of concerns about lawsuits.

He told me about Rachel Swanson, a middle-aged woman with ovarian cancer whose disease was clinically well controlled on chemotherapy; her tumors were relatively small and had not grown significantly for a long time. During a yearly visit to her internist, she was referred to a gastroenterologist for a routine colonoscopy. The gastroenterologist noted a metastasis that had deposited on the surface of the colon. "Rachel had no symptoms whatsoever from this," Tepler said. "We usually don't perform colonoscopies on women with known metastatic ovarian cancer unless they have bleeding or some other problem. This was really an incidental finding. There was no reason to think, given that her tumor was well controlled, that it would perforate the bowel." Nonetheless, the gastroenterologist referred her to a surgeon who advised removing the metastasis and adjoining segment of colon. Once this recommendation was made, subsequent consultants were reluctant to challenge it, because, if on the off chance that in the future it did cause a problem, particularly perforation of the bowel, then they could be sued. "I can understand their thinking," Tepler said, "but you can't be guided by fear of lawsuits. You can't practice defensive medicine like this, particularly when it involves subjecting a woman to major surgery."

Tepler continued to advise Mrs. Swanson against the operation, but she was persuaded by the surgeon that it was important to remove the metastasis even though she'd had no symptoms from it. Again, as Tepler pointed out, it is very hard for people to live with the knowledge that tumors in their body could pose a future threat, despite the fact that those tumors are being controlled by chemotherapy. "Rachel wanted the surgery," Tepler said, "and this was communicated to the doctors that she saw. In fact, one excellent gynecological surgeon saw her initially and told me that he agreed with me, that there was no real basis for an operation in her case, but then he changed his mind — probably to satisfy her want." Although the bowel was successfully removed with the metastasis, the surgeon noted several other tumors in the abdomen that could not be excised. Tepler had explained to Mrs. Swanson that regular cycles of chemotherapy that were keeping her ovarian cancer in check would have to be delayed by the operation. And, alas, "her disease just exploded," he said. "She was in terrible pain from the bowel resection, and then the ovarian cancer started to spread aggressively.

"Rachel came back to me, and I felt awful for her," Tepler said. "And she said that she knew I must be angry, that I had told her not to do this. Yes, I said, I had disagreed, but I also pointed out, honestly, that no one can predict what is going to happen in any particular instance." This fundamental truth is too rarely expressed by doctors, and it shows Tepler's humility. Although he has confidence in his own clinical judgment, he accepts that sometimes he may be wrong or that he cannot definitively predict an outcome. In this case, Tepler accepted that there were shades of gray: Mrs. Swanson could have had the tumor successfully removed without the postoperative complications and the explosion of growth in the other metastases; in fact, the resection would have proved to be prudent if in the coming months the tumor had perforated the bowel. The patient's choice, Tepler told me, was in keeping with her character. She wanted to be "proactive" with her cancer. "Understandably, people want the home run," he said. "But often in oncology what we achieve is less than that. And the risk is, by going for the home run, you can strike out."

When Tepler believes that any further chemotherapy is futile, he promises patients that he will be there for them until the end, and he further promises that they will be comfortable with the time they have left. When they press him for numbers — weeks or months — he gently invokes Stephen J. Gould's remark, "The median is not the message."

Many people seek out Memorial Sloan-Kettering based on its well-deserved reputation as a preeminent center for cancer treatment. But often the doctor matters more than the hospital. A friend of mine, an artist in her fifties with bladder cancer who went to Memorial, saw this for herself. She'd had surgery there, and she adored her surgeon. Even after her metastases appeared and there was no reason for further surgery, he visited her in the hospital. She was not a celebrity, not wealthy, so there appeared to be no ulterior motive on his part; she was warm, outgoing, a sparkling person, and the doctor was showing how much he cared, how much he enjoyed her company and the company of her husband, a novelist, by visiting them.

Her distress came from her interaction with her oncologist. He had treated her with what he said was the "best protocol" available, and when her cancer returned after a brief remission, his response to her queries about further treatment left her frightened and paralyzed. I spoke with the oncologist about her case. "She has a projected seven-month survival," he said. "There are no data that any other drugs have more than a ten to fifteen percent response rate — at best." I asked about several drugs in development. "There are phase-two studies," he said, referring to the second phase of evaluation, which is designed to assess the benefit in patients following the first phase, when toxicity is defined. I knew that several patients with bladder cancer had responded well to the drugs in these phase-two studies. "It's much too early to know whether those responses were meaningful," he said, "and no one knows the optimal duration of therapy or the optimal dose." What the oncologist said to me was precisely what he had told the artist and her husband — in his flat, direct way. "She should go home and live out her life. There are no data to support treating her at this point," he concluded.

"I am fifty-six years old," the artist told me. "I am not ready to go home and die in seven months. I have two sons and a husband I adore." She consulted an oncologist at another Manhattan hospital. He gave her one of the drugs that was still in phase-two testing. She had a dramatic response and lived well for more than a year. When the cancer returned, causing a bowel obstruction, she decided that she was ready to die, that there was no real likelihood of sustaining her quality of life. She passed away at home with her family at her side.

"Fundamentally, it's not about the hospital," said Karen Delgado, "although there are those with better support services, better nursing, and more expertise in certain diseases. All of that matters, but what matters most is the doctor. And, I tell people that a physician might be the right doctor for you but not the right doctor for another individual."

Delgado's words rang true. Before George Franklin met Stephen Nimer, he was treated by another specialist at Memorial Hospital. The two did not click; in fact, Franklin and his family took a deep dislike to the oncologist. But a journalist friend of mine who also had an aggressive lymphoma adored the specialist that Franklin could not abide. "There are times I feel like strangling him," the journalist said. "But that's part of why I like him so much. He is incredibly direct. He never pulls any punches. He tells me exactly what he is thinking and why. He can be infuriating, but he is a great doctor for me."

A physician is definitely not great, however, if he abandons any person or family when things go sour clinically. Another friend of mine, who worked in the intelligence services and was a heavy smoker, developed widespread lung cancer in his early sixties. He had retired from the spy business, but prided himself on being an acute observer of people. Yet when he fell ill, he became blind to reading certain doctors' personalities. He was hell-bent on being cared for at Memorial Sloan-Kettering, convinced that some magic there could reverse his dire disease. He finally secured an appointment with a young doctor on the staff, whom at first he found charming. But when the lung cancer grew after several cycles of intensive chemotherapy, the oncologist wouldn't return his calls. When he was admitted to the hospital with complications, the oncologist spent a few fleeting minutes at his bedside and then seemed to disappear entirely. His office said that he was traveling a lot. My friend was in the hospital for days without his oncologist visiting or even telephoning. He was emotionally devastated, afraid and alone. My friend ultimately sought an outstanding oncologist in his hometown in New Jersey who was attentive and made sure that his final days were as comfortable as possible.

My novelist friend theorized that the oncologist who treated his artist wife but would not consider treatment beyond statistics and protocols, and the oncologist who abandoned the intelligence operative, both suffered from fear of failure, and probably fear of death. "I know it sounds strange," he said, "supposing that an oncologist who sees so much death would flee from it. But I think posing as highly rational, acting only when all the numbers are in hand, is in fact an irrational way to care for people with cancer. You refuse to try anything creative, refuse to put yourself on the line. He must have known that we would leave him, that we would seek another doctor at this most difficult point in our lives, when we were facing death. It is a more subtle form of abandonment than what happened to your friend with lung cancer."

This is a fundamental schism in the field of oncology, between those who are driven almost entirely by data and those who are willing to treat patients outside of proven protocols. Sometimes veering too far from widely tested therapies can result in unnecessary toxicity and suffering. But I found a deep resonance in what the novelist said — that what appeared to be a rational form of thinking was actually irrational when applied to a patient's needs and goals, and might reflect the emotional state of the oncologist more than the clinical needs of the patient.

Nimer and Tepler try to understand a patient's character and factor this understanding into their clinical judgments. My novelist friend showed me how patients and their families can understand their oncologists' character and weave that understanding into their decisions. People with cancer and other serious diseases can face a dizzying array of choices. Which path they take pivots on clinical facts and the dimension of character — their own and their doctors'. This applies not only to oncology but to all of medicine, a mix of science and soul.

Epilogue: A Patient's Questions

L ET'S IMAGINE you are sitting in a doctor's office. For several weeks you've had a symptom that has not gone away — say, discomfort in the center of your chest, beneath the breastbone. The doctor has taken the history, performed a physical examination, and ordered some tests. He reviews with you the information he has gathered and believes that you have acid reflux, a common problem when the irritating juices from the stomach move up into the esophagus.

In most cases, a physician arrives at the correct diagnosis and offers appropriate treatments. But not always. If, after a while, you are not getting better, the discomfort persists or has worsened, then it is time to rethink the diagnosis. Recall that most misguided care results from a cascade of cognitive errors. Different doctors have different styles of practice, different approaches to problems. But all of us are susceptible to the same mistakes in thinking.

How to make the correct diagnosis? There is no single script that every doctor or patient should follow. But there are a series of touchstones that help correct errors in thinking. Doctor and patient will start again searching for clues to solve the problem. The first detour away from a correct diagnosis is often caused by miscommunication. So a thinking doctor returns to language. "Tell me the story again as if I'd never heard it — what you felt, how it happened, when it happened." If he doesn't ask you to do this, then you can offer to retell your story. Telling the story afresh can help you recall a vital bit of information that you forgot. Telling the story again may help the physician register some clue that was, in fact, said the first time but was overlooked or thought unimportant. This will prompt him to look in new directions for answers.

These days, when we are not getting better, most of us return to see the doctor with ideas about what might be wrong. Our notions sometimes come from knowing a friend or relative with a similar symptom, or ideas may have been sparked by looking on the Internet. Our thoughts about our unrelieved symptoms often focus on the worst-case scenario. Such self-diagnosis is a reality that neither patient nor physician should ignore. Since the doctor may not address it, you should. "I'm most worried that what seemed like acid reflux could be the first sign of cancer," one patient might say. Or another might recount to the doctor how her friend was told she had indigestion but it was actually a brewing heart attack. For some, articulating such fears is exceedingly difficult to do because of magical thinking — the notion that saying it might make it real. I recall one middle-aged woman with discomfort in the chest whose face was a mask of worry when we were searching for a diagnosis. "Tell him what is really frightening you," her husband said with loving firmness. A relative had died of a pulmonary embolus, and she was terrified that this was the cause of her chest pain. After she told me, she admitted that she'd been scared to say it, since doing so might make it true.

A thoughtful doctor listens closely to these worries. Alerted to your deepest concerns, he may be prompted to ask more probing questions, to have you describe your symptoms in greater detail.

This expands the breadth of your dialogue with him and removes inhibitions that could hide clues.

But the answer may not be revealed quickly by a fresh dialogue. The doctor may need to repeat your physical examination, focusing more intensively on one or another part of your body. Or he may begin to doubt the value of a particular laboratory test, or the reading of your x-ray. As we've seen throughout this book, physicians tend to go with their first impressions. The initial biases in a physician's thinking are often reinforced by his selective survey of diagnostic data. We all are inclined to seize on an apparently positive finding and ignore what may be negative and contradictory.

Sometimes he may need to repeat laboratory tests and sophisticated scans. This can be costly. In the current environment of medical practice, repeating tests is strongly discouraged as not being cost effective. The imperative from hospital and managed care administrators is to be economical. And arriving at the correct diagnosis may not require actually repeating tests, only doubting them. As we saw, there can be significant differences in how different radiologists read the same image, how different pathologists assess the same biopsy. Revisiting the diagnosis means the doctor returns with a sharp and discerning eye to inspect all the results to date — blood tests and x-rays and pathology reports.

Yet there are times when repeating a test is essential. There are instances when the first CT scan was not correctly calibrated, as Dr. Herb Kressel recounted in the case of the woman with chest pain believed to have a pulmonary embolus but actually suffering from a tear in her aorta. There are times when the first biopsy misses the lesion. In my field of hematology, more than one bone marrow examination may be needed to find a malignancy like a lymphoma, because tumors are not uniformly present in the bones, and I may have placed the biopsy needle in an area of the marrow that did not contain the tumor. After review or repetition, the tests still may not give the answer.

"What else could it be?" is now the question you or your loved one should ask the physician. The cognitive mistakes that account for most misdiagnoses are not recognized by physicians; they largely reside below the level of conscious thinking. When you or your loved one asks simply, "What else could it be?" you help bring closer to the surface the reality of uncertainty in medicine. "What else could it be?" is a key safeguard against these errors in thinking: premature closure, framing effect, availability from recent experience, the bias that the hoofbeats are horses and not zebras. Each cognitive error constrains the pursuit of answers, and correcting the error helps the doctor think of a test or procedure that he didn't previously consider and can make the diagnosis.

"Is there anything that doesn't fit?" may be your next question. This follow-up should further prompt the physician to pause and let his mind roam more broadly. He will begin to survey more of the clinical territory, aided by a vision that comes from doubt. "Is there anything that doesn't fit?" was the question underpinning Rachel Stein's insistence that her infant daughter Shira's atypical case might not be atypical at all, but something altogether different.

"Is it possible I have more than one problem?" We are taught in medical school and residency to be parsimonious in our thinking, to apply Ockham's razor, to seek one answer to a patient's many complaints. Usually this turns out to be the correct approach. But, again, not always. Posing this question is another safeguard against one of the most common cognitive traps that all physicians fall into: search satisfaction. Your question about multiple causes for your problems should trigger the doctor to cast a wider net, to begin to ask questions that he didn't pose before, to order tests that might not have seemed necessary based on his initial impressions. You might have acid reflux but also angina — both are common; or acid reflux and a tear in your aorta, a rarer condition. As we saw in the Introduction, Dr. Myron Falchuk reframed

Anne Dodge's case to encompass two pictures, and, by doing so, saved her life.

Sometimes I come to the end of my thinking and am not sure what to do next. This may mean I made a cognitive error and don't realize it. In retrospect, analyzing my own misdiagnoses, sometimes I failed to ask the right questions, failed to find the abnormality during the physical examination, failed to identify a key bit of data because I didn't order the right tests. I had fallen unawares into a cognitive trap. At such times, ego can form another cognitive pitfall. I have learned to say to my patient, "I believe when you say something is wrong, but I haven't figured it out." And since I can't figure out your problem, I continue, I should send you elsewhere, to a physician with an independent mind who likes to tackle complicated cases. The internist caring for Anne Dodge didn't want to do this because she believed there was nothing new to find; she had exhausted all possibilities. If a loved one had not insisted, Anne Dodge would still be suffering, or worse.

When a patient tells me, "I still don't feel good. I'm still having symptoms," I have learned to refrain from replying, "Nothing is wrong with you." The statement "Nothing is wrong with you" is dangerous on two accounts. First, it denies the fallibility of all physicians. Second, it splits the mind from the body. Because sometimes what is wrong is psychological, not physical. This conclusion, of course, should be reached only after a serious and prolonged search for a physical cause for the patient's complaint.

The lingering stigma that exists in medicine, and in the larger society, about psychological distress and its ramifications through the body, stands as a roadblock to relieving the pain and misery of so many patients. Many doctors, as we have seen, dislike patients whom they stereotype as neurotic and anxious. These patients pose one of the greatest challenges to even the most caring physicians. They may relate their story in a scattershot way, hypersensitive to every ache and pain, and make it difficult for the doctor to focus his mind so that he finds the tumor in the breast or the nodule in the thyroid gland. A patient's insight into his own thinking and emotional state can be enormously helpful to a physician. Recall how one of Karen Delgado's patients told her that she knew she was a little bit "kooky," but that her complaints should not be ignored for this reason. Sometimes, of course, patients are not kooky, just terrified, but are labeled hypochondriacs by the doctor. A close friend in Los Angeles, a hard-driving businesswoman in the entertainment industry, repeatedly told her doctor about the aches in her breasts. Her mammogram was read by the radiologist as normal, and her persistent complaints were dismissed. She was told "Nothing is wrong with you." Her aches, the doctor said, were caused by stress. Only after going to another doctor, who performed more tests, was the cancer identified. Her diagnosis was delayed by nearly two years, and the cancer was found in more than a dozen lymph nodes.

We've all heard stories like this, and patients and physicians alike dread them. But if, in another woman's case, it turned out the discomfort in her breasts was not cancer but the result of psychological distress, the statement "Nothing is wrong with you" would still be misguided. She should be reassured and, if her distress and symptoms continue, be referred to a psychologist or psychiatrist who can help her.

When I was undergoing tests to diagnose the pain and swelling in my right hand, one of the surgeons sent me for a bone scan. This scan evaluates all of the bones in the body, not just those in the wrist. The radiologist who looked at the scan saw some spots over my ribs. The surgeon called me at home in the evening. I was alone; my family was away on a skiing trip. The surgeon said that there was no rush to operate on my hand because the spots on the scan looked like metastatic cancer in my ribs. I generally think of myself as reasonably well put together psychologically, but within moments my chest began to ache. When I touched my ribs, they hurt. As an oncologist, I know it is unlikely my bones would be riddled with tumors without any symptoms. But, at that moment, I was suddenly not a doctor. I was completely a patient. My mind froze. I desperately tried reaching my wife. After several hours, I found her. Pam told me not to panic. She said I should go for further x-rays the next morning. Her words, that the radiologist might be wrong, did not hold sway. I spent a sleepless night, imagining a slow death from an incurable cancer. Despite all my training and experience, I was overcome by fear. The pain in my chest was real.

I was first in line the next day and had a series of x-rays that showed my ribs were normal. A second radiologist looked at the bone scan and concluded that it had been overread, that there were no spots. It took several hours until the ache in my chest fully subsided and my ribs were no longer tender to my touch.

I learned two lessons from this episode. First, after shocking news was delivered in a blunt and absolute way, I needed someone to guide me, to provide balance, to raise doubt, to highlight uncertainty — to think for me and with me — because even though in another setting I would intellectually consider that the spots might be artifacts, I couldn't grasp it viscerally. Second, I experienced the power of the mind over the body, of psychosomatic symptoms.

Of course, persistent but elusive symptoms sometimes are not psychosomatic, and finally a correct physical diagnosis is made. The doctor treats you, but you don't get better with the treatment. Before launching into a new therapy, the physician should talk with you and consider, as Dr. JudyAnn Bigby teaches, the context — where and how and when you are taking the therapy. Recall the study of forty-five doctors in California caring for more than nine hundred patients. Two thirds did not tell the patients either how long to take the new medicine or what its side effects could be. Nearly half failed to specify the dose of the drug and how often it should be taken. It is not enough to assume that a pharmacist or other health professional will fill in these gaps. There must be a clear mutual understanding between you and your doctor about the therapy, its rationale, and its specifics. Furthermore, as Bigby emphasizes, the doctor who pays attention to your social setting will think about the nonmedical reasons the treatment seems to be failing.

There can be other considerations as well. Karen Delgado told me that, although medicines are now color-coded, miscommunication can still occur. Delgado was concerned when an elderly female patient with an underactive thyroid was not responding to treatment. "Check the pills that the pharmacist gave you," Delgado said. "Are they purple?" The woman replied, "Yes, they're purple." For a while Delgado couldn't figure out what was wrong, why the woman was still sluggish. Then she asked the woman to bring in all her medications. It turned out one pill containing 175 micrograms of thyroid hormone was one shade of purple, and another pill containing 75 micrograms was a slightly different shade of purple. The patient was in no position to distinguish between subtle shades of purple.

In other instances, the treatment, although correctly prescribed and taken, simply doesn't work. Each of us is unique in our biology, and there can be important differences in both the side effects we suffer and the benefits we gain from the same medication. We can share a single illness but not share its remedy, despite receiving the same drug or undergoing the same procedure. How long to persist with a treatment that has not quickly worked, and which treatment to choose as the second option, reflect the science and the art of medicine. Dr. Stephen Nimer immediately changed George Franklin's chemotherapy regimen, while other oncologists wanted to continue the protocol. Recognizing failure early and switching therapies extended Franklin's life by years.

Good treatments are the products of a robust pharmaceutical industry, and many diseases that were once incurable have now been brought to heel with new medicines. But when a physician and patient make decisions about treatment, they should be mindful of the benefits and risks, the needs and goals they share. Their choices should be free of the influences of financial gain and the biases introduced by corporate marketing.

All of this takes time, and time is the greatest luxury in today's medical care. Those who see medicine as a business rather than a calling push for care to be apportioned in fixed units and tout efficiency. A doctor's office is not an assembly line. Turning it into one is a sure way to blunt communication, foster mistakes, and rupture the partnership between patient and physician. A doctor can't think with one eye on the clock and another on the computer screen. But a thinking doctor does need to allot his time wisely. Problems that are well defined and straightforward can be addressed with clarity in fifteen or twenty minutes, and a patient and family can leave the visit feeling informed and satisfied. Complicated problems cannot be solved in a rush. The inescapable truth is that good thinking takes time. Working in haste and cutting corners are the quickest routes to cognitive errors.

For three decades practicing as a physician, I looked to traditional sources to assist me in my thinking about my patients: textbooks and medical journals; mentors and colleagues with deeper or more varied clinical experience; students and residents who posed challenging questions. But after writing this book, I realized that I can have another vital partner who helps improve my thinking, a partner who may, with a few pertinent and focused questions, protect me from the cascade of cognitive pitfalls that cause misguided care. That partner is present in the moment when flesh-and-blood decision-making occurs. That partner is my patient or her family member or friend who seeks to know what is in my mind, how I am thinking. And by opening my mind I can more clearly recognize its reach and its limits, its understanding of my patient's physical problems and emotional needs. There is no better way to care for those who need my caring.

ACKNOWLEDGMENTS

Three years ago, when I returned from rounds filled with questions about how doctors think, I first shared my desire to find out with Pam, my wife and soul mate. It is a gift to live your life with a person you love who is wiser than you. As a consummate physician, Pam brought to bear knowledge and insight into clinical judgment and misjudgment that had escaped me. As the wife of a man who had been a desperate patient, as a mother of children who had been ill, and as the daughter of still vigorous but aging parents, Pam helped me see physicians' thinking and behavior from inside and outside our shared professional world. Her contributions were extraordinary, and her imprint is on every page of this book.

Suzanne Gluck at the William Morris Agency is more than my agent; she is a friend and comrade and advocate. Her keen intelligence and constructive criticisms were vital in refining the project and finding the best home for it.

Eamon Dolan, my editor at Houghton Mifflin, pushed me to probe deeper and explore more widely the questions raised in this book. He reined me in with an expert hand when I went astray. His talent in sharpening ideas and sculpting prose is something to behold. The team at Houghton Mifflin worked with unique intensity and commitment, and I am deeply indebted to Bridget Marmion, Lori Glazer, Anne Seiwerath, Sasheem Silkiss-Hero, Larry Cooper, and Janet Silver.

Youngsun Jung, my assistant of twenty-one years, never flinched from the immense burdens of fact-checking, manuscript preparation, and dead-lines. She brings more than diligence to each project; Youngsun applies her intelligence to the ideas that I seek to express.

I am fortunate to have friends who lead literary lives and who gener-ously gave their time and expertise, offering critiques that were always to the point. Foremost among these is Keith Johnson, a wordsmith par ex-cellence. Jonathan Alter, who emerged strong and ready to reengage the world after a bone marrow transplant for lymphoma, and Emily Lazar, an accomplished TV producer, not only expressed enthusiasm for the project but also introduced me to physicians and surgeons they know around the country, some of whom appear in these pages. Although I've been writing regularly for more than a decade, I still see myself as primar-ily a physician and scientist, and I rely on friends who are pros for guid-ance and feedback. In this project I turned to Ron Chernow, Nora Ephron, Ann Godoff, Annik LaFarge, Norman Manea, Tim Noah, Fran-cine Pascal, Nick Pileggi, Dorothy Rabinowitz, Frank Rich, David San-ford, Alvin Sargent, Stuart Schoffman, Andrew Sullivan, Melanie Thern-strom, Elizabeth Weymouth, Sarah Elizabeth Button White, Jay Winik, Alex Witchel, Rafael Yglesias, and Laura Ziskin.

While writing this book, several patients whom I counted as friends encouraged me and taught me lessons about communication, critical thinking, and the paramount importance of a person's values and spiri-tual needs. Marjorie Williams confided that she was keeping a running list of all of the obtuse remarks physicians had made to her, but wouldn't disclose how many times my name and words appeared in her compen-dium. Margaret Joskow, an elegant artist, explained how honesty is key to caring. When I visited Margaret in her hospital room, she rewarded me with a cache of pens with a wide grip to assist my injured hand; I still use them. Betty Tzafrir was an *ayshet chayil,* a woman of valor, who made sure her doctors thought about the impact of her illness on her family, not just on her. Jim Young, an ex-marine with a sharp sense of humor, wanted to know what I was thinking without any filter between us so he could deploy his forces strategically; Jim ended each conversation with "Semper Fi." Valerie Chernow, a professor of Romance languages, showed me the power of words in sustaining grace and poise despite dire circumstances, and reminded me of the value of honoring the wishes of a person in her last days. Barry Bingham, a retired publisher, made sure that we spoke first about the day's headlines before discussing his symptoms; he was telling me that he remained who he was despite his malady. As his illness overtook him, his dedicated family served as his interlocutor and taught me about the role of loved ones in making a patient's most difficult decision. Julia Thorne was writing a novel, and reminded me time and again that narrative is the most compelling form of learning and teaching. Ruth Gay sustained *joie de vivre* in the face of sustained uncertainty, invoking Yiddish aphorisms that capture the fun and folly of life. Johnny Apple, with the discerning mind of a political reporter, posed hard questions and made sure that the answers from his multiple medical sources made sense. Johnny told me that only he, a Lutheran from the Midwest, knew the best kosher restaurant in the cosmos, and that my incentive to finish the book was dinner at this unnamed place. There are many others, and I hold them in my heart. If indeed there is a heaven, I hope they can hear my thanks.

I was regularly encouraged in my work by Ron Ansin, Betsey Apple, Barbara Bierer, Arthur Cohen, Everett Fahey, Lisa Goldberg, Lenny Groopman, Rabbi William Hamilton, Francine and Harry Hartzband, Margo Howard, Steve Hyman, Ben Mizell, Daryl Otte, Anne Peretz, Michael Share, Abe and Cindy Steinberger, and Liz Young.

For a decade, *The New Yorker* has been the laboratory where I experiment with writing about medicine and biology. Although my editors there were not directly involved in the crafting of this book, they continue to instruct me in the elements that make for quality writing. I learn so much from Emily Eakin, Dorothy Wickenden, Daniel Zalewski, Henry Finder, and of course David Remnick. I've also benefited over the years from lively interactions with Marty Peretz and Leon Wieseltier at the *New Republic*.

The candor and insights offered by patients and physicians in these pages have made me understand medicine in an entirely new way. By opening up their lives to me, they have given me gifts of knowledge that I am privileged to share with those who are ill and in need. Any shortcomings in substance or style reflect my own deficiencies.

Introduction

Two recent articles about the shortcomings of algorithms and practice guidelines are Mary E. Tinetti, "Potential pitfalls of disease-specific guidelines for patients with multiple conditions," *New England Journal of Medicine (NEJM)* 351 (2004), pp. 2870–2874, and Patrick J. O'Connor, "Adding value to evidence-based clinical guidelines," *Journal of the American Medical Association (JAMA)* 294 (2005), pp. 741–743.

Those interested in the Bayesian approach can read Baruch Fischhoff and Ruth Beyth-Marom, "Hypothesis evaluation from a Bayesian perspective," *Psychological Review* 90 (1983), pp. 239–260; Fredric M. Wolf et al., "Differential diagnosis and the competing-hypotheses heuristic: A practical approach to judgment under uncertainty and Bayesian probability," *JAMA* 253 (1985), pp. 2858–2862. The observation by Robert Hamm that few physicians work in such a mathematical mode comes from "Clinical intuition and clinical analysis: Expertise and the cognitive continuum," in *Professional Judgment: A Reader in Clinical Decision Making,* ed. Jack Dowie and Arthur Elstein (Cambridge: Cambridge University Press, 1988), pp. 78–105.

The varied clinical manifestations of celiac disease are presented in Richard J. Farrell and Ciaran P. Kelly, "Celiac sprue," *NEJM* 346 (2002), pp. 180–188; Alessio Fasano, "Celiac disease — How to handle a clinical chameleon," *NEJM* 348 (2003), pp. 2568–2570; Ross McManus and Dermot Kelleher, "Celiac disease — The villain unmasked?," *NEJM* 348 (2003), pp. 2573–2574.

The work of Judith Hall and Debra Roter is extensive and scholarly. Their recent book is a comprehensive analysis of the field: *Doctors Talking with Patients / Patients Talking with Doctors: Improving Communication in Medical Visits,* 2nd ed. (Westport, Conn.: Praeger Publishers, 2006). Publications relevant to their remarks in this chapter include "Task versus socioemotional behaviors in physicians," *Medical Care* 25 (1987); "Physicians' psychosocial belief correlate with their patient communication skills," *Journal of General Internal Medicine* 10 (1995), pp. 375–379; "Communication patterns of primary care physicians," *JAMA* 277 (1997), pp. 350–356; "Relations between physicians' behaviors and analogue patients' satisfaction, recall, and impressions," *Medical Care* 25 (1987), pp. 437–451; "Liking in the physician-patient relationship," *Patient Education and Counseling* 48 (2002), pp. 69–77; "Physician gender and patient-centered communication: A critical review of empirical research," *Annual Review of Public Health* 25 (2004), pp. 497–519. Other useful sources include E. J. Emanuel and L. L. Emanuel, "Four models of the physician-patient relationship," *JAMA* 267 (1992), pp. 2221–2226; G. L. Engel, "How much longer must medicine's science be bound by a seventeenth-century world view?," in *The Task of Medicine: Dialogue at Wickenburg. Menlo Park, California,* ed. K. White Donald (Henry J. Kaiser Foundation, 1988). Redelmeier has also examined the importance of clinical dialogue. See "Problems for clinical judgment: Eliciting an insightful history of present illness," *Canadian Medical Association Journal* 164 (2001), pp. 647–651; "Problems for clinical judgment: Obtaining a reliable past medical history," *Canadian Medical Association Journal* 164 (2001), pp. 809–813.

Studies of expertise have been greatly advanced by K. Anders Ericsson, and the interested reader is directed to "The role of deliberate practice in the acquisition of expert performance," *Psychological Review* 100 (1993), pp. 363–406; "Deliberate practice and the acquisition and maintenance of expert performance in medicine and related domains," *Academic Medicine* 79 (2004), pp. S70–S81. Geoff Norman is another leader in this area, and he recently reviewed how doctors can improve their skills in Geoff Norman et al., "Expertise in medicine and surgery," in *The Cambridge Handbook of Expertise and Expert Performance*, ed. K. Anders Ericsson et al. (Cambridge: Cambridge University Press, 2006), pp. 339–353.

The Institute of Medicine report is a landmark book: *To Err Is Human: Building a Safer Health System* (Washington, D.C.: National Academy Press, 1999). Donald Berwick has done wonderful work about system errors and how hospitals can protect patients from technical mistakes; a good example is "Taking action to improve safety: How to increase the odds of success," in *Enhancing Patient Safety and Reducing Errors in Health Care* (Chicago: National Patient Safety Foundation, 1999), pp. 1–11.

Arthur Elstein studied clinical reasoning, testing physicians' acumen with written descriptions of cases as well as with actors posing as patients with various diseases. Overall, Elstein estimated the rate of error in diagnosis at 15 percent, meaning one in six to seven patients was incorrectly assessed. Elstein's estimate agrees with classic studies of diagnostic errors of 10 to 15 percent, based on autopsies that revealed the missed diagnosis: A. S. Elstein, "Clinical reasoning in medicine," in *Clinical Reasoning in the Health Professions,* ed. J. Higgs and M. A. Jones (Woburn, Mass.: Butterworth-Heinemann, 1995), pp. 49–59; W. Kirch and C. Schafil, "Misdiagnosis at a university hospital in 4 medical eras," *Medicine* 75 (1996), pp. 29–40; K. G. Shojania et al., "Changes in rates of autopsy-detected diagnostic errors over time," *JAMA* 289 (2003), pp. 2849–2856; L. Goldman et al., "The value of the autopsy in three different eras," *NEJM* 308 (1983), pp. 1000–1005. Of note, the frequency of diagnostic errors did not change between 1960 and 1980 at an American university teaching hospital despite the introduction of new technologies like CT scans. In fact, overreliance on new procedures sometimes was the cause of serious missed diagnoses. Similar data were found in a study in a German teaching hospital. In the United States and Canada, more than one million people die in the hospital each year; missed diagnoses of a serious nature accounted for about fifty thousand deaths that could have been prevented if the actual case had been identified.

Although the frequency of misdiagnosis has been studied, few researchers have focused on its relationship to physician cognition. One of the first articles to do so was Jerome P. Kassirer and Richard I. Kopelman, "Cognitive errors in diagnosis: Instantiation, classification, and consequences," *American Journal of Medicine* 86 (1989), pp. 433–441. Pat Croskerry has worked with great commitment to categorize cognitive errors, particularly in his specialty of emergency medicine. Several of his important articles are "The importance of cognitive errors in diagnosis and strategies to minimize them," *Academic Medicine* 78 (2003), pp. 775–780; "Achieving quality in clinical decision making: Cognitive strategies and detection of bias," *Academic Emergency Medicine* 9 (2002), pp. 1184–1204; "When diagnoses fail: New insights, old thinking," *Canadian Journal of CME,* November 2003. Donald Redelmeier recently wrote about detours in doctors' thinking in "The cognitive psychology of missed diagnoses," *Annals of Internal Medicine* 142 (2005), pp. 115–120. Mark Graber, at the State University of New York, Stony Brook, raised the question of how to teach physicians to think about their thinking in "Metacognitive training to reduce diagnostic errors: Ready for prime time?," *Academic Medicine* 78 (2003), p. 781.

Most physicians are not aware of their cognitive mistakes; in addition, the medical system affords only inconsistent feedback to physicians about diagnostic errors and why they occurred. Thus, data on the frequency of flawed thinking come from retrospective analyses of medical records, from autopsies, and from hindsight physician interviews. Tejal K. Gandhi concluded that the majority of serious errors that led to malpractice claims were cognitive in nature; see "Missed and delayed diagnoses in the ambulatory setting: A study of closed malpractice claims," *Annals of Internal Medicine* 145 (2006), pp. 488–496. Mark Graber presented a study of one hundred misdiagnoses highlighting the high frequency of cognitive pitfalls in "Diagnostic error in internal medicine," *Archives of Internal Medicine* 165 (2005), pp. 1493–1499.

Studies of the use of computers to improve diagnosis have shown relatively small benefits, primarily among students rather than medical residents or attending physicians. In some instances the "computer consultation" was detrimental and caused the clinician to latch on to a misdiagnosis: Charles P. Friedman et al., "Enhancement of clinicians' diagnostic reasoning by computer-based consultation: A multiple study of 2 systems," *JAMA* 282 (1999), pp. 1851–1856.

1. Flesh-and-Blood Decision-Making

Robert Hamm's comments can be found in his chapter "Clinical intuition and clinical analysis: Expertise and the cognitive continuum," in *Professional Judgment: A Reader in Clinical Decision Making*, ed. Jack Dowie and Arthur Elstein (Cambridge: Cambridge University Press, 1988), pp. 78–105. Donald A. Schön presents his views in "From technical rationality to reflection-in-action," in *Professional Judgment*, pp. 60–77. "Flesh-and-blood decision-making," the phrase that Croskerry used, is explored in James Reason's seminal work *Human Error* (Cambridge: Cambridge University Press, 1990), p. 38. The use of heuristics is well articulated in two of Croskerry's articles: "Achieving quality in clinical decision making: Cognitive strategies and detection of bias," *Academic Emergency Medicine* 9 (2002), pp. 1184–1204, and "The theory and practice of clinical decision-making," *Canadian Journal of Anesthesia* 52 (2005), pp. R1–R8. The Yerkes-Dodson law was published nearly a hundred years ago in Robert M. Yerkes and John D. Dodson, "The relation of strength of stimulus to rapidity of habit-formation," *Journal of Comparative Neurology and Psychology* 18 (1908), pp. 459–482.

There is considerable interest in using simulation to train physicians. The encounter with Stan is described in my article "A model patient: How simulators are changing the way doctors are trained," *New Yorker,* May 2, 2005.

The research on physicians' attitudes toward patients with psychological problems is included in an article by Judith Hall and Debra Roter, "Liking in the physician-patient relationship," *Patient Education and Counseling* 48 (2002), pp. 69–77. Physicians in training are often directed to an article by J. E. Groves, "Taking care of the hateful patient," *NEJM* 298 (1978), pp. 883–887. Of course, there is an extensive literature related to mental health care, which is beyond the scope of this book. The interested reader can consult R. A. Flood and C. P. Seager, "A retrospective examination of psychiatric case records of patients who subsequently committed suicide," *British Journal of Psychiatry* 114 (1968), pp. 443–450; W. Ironside, "Iatrogenic contributions to suicide and a report on 37 suicide attempts," *New Zealand Medical Journal* 69 (1969), p. 207; John Maltsberger and Donald Buie, "Countertransference hate in the treatment of suicidal patients," *Archives of General Psychiatry* 30 (1974), pp. 625–633.

The connections between cognition and emotion are beautifully described in Antonio Damasio's *Descartes' Error: Emotion, Reason, and the Human Brain* (Itasca, Ill.: Putnam, 1994).

2. Lessons from the Heart

Amos Tversky and Daniel Kahneman were the pioneers in categorizing cognitive biases. Kahneman was awarded a Nobel Prize for their work; alas, Tversky died before the Nobel Committee's decision. Valuable articles by these researchers on errors include "Availability: A heuristic for judging frequency and probability," *Cognitive Psychology* 5 (1973), pp. 207–232, and "Judgment under uncertainty: Heuristics and biases," *Science* 185 (1974), pp. 1124–1131. Again, Pat Croskerry's "Achieving quality in clinical decision making: Cognitive strategies and detection of bias," *Academic Emergency Medicine* 9 (2002), pp. 1184–1204, is a compendium of thinking errors with special reference to the emergency department. Redelmeier's self-awareness about his feelings is found in his published work, including "Problems for clinical judgment: Introducing cognitive psychology as one more basic science," *Canadian Medical Association Journal* 164 (2001), pp. 358–360. Wilson's disease is a disorder involving copper metabolism resulting in a buildup of the metal in the liver and other organs.

About 5 percent of people who go to the emergency room with what is, in fact, a myocardial infarction, or who are on the cusp of developing one ("crescendo angina"), are mistakenly sent home. Thus, McKinley's case is not at all rare. Twenty percent of patients with myocardial infarction in the ER have a normal EKG, and 25 percent do not have such classic symptoms as pain radiating down the arm or shortness of breath. Blood tests, like the cardiac enzymes that Croskerry ordered, often don't show a myocardial infarction or worsening angina even though there is blockage of the coronary artery; these enzymes may only rise to abnormal levels many hours after the onset of the chest pain.

A number of cardiologists have spent years trying to perfect algorithms that would identify chest pain specifically due to increasing angina or a full-blown heart attack as opposed to the many other causes of the symptom. Dr. Lee Goldman, a friend and colleague of mine, recently concluded, after two decades of trying, that an algorithm could not be perfected. Numerous studies have addressed how to more accurately identify those patients with a cardiac cause of their chest pain. A good discussion with a comprehensive bibliography is found in Lee Goldman and Ajay J. Kirtane, "Triage of patients with acute chest pain and possible cardiac ischemia: The elusive search for diagnostic perfection," *Annals of Internal Medicine* 139 (2006), pp. 987–995. Goldman, currently the vice president of health affairs at my alma mater, Columbia, said, "One lesson, which is probably a good one for us all, is to remain humble and open to changes in our thinking." It is better to err on the side of caution and admit patients like McKinley for observation rather than discharge them from the ER. But, of course, some patients should be sent home rather than kept under observation. It will always be impossible to predict 100 percent of the time whether the chest pain is due to coronary artery disease, but the ER doctor's decision to admit the patient or send him home should be made with attention to potential cognitive pitfalls.

The role of prototypical and attribution errors in the doctor's assessment of patients is well covered in Croskerry, "Achieving quality in clinical decision making," cited above, and Donald A. Redelmeier, "The cognitive psychology of missed diagnoses," *Annals of Internal Medicine* 142 (2005), pp. 115–120. Currently, cardiologists use computer programs to help them analyze EKGs. "Computer EKG diagnosis of life-threatening conditions, e.g., acute myocardial infarction or high-degree AV blocks [arrhythmia] are frequently not accurate (40.7% and 75.0% errors respectively)." Maya Guglin et al., "Common errors in computer electrocardiogram interpretation," *International Journal of Cardiology* 106 (2006), pp. 232–237. A cogent article advocating that physicians should develop strategies to enhance self-awareness is Ronald M. Epstein, "Mindful practice," *JAMA* 282 (1999), pp. 833–839.

Although first impressions may be correct, medical decision-making is not a process that should rely primarily on intuition. Recently, the lay media widely reported a study from the Netherlands that concluded that first impressions are superior to deliberate analysis: Ap Dijksterhuis et al., "On making the right choice: The deliberation-without-attention effect," *Science* 311 (2006), pp. 1005–1007. This study involved consumer choices, like buying furniture. The publication was followed by an important letter from Hilary L. Bekker, "Making choices without deliberating," *Science* 312 (2006), p. 1472. Bekker, who studies healthcare in the United Kingdom, pointed out that it is dangerous to go with your gut when it comes to clinical choices. The Dutch researchers strongly agreed that their work should not be glibly generalized to include clinical decision-making.

For those interested in the life and work of Dr. Francis Weld Peabody, the biography by Oglesby Paul, *The Caring Physician: The Life of Dr. Francis W. Peabody* (Cambridge, Mass.: Harvard University Press, 1991), is an excellent source. Dr. Peabody's contributions were also celebrated in "The care of the patient," *JAMA* 88 (1927), pp. 877–882.

3. Spinning Plates

Harrison Alter's ABCs of emergency care form the kind of mnemonic that can be lifesaving when immediate action must be taken. It provides a mental checklist that is readily retrieved from one's memory in an urgent and stressful situation. Its simplicity and comprehensiveness make it a useful aid that can move a doctor away from the far end of the Yerkes-Dodson curve where anxiety impairs performance. I wish that I'd learned these ABCs before my first day of internship when I froze in front of Mr. Morgan.

Earlier, I cited the extraordinary insights of Amos Tversky and Daniel Kahneman. Their exploration of availability errors is found in "Availability: A heuristic for judging frequency and probability," *Cognitive Psychology* 5 (1973), pp. 207–232.

Note how incomplete communication and cognitive pitfalls are linked in the case of Blanche Begaye. Once Alter had anchored his assumption that she had a viral infection, he limited his dialogue with her. In revisiting the reasons for missing the diagnosis of aspirin toxicity, he pinpointed that he did not define what "a few" meant. Alter is now an expert in emergency medicine, and that level of performance comes from listening to feedback and understanding past mistakes. This is consistent with the studies of Ericsson and Norman referred to previously:

K. Anders Ericsson et al., "The role of deliberate practice in the acquisition of expert performance," *Psychological Review* 100 (1993), pp. 363–406; Geoff Norman et al., "Expertise in medicine and surgery," in *The Cambridge Handbook of Expertise and Expert Performance,* ed. K. Anders Ericsson et al. (Cambridge: Cambridge University Press, 2006), pp. 339–353.

A physician considering which test to order is aided by a knowledge of its predictive value, and this is one instance where Bayesian analysis works well, so long as there is a solid database about how the test performs in populations with the specific symptoms or findings on physical examination.

Many of the technical errors that have plagued clinical care, like mislabeling an x-ray with the wrong patient's name or incorrectly transcribing the dose of a medication, have been remedied since the Institute of Medicine report referred to earlier. Nearly all hospitals have adopted procedures with checks and double checks to help safeguard against such mistakes. Recently, after an injury to my hand, the nurse practitioner made sure to mark the injured limb with an X so that the technician would place the correct hand on the x-ray plate to generate the film. Similarly, in my own field of hematology, patients who are anemic and need a blood transfusion wear bracelets with their name, hospital identification number, and date of birth. The nurse asks the patient to say his or her name and birthday, and then the nurse reads the bracelet to check that the spoken name and birthday match it, as well as the name and date of birth on the unit of blood that the patient will receive.

Maxine Carlson's story echoes, in some ways, that of Anne Dodge. The work of Roter and Hall is again relevant with regard to how doctors and nurses feel about patients who are characterized as neurotic or hypochondriacal. When such patients have been extensively evaluated in the past, and their medical records weigh several pounds, the physician's challenge is to think about what has not been examined. All of us tend to rely on previous laboratory tests and x-rays, but we should be equally attentive to the patient's current words. In both Anne Dodge's and Maxine Carlson's case, they were telling the doctors that something was different, that they were getting worse rather than better. The benefit of the doubt, meaning taking them at their word, can be a key trigger to thinking afresh about their symptoms and distinguishing them from their long-standing illnesses and prior complaints.

The disturbing story about the resident acting spitefully highlights the points made by Ronald M. Epstein, "Mindful practice," *JAMA* 282 (1999), pp. 833–839. Among senior clinical staff, there is increasing attention to providing constructive feedback to residents who behave inappropriately, with patients or with other healthcare providers, like nurses, technicians, and fellow physicians. Alter and the senior staff at Highland Hospital did provide such feedback in this case.

4. Gatekeepers

For readers interested in more details about how our first child, Steve, almost died, see Jerome Groopman, *Second Opinions: Stories of Intuition and Choice in the Changing World of Medicine* (New York: Viking, 2000), pp. 9–37.

A study of the issues raised by McEvoy about communication is L. S. Wissow et al., "Pediatrician interview style and mothers' disclosure of psychosocial issues," *Pediatrics* 93 (1994), pp. 289–295.

Dr. McEvoy's article appeared in "They are fearless, they're mighty, they're . . . The Incredibles," *Harvard Medical Alumni Bulletin,* Winter 2006.

An engaging book about cultural differences and medical care is Anne Fadiman, *The Spirit Catches You and You Fall Down: A Hmong Child, Her American Doctors, and the Collision of Two Cultures* (New York: Farrar, Straus and Giroux, 1997). Her book should be required reading for every healthcare provider.

The study of forty-five physicians based in Sacramento, California, practicing in either a university center or community clinic is cited in Derjung M. Tarn et al., "Physician communication when prescribing new medications," *Archives of Internal Medicine* 166 (2006), pp. 1855–1862.

Dr. JudyAnn Bigby wrote an important book about context: *Cross-Cultural Medicine* (Philadelphia: American College of Physicians, 2003). A few months after I interviewed her, Dr. Bigby was appointed to head the Massachusetts Department of Health and Human Services.

Dr. Eric Cassell's book is an illuminating exploration of the art of medicine: *Doctoring: The Nature of Primary Care Medicine* (New York: Oxford University Press, 1997), pp. 16, 27, 28, 34, 38.

There is no simple way to find a physician who is right for you. Competence and character are the key criteria. Dr. Kent Sepkowitz addressed this in his lively article "A few good doctors: Don't look for them on a magazine top-10 list," *Slate,* June 13, 2006.

5. A New Mother's Challenge

More information about ECMO can be obtained from reliable Internet sources that explain the machine, its uses, and risks. Among these are

> www.nichd.nih.gov/cochrane/Elbourne/Elbourne.htm
> www.childrenshospital.org/clinicalservices/Site459/
>   mainpageS459P4.html
> www.vanderbiltchildrens.com/interior.php?mid=959&mod

Pat Croskerry's phrase "zebra retreat" is found in his taxonomy of cognitive errors: "Achieving quality in clinical decision making: Cognitive strategies and detection of bias," *Academic Emergency Medicine* 9 (2002), pp. 1184–1204.

Harold Koenig, Michael McCullough, and David Larson have assembled a comprehensive and scholarly review of how faith influences patients: *Handbook of Religion and Health* (New York: Oxford University Press, 2001).

6. The Uncertainty of the Expert

A review of congenital heart disease is found in Ariane J. Marelli, "Congenital heart disease in adults," in *Cecil Textbook of Medicine,* 22nd ed., ed. Lee Goldman and Dennis Ausiello (Philadelphia: Saunders, 2004), pp. 371–383.

There are numerous biographies and Web sites devoted to the life of Arthur Conan Doyle. I particularly enjoyed reading the material at www.sherlockholmesonline.org.

The illustration of the heart is adapted from Enchanted Learning, LLC. www.enchantedlearning.com/subjects/anatomy/heart/labelinterior /labelanswers.shtml.

The story about the medical meeting where cardiologists voted is derived from my interview with Dr. James Lock.

Lock's perspective on what is needed to achieve a high level of expertise in cardiac catheterization and other procedures is supported by the work of K. Anders Ericsson et al., "The role of deliberate practice in the acquisition of expert performance," *Psychological Review* 100 (1993), pp. 363–406; Geoff Norman et al., "Expertise in medicine and surgery," in *The Cambridge Handbook of Expertise and Expert Performance,* ed. K. Anders Ericsson et al. (Cambridge: Cambridge University Press, 2006), pp. 339–353.

For those interested in learning more about fetal distress and how the aspiration of meconium can injure the newborn, see Michael G. Ross, "Meconium aspiration syndrome — More than intrapartum meconium," *NEJM* 353 (2005), pp. 946–948.

The challenges that pediatric cardiologists like James Lock face in caring for such patients as Baby O'Connell, particularly the lack of instruments designed for these children, is explored in my article "The pediatric gap: Why have most medications never been properly tested in kids?," *New Yorker,* January 10, 2005.

The lack of awareness among most physicians that they have made cognitive errors is supported by Mark L. Graber et al., "Diagnostic error in internal medicine," *Archives of Internal Medicine* 165 (2005), pp. 1493–1499; Tejal K. Gandhi et al., "Missed and delayed diagnoses in the ambulatory setting: A study of closed malpractice claims," *Annals of Internal Medicine* 145 (2006), pp. 488–496; Pat Croskerry, "Cognitive errors in clinical decision-making: A cognitive autopsy," *Quality Healthcare Network,* May 2004; Donald A. Redelmeier et al., "Problems for clinical judgment: Introducing cognitive psychology as one more basic science," *Canadian Medical Association Journal* 164 (2001), pp. 358–360; Donald A. Redelmeier, "The cognitive psychology of missed diagnoses," *Annals of Internal Medicine* 142 (2005), pp. 115–120.

Arthur Elstein, as mentioned earlier, is one of the pioneers in the field of medical decision-making. His book edited with Jack Dowie presents a remarkable range of opinions on the subject and is well worth consulting for those who wish to learn more: *Professional Judgment: A Reader in Clinical Decision Making* (Cambridge: Cambridge University Press, 1988). The quotes from Donald A. Schön are from "From technical rationality to reflection-in-action," in *Professional Judgment,* pp. 60–77. The quote from David Eddy of Duke University is from "Variations in physician practice: The role of uncertainty," in *Professional Judgment,* pp. 45–59. Similarly, the chapter by Jay Katz refers to the work of Renée Fox on uncertainty and describes Katz's own experiences during his medical training: "Why doctors don't disclose uncertainty," in *Professional Judgment,* pp. 544–565.

7. Surgery and Satisfaction

"The best doctors in . . .": see, again, Kent Sepkowitz, "A few good doctors: Don't look for them on a magazine top-10 list," *Slate,* June 13, 2006.

Richard Selzer's book *Letters to a Young Doctor* (New York: Simon and Schuster, 1982) is a wonderful collection and worth reading for both the general reader and professionals. Dr. Sherwin Nuland writes beautifully about the experience of the seasoned surgeon in *How We Die: Reflections on Life's Final Chapter* (New York: Knopf, 1994), and *How We Live* (New York: Vintage, 1998). For those interested in the perspective of a surgical resident in training, see a book by my colleague at *The New Yorker* Atul Gawande, *Complications: A Surgeon's Notes on an Imperfect Science* (New York: Metropolitan Books, 2002). Dr. Light's comments about every patient coming in with a story might strike the reader as unusual, since surgeons are often depicted as being interested only in working with their hands. But as Roter and Hall said, the best ones have the full package.

Satisfaction of search as a cognitive error is well described in Pat Croskerry, "Achieving quality in clinical decision making: Cognitive strategies and detection of bias," *Academic Emergency Medicine* 9 (2002), pp. 1184–1204.

A terrific and amusing article about the world of orthopedics is Donald Berwick, "My right knee," *Annals of Internal Medicine* 142 (2005), pp. 121–125.

8. The Eye of the Beholder

A special issue of the *Journal of the American College of Radiology* (vol. 3, 2006) had a number of articles that provided considerable data and a bibliography for this chapter: Harold L. Kundel, "History of research in medical image perception," pp. 402–408; Craig A. Beam et al., "The place of medical image perception in 21st-century health care," pp. 409–412; E. James Potchen, "Measuring observer performance in chest radiology: Some experiences," pp. 423–432; Elizabeth A. Krupinski, "Technology and perception in the 21st-century reading room," pp. 433–440; Matthew Freedman and Teresa Osicka, "Reader variability: What we can learn from computer-aided detection experiments," pp. 446–455; Bradley J. Erickson et al., "New opportunities in computer-aided diagnosis: Change detection and characterization," pp. 468–469; Dulia Ortega and César García, "Communication between radiologists and patients: An unsolved issue," pp. 472–477; Ehsan Samei, "Why medical image perception?," pp. 400–401.

The estimate of the number of cases being read by radiologists comes from Dr. Herbert Kressel, who served as the president of Beth Israel Deaconess Medical Center, Boston, in addition to being the Stoneman Professor of Radiology at Harvard.

The error rates in observing cyanosis, the misinterpretation of EKGs, and disagreement about cervical biopsies are from David Eddy, "Variations in physician practice: The role of uncertainty," in *Professional Judgment: A Reader in Clinical Decision Making*, ed. Jack Dowie and Arthur Elstein (Cambridge: Cambridge University Press, 1988), pp. 45–59.

There are numerous studies about the accuracy of mammography. Interested readers may consult the following to gain a sense of the data: Craig A. Beam et al., "Association of volume and volume-independent factors with accuracy in screening mammogram interpretation," *Journal of the National Cancer Institute* 95 (2003), pp. 282–290; Joann G. Elmore et al., "Variability in radiologists' interpretations of mammograms," *NEJM* 331 (1994), pp. 1493–1499; Yulei Jiang et al., "Potential of computer-aided diagnosis to reduce variability in radiologists' interpretations of mammograms depicting microcalcifications," *Radiology* 220 (2001), pp. 787–794; Daniel B. Kopans, "Mammography screening is saving thousands of lives, but will it survive medical malpractice?," *Radiology* 230 (2004), pp. 20–24.

More detail about Kundel's studies, particularly his seminal work, is found in his article in the *Journal of the American College of Radiology* cited above, as well as in G. Revesz and H. L. Kundel, "Psychophysical studies of detection errors in chest radiology," *Radiology* 123 (1977), pp. 559–562. Similarly, Ehsan Samei studied the challenge of detecting lung nodules: Ehsan Samei et al., "Subtle lung nodules: Influence of local anatomic variations on detection," *Radiology* 228 (2003), pp. 76–84.

Dr. Vickie Feldstein was a numbers whiz as a student, a valued member of the Newton South High School math team in Newton, Massachusetts. Her understanding of how to apply numbers to medical decision-making, as epitomized in this chapter, is a model for the modern physician who can look to metrics but also recognize their shortcomings.

An interesting paper about defensive medicine, meaning medical decisions made because of concerns about potential litigation, is David M. Studdert et al., "Defensive medicine among high-risk specialist physicians in a volatile malpractice environment," *JAMA* 293 (2005), pp. 2609–2617.

9. Marketing, Money, and Medical Decisions

There has been considerable controversy about the relationship among pharmaceutical companies, their educational programs, marketing to doctors, advertising to the public, scientific research, and clinical decision-making. Articles and books reflecting a diversity of opinion about these issues include Ashley Wazana, "Physicians and the pharmaceutical industry: Is a gift ever just a gift?," *JAMA* 283 (2000), pp. 373–380; Troyen A. Brennan et al., "Health industry practices that create conflicts of interest," *JAMA* 295 (2006), pp. 429–433; Jason Dana and George Loewenstein, "A social science perspective on gifts to physicians from industry," *JAMA* 290 (2003), pp. 252–255; David Blumenthal, "Doctors and drug companies," *NEJM* 351 (2004), pp. 1885–1890; Jerry Avorn, *Powerful Medicines: The Benefits, Risks, and Costs of Prescription Drugs* (New York: Knopf, 2004); Marcia Angell, *The Truth about the Drug Companies: How They Deceive Us and What to Do about It* (New York: Random House, 2004); Thomas Stossel, "Free the scientists!: Conflict-of-interest rules purport to cure a problem that doesn't exist — and are stifling medical progress," *Forbes,* February 14, 2005; Thomas Stossel and David Shaywitz, "What's wrong with money in science?," *Washington Post,* July 2,

2006; and an article by my colleague at *The New Yorker* Malcolm Gladwell, "High prices: How to think about prescription drugs," *New Yorker*, October 25, 2004.

Robert Steinbrook highlighted drug companies' access to physicians' prescribing habits in "For sale: Physicians' prescribing data," *NEJM* 354 (2006), pp. 2745–2747, so now Karen Delgado and her colleagues no longer need to learn this information from readers of business magazines, like her husband.

Recently, practice guidelines that were written by a panel of experts were criticized because a drug company that made a questionable product recommended in the guidelines financially supported the writing: Peter Q. Eichacker et al., "Surviving sepsis — Practice guidelines, marketing campaigns, and Eli Lilly," *NEJM* 355 (2006), pp. 1640–1642.

The controversy over androgen replacement for aging men is nicely summarized in Paul M. Stewart, "Aging and fountain-of-youth hormones," *NEJM* 355 (2006), pp. 1724–1726, which was based on a recent study by K. Sreekumaran Nair et al., "DHEA in elderly women and DHEA or testosterone in elderly men," *NEJM* 355 (2006), pp. 1647–1659.

My article on cox-2 inhibitors was published in *The New Yorker* on June 15, 1998: "Superaspirin: A new kind of drug could make Motrin and Aleve obsolete."

The debate about hormone replacement therapy in women has been widely covered. The article by Francine Grodstein et al., "Hormone therapy and coronary heart disease: The role of time since menopause and age at hormone initiation," *Journal of Women's Health* 15 (2006), pp. 35–44, sparked considerable news coverage. For insight into how the lay press reports laboratory and clinical studies, see Edward W. Campion, "Medical research and the news media," *NEJM* 351 (2004), pp. 2436–2437. In the chapter, the *New York Times* article "Rethinking hormones, again," by Roni Rabin, appeared on January 31, 2006, and the *Wall Street Journal* article "In study of women's health, design flaws raise questions," by Tara Parker-Pope, on February 28, 2006.

Numerous articles in newspapers and magazines have alerted patients to marketing practices and the influence of consulting fees and gifts on physicians' advice: Abigail Zuger, "How tightly do ties between doctor and drug company bind?," *New York Times,* July 27, 2006; Gina Kolata, "Spinal cement draws patients and questions," *New York Times,* August 28, 2005; Gina Kolata, "With costs rising, treating back pain often seems futile," *New York Times,* February 9, 2004; Reed Abelson, "Whistle-blower suit says device maker generously rewards doctors," *New York Times,* January 24, 2006; Gardiner Harris, "In article, doctors back ban on gifts from drug makers," *New York Times,* January 25, 2006; Carl Elliott, "The drug pushers," *Atlantic Monthly,* April 2006; Gwen Ifill interview with Dr. David Blumenthal, "Debating drug company gifts," *PBS Online,* January 25, 2006.

The debate about the proper diagnosis and treatment of back pain can be found in the excellent review by Richard A. Deyo and James N. Weinstein, "Low back pain," *NEJM* 344 (2001), pp. 363–370. Also see Peter Fritzell et al., "Lumbar fusion versus nonsurgical treatment for chronic low back pain," *Spine* 26 (2001), pp. 2521–2534; Judith A. Turner et al., "Patient outcomes after lumbar spinal fusions," *JAMA* 268 (1992), pp. 907–911; Daniel C. Cherkin et al., "Physician variation in diagnostic testing for low back pain: Who you see is what you get," *American College of Rheumatology* 37 (1994), pp. 15–22. In the lay press, see Judy Foreman, "Aching spine," *Boston Globe,* May 3, 2005. An important study about informed decision-making can be found in Richard A. Deyo et al., "Involving patients in clinical decisions: Impact of an interactive video program on use of back surgery," *Medical Care* 38 (2000), pp. 959–969.

10. In Service of the Soul

Stephen Hall's book is *A Commotion in the Blood: Life, Death, and the Immune System* (New York: Owl Books, 1998).

Readers interested in the history of medical philanthropy by the Rockefeller family should read Ron Chernow, *Titan: The Life of John D. Rockefeller, Sr.* (New York: Random House, 1998).

The IPSS was published in Peter Greenberg et al., "International scoring system for evaluating prognosis in myelodysplastic syndromes," *Blood* 89 (1997), pp. 2079–2088.

Epilogue

Dr. Arthur J. Barsky has written extensively about somatic symptoms caused by psychological distress. His work and that of others is featured in my article "Sick with worry: Can hypochondria be cured?," *New Yorker,* August 11, 2003. Barsky and Emily C. Deans recently published a book for people suffering from hypochondria which sets out a program in cognitive behavioral therapy to ameliorate their suffering: *Stop Being Your Symptoms and Start Being Yourself* (New York: HarperCollins, 2006).

The study of forty-five doctors is by Derjung M. Tarn et al., "Physician communication when prescribing new medications," *Archives of Internal Medicine* 166 (2006), pp. 1855–1862.

The vignette told by Karen Delgado about the purple pills shows that system-wide solutions still require communication and are not default remedies for errors in care. Doctors have to keep thinking until they find the answer.

INDEX

Acromegaly, 204
Active listening, 18
ADHD, 133, 157
Adriamycin, 49–50, 51–52, 53
Affective error, 47, 65–66
  in case of cancer patient, 58
Agency for Health Care Policy and
    Research, spinal fusion panel
    convened by, 229–30
Aging
  and estrogen, 218–19
  medicalizing of, 206, 209–10
  and testosterone, 209
AIDS, and Shira Stein, 109, 115
Alcoholic(s)
  Charles Carver seen as, 44–46
  with ischemic bowel, 183–84
  as numerous in inner city, 65
Algorithms, and diagnosis, 5, 6
  overreliance on, 238, 239
  risks in, 88
  See also Bayesian analysis
Alter, Harrison, 59–66, 67, 68, 72–75, 78,
    86
Alzheimer's disease, and COX-2 inhibitors,
    213
American College of Physicians, and
    Agency for Health Care Policy
    and Research, 230

American Hospital Association, and
    Agency for Health Care Policy
    and Research, 230
American Journal of Cardiology, shunt
    criterion published in, 140
American Medical Association, and
    Agency for Health Care Policy
    and Research, 230
Anchoring, 65, 75
Andropause, 208, 209, 211
Anemia
  and ankle pain case, 67
  and babesiosis case, 251
  in case of Anne Dodge, 13
  in case of George Franklin, 241
  in case of Vincent Rivera, 248, 249
  from lack of vitamin B_{12}, 128
Angina, 30
  and case of Gloria Manning, 91
  and case of Evan McKinley, 43, 44,
    68
  and case of William Morgan, 30
  illusory procedure for, 223–24
  and possibility of missed diagnosis,
    263
Annals of Internal Medicine, 215
Anorexia nervosa, and case of Anne
    Dodge, 2, 12, 22
Antithymocyte globulin (ATG), 248

Anxiety, productive, 37
Aortic aneurysm, misdiagnosis of, 75–76
Aortic dissection, missed diagnosis of, 25
Aortic stenosis, 147
Apoplexy, pituitary, 205
Arthritis
    and author's hand, 160, 173
    in case of Gloria Manning, 91
    in communication example, 94–95
    cox-2 inhibitors for, 212
    popularity of new medications for,
        220
Aspirin toxicity, misdiagnosis of, 63–64
Atrium, 138, 139, 143
Attribution error, 44
    and case of apparent alcoholic, 44
    in case of Ellen Barnett, 56–57
    in diabetes case (Delgado), 55
Atypical presentations, short shrift to,
    126
Autism
    in McEvoy's patient, 83
    parents' fear of, 82, 84
Availability heuristic and error, 64–65, 75,
    188, 196

Babesiosis, 251
Back pain, chronic, surgery for, 223, 224–
    29. See also Spinal fusion
Bactrim, 108
"Bad blood," 94
"Bad disease," 239–40
    T-cell lymphoma as, 241
Barnett, Ellen (patient), 56–58
Bayesian analysis, 11–12, 61–62, 89, 150–51
    and unique situations, 151
Bedside manner, 19. See also Doctor-
        patient relationship
Begaye, Blanche (patient), 63–64, 66, 76
Behavioral change, as primary care goal,
        90
Bigby, JudyAnn, 88–95, 96, 266–67
Bilezikian, John, 245
Biopsy, need to repeat, 262
Bladder cancer, 256, 257
Blood (publication), 215

Blood pressure control, existing drugs sat-
        isfactory for, 220
Body language (nonverbal behavior), 17,
        19
    in case of Anne Dodge, 11
Boilerplate schemes, 238
Bone marrow transplantation, 118–19,
        242
    and case of Max Bornstein, 238
    and case of George Franklin, 242, 243–
        44
    and case of Shira Stein, 120, 124, 125
Bornstein, Max (patient), 236–38
Breast cancer
    in chemoembolization case (Diane
        Waters), 253–54
    gemcitabine for, 211
    and hormone replacement, 214, 217, 218
    lumpectomy vs. radical mastectomy for,
        224
    and mammography, 188, 195
Brigham Hospital, and Falchuk's picture,
        16
Brigham and Women's Hospital, 92
    Bigby at, 89, 92
    Manning in, 91
    West in, 93
Brown, Paul (surgeon), 168
Bulimia, and case of Anne Dodge, 2, 12,
        22
Burnside, John, 31–32, 34, 39

Cancer, 10
    and ankle pain case, 67
    author's feared case of, 265–66
    and case of Brad Miller, 49–54
    control vs. eradication of, 252–53
    expanded uses of drugs for, 211
    and false conclusion from x-ray, 92–93
    Memorial Sloan-Kettering as treatment
        center for, 234, 256
    and Orwig on mammograms, 187
    and outcome bias (case), 58
    tardy identification of, 265
    and treatment choice
        in contrasting examples, 247–48

Cancer (*cont.*)
　for George Franklin, 241–42, 243–44,
　　267–68
　for Naomi Freylich, 250
　and long vs. short term, 246
　and need for eradication (Alex Woo),
　　253
　for Vincent Rivera, 248–49
　for Rachel Swanson, 254–56
　in unproven drug example, 256–57
　for Diane Waters, 253–54
　types of
　　bladder, 256, 257
　　breast, 188, 195, 211, 214, 217, 218,
　　　224, 253–54
　　colon, 67, 193, 242, 253, 254
　　ovarian, 211, 254, 255
　　pancreatic, 192, 211
　　prostate, 154, 240
　　thyroid, 58
　See also Leukemia; Lymphoma
Candida albicans (fungus), 115, 118
Cardiac tamponade, 136
　procedure for remedy of, 136–38
Cardiology
　radiology as changing, 192
　See also Pediatric cardiology
Carlson, Maxine (patient), 69–72, 76
Carver, Charles (patient), 44–46
Cassell, Eric J., 97–98, 99
Catecholamines, 57
Celebrex, 212, 213, 220
Celiac disease (Anne Dodge case), 15–16
Cerebral ventricle, 200
Chemoembolization, 253–54
Chemotherapy
　in case of George Franklin, 241–42, 243
　in case of Brad Miller, 49–50, 51–52
　in case of Rachel Swanson (metastasis
　　in colon), 254–55
　in case of Diane Waters
　　(chemoembolization), 253–54
　as cause of bone marrow stem-cell
　　injury, 236–37
　difficult choice over, 238
　in example of colon cancer, 242

　as more beneficial choice (acute leuke-
　　mia), 244–45
　point of futility of, 256
　short-term beneficial treatment chosen
　　over, 248–49
　side effects from, 245, 246
　　in contrasting cancer cases, 247–48
Cherry-picking of symptoms, 65
Chicago White Sox, Light as hand sur-
　geon for, 156
Children's Hospital, Boston, 105, 109, 113,
　125–26, 132
Chondrocalcinosis, as hand-problem diag-
　nosis, 164, 165, 172
Chronic lymphocytic leukemia, in case of
　Naomi Freylich, 250–51
Cisplatin, 211
Clark, Holly, 135–37, 138
Classification schemes, 238
Clinical conference, 125
　on Shira Stein, 124–25, 127
Clinical decision-making. *See* Decision-
　making, medical
Cognition, and emotion, 39–40
Cognitive cherry-picking, 65
Coley, William, 235, 236
Colon cancer, 67, 193, 253
　case of metastasis as, 254
　in example of survival-rate presenta-
　　tion, 242
Colonoscopy, in ovarian cancer case, 254
Commission bias, 169
Commodity view of medical care, 99. *See
　also* Hospital administrators; In-
　surance companies; Managed care
Commotion in the Blood, A (Hall), 234
Communication, 17, 94–95
　and "bad blood" example, 93–94
　between clinician and radiologist, 192,
　　193–94
　and competence, 19–20
　in diagnosis, 261
　ignorance as inhibiting, 8
　as impaired, 86, 266–67
　phrasing of recommendations, 242–43
　time needed for, 88

and tragic-sounding diagnoses, 95
  about treatment choices, 266–67
  See also Language
Compatibility between doctor and
    patient, 25–26. *See also* Doctor-
    patient relationship
Compliance, 23
  and Anne Dodge, 23
  and noncompliance
    doctors' dislike of, 91
    inability to read as cause of, 91–92
Computer-aided diagnostic system, 198
  for ultrasonography, 200
Concierge medical practices, 81
Conference, clinical, 125
  on Shira Stein, 124–25, 127
Confidence
  of patients, 155, 172
  of radiologists
    and computer-assisted detection, 199
    in inaccurate diagnoses, 180
  surgeon's need of, 169
Confirmation bias, 65–66, 154
Congenital heart disease. *See* Heart dis-
    ease, congenital
"Consistent with . . . ," and diagnosis mo-
    mentum (Shira Stein), 128
Cooperation, physicians' need of, 45
Coronary artery disease, illusory proce-
    dure for, 223–24
Corporate influence
  and clinical care vs. laboratory research,
    232
  and financing of surgeons' trips, 223,
    230
  vs. findings of panel on spinal fusion,
    230
  hospitals against, 231
  JAMA article against, 231–32
  need to be free of, 268
  See also Pharmaceutical industry mar-
    keting
Cost control, as insurance/HMO aim, 97
cox-2 inhibitors, 212–14
Croskerry, Pat, 34
  and Alter, 59

and availability error, 188
and case of Maxine Carlson, 70–71
and case of Evan McKinley (representa-
    tiveness error), 41–44, 46–47, 58,
    68
and doctors' feelings, 36
as emergency physician, 66, 75–76, 78,
    86
and heuristics, 35
on pattern recognition, 34–35
on satisfaction of search, 170
on temperament, 181
on "zebra retreat," 127
Crowley, William, 209
CT scan, 177, 178, 188–89, 191
  incorrect calibration of, 262
  increase in number of, 190
  ischemic bowel found by (Orwig),
    183–85
  and surgery for chronic back pain, 224,
    225
Cyanosis, diagnosis of, 181–82
Cyclosporine, 248–49
Cytomegalovirus (CMV), 115, 118

Dalhousie University Medical School, 59,
    127
Dashiell, Elizabeth, 234–36
Decision-analysis viewpoint, 151. *See also*
    Bayesian analysis
Decision-making, medical
  Bayesian, 11–12, 61–62, 89, 150–51
  and Bigby's training in internal medi-
    cine, 89
  decision trees in, 5
  in didactic exercises vs. clinical crisis,
    34
  doctors' feelings in, 36
    immature resentment (example of
        resident), 74
  in emergency room, 66–69
    "studied calm" in (Alter), 74–75
  and "last bad experience" (Potchen),
    188
  medical school memorization for, 28
  "optimal," 7

Decision-making, medical (*cont.*)
 through pattern recognition, 34–35, 38, 39 (*see also* Pattern recognition)
 See also Diagnosis; Doctors' thinking; Treatment choice
Decision trees, and diagnosis, 5, 6
Defensive medicine, 254–55. *See also* Legal ramifications and lawsuits
Delgado, Karen, 54–58, 233
 and hormone therapy, 215, 217–18
 on importance of doctors vs. hospitals, 257
 lateral thinking of, 171
 on misunderstanding about medicines, 267
 on patient empowerment, 247
 patient of as "kooky," 57, 265
 and drug companies, 203–7, 208, 209, 213–14, 216–17
Deyo, Richard, 226, 229
Diabetes, in case of attribution error, 55
Diagnosis, 260–61
 of author's hand problem, 160, 161, 164, 166
 and Bigby's training in internal medicine, 89
 coherent picture needed in, 167
 common vs. arcane, 126–27
 decision trees in, 5, 6 (*see also* Bayesian analysis)
 through dialogue with patient, 17, 18–19, 67, 261–62 (*see also* Questioning)
 in didactic exercises vs. clinical crisis, 33–34
 and doctors' temperaments, 181
 and elusive symptoms, 264–66
 and example of patient's casual remark, 87–88
 extra care in (Tepler), 251–52
 by Falchuk (case of Anne Dodge), 14
 friendly critique in, 268–69
 of heart disease
  in Baby O'Connell, 144–46
  without preconceptions (Lock), 146

heuristics in, 35–36
hypotheses in, 11–12, 35
as influenced by specialty, 225–26
lateral thinking in, 170–71
need for repetition in, 262
need to rethink, 260, 263
patient's questioning in, 23, 76, 263–64
and patients' reports, 67–68
patient templates for, 98–99
in pediatric medicine, 78–79, 83
probability in, 155 (*see also* Probability)
through radiology, 185–94
 computer-aided systems for, 198–99
 and issue of informing of fetal abnormality, 201–2
 systematic approach to (Orwig), 182–85
 ultrasonography, 200–202
 uncertainty in, 195–97
and rapport, 20
self-diagnosis, 261
as "thought-in-action," 35
variability and error in
 for cyanosis, 181–82
 with EKGs, 182
 among pathologists, 182
 among radiologists, 179–81
 and "We see this sometimes," 62, 63
See also Decision-making, medical; Doctors' thinking; Misdiagnosis
Diagnosis momentum, 128, 154
Differential diagnosis, 33–34
 by Bigby on chest x-ray, 93
 in case of Shira Stein, 124
Discectomy, 225, 226, 228, 229, 232
Distorted pattern recognition, 65
Doctoring: The Nature of Primary Care Medicine (Cassell), 97
Doctor-patient relationship
 and admission of uncertainty, 159, 172
 and avoidance of outcome bias, 58
 and avoidance of stereotypes, 56
 commission bias furthered by, 169
 communication in, 94–95

as crucial factor (cancer treatment),
256, 259
and doctor's liking patient, 18–19, 25,
46
and doctors' thinking, 7–8, 10, 25–26,
76
and ER physician's pace, 75
and informed choice, 233
and language, 10
matching personality types in, 251
in oncology (Tepler), 250
and "patient activation and engagement," 17
and patient's compliance, 23, 91–92
and patient's emotions, 18–19
and patient's plea to live, 243
in pediatric medicine, 121
as partnering, 114
and Rachel Stein's interventions, 119,
121–22, 128, 129, 263
questioning in, 18, 76, 175, 263–64 (see
also Questioning)
realistic expectations presented in, 173
thinking in sync, 174
and time management, 88, 268
and treatment choice, 243–44, 247–49,
266–67
Doctors' thinking, 6–7
and "bad disease," 239–40
and crisis of patient Morgan, 33
as decided by group vote (two-to-one
shunt), 140
as decided by tradition (cardiac
tamponade relief), 137–38
and demand for prescription, 209,
222
and doctor-patient relationship, 7–8,
10, 25–26
patient as guide, 76
drug companies' attempts to influence,
209–11, 212
and emotions of doctor, 8, 25, 39–40
and caring (Peabody), 54
in case of Brad Miller, 52–53, 58
and heuristics, 36

negative (unattractive patients), 19,
45, 57–58
and overreliance on conventional,
259
positive (attractive patients), 46–48,
58
as following eminent physicians,
163–64
and gift-giving by business, 231
and Sherlock Holmes's deductions, 134
and honesty about possible achievement, 173
individual and novel approaches disre-
garded (oncology)
and classification schemes, 238–39
and fear of failure, 258–59
phase-two drugs rejected (bladder
cancer case), 257
as influenced by desire to believe, 207,
212, 216–17
as influenced by "opinion leaders," 206,
211
as influenced by specialty, 216, 225–26
inner monologue to guide (Falchuk),
20
and mistakes, 7, 10, 24, 260 (see also
Errors, medical)
need to question foundations of (Lock),
135
and patients' personalities, 259
in primary care, 100
and social context, 92
under uncertainty, 149–50, 151, 152–54
See also Decision-making, medical;
Diagnosis
Dodge, Ann (patient), 1–3, 8, 10–16, 17–
20, 22–24, 39
anorexia with bulimia as diagnosis for,
2, 12, 22
celiac disease as true diagnosis for, 15–16
and cognition-emotion relation, 39–40
and diagnosis momentum, 128
doctor's failure to send elsewhere, 264
and doctors' past mistakes, 21
and doctors' way of thinking, 7

Dodge, Ann (patient) (*cont.*)
  and psychiatric stereotype, 45
  reframing case of, 263–64
Dole, Bob, 221
Dowie, Jack, 150
Down syndrome, and heart malformation, 147
Doyle, Arthur Conan, 133–34, 187
Drug companies. *See* Pharmaceutical industry marketing
Duggan, Rick, 203–4, 205–7, 210
Dynamic scaphoid-lunate instability, 167–68

ECMO (extracorporeal membrane oxygenation, 111
  in case of Baby O'Connell, 142–43, 146
  in case of Shira Stein, 111–12
Economics, in contrast with medical decision-making, 35
Eddy, David M., 151, 154–55, 181
Education, medical. *See* Medical training
EKGs, variability in interpreting of, 182
Electromyograms (EMGs), 225–26, 228
Electronic technology, 99
Elstein, Arthur, 150
Emergency room, 9
  basic examination essentials in, 61
  and case of Nathan Talumpqewa, 61, 62
  chest pain as reason for visiting, 43
  decision-making in, 66–69
    basic question for, 78
    pattern recognition in (Croskerry), 34–35
    "studied calm" in (Alter), 74–75
  ecology of, 72
  similarity among diverse examples of, 59
Emotion, and cognition, 39–40
Emotions of doctor, 8, 25, 39–40
  and caring (Peabody), 54
  in case of Brad Miller, 52–53, 58
  and heuristics, 36
  negative (unattractive patients), 45, 57–58

and overreliance on conventional, 259
positive (attractive patients), 46–48, 58
Endoscopy, for Anne Dodge, 14–15
Epistemology, Lock on, 134, 150
Errors (mistakes), medical, 7, 10, 260
  from anchoring, 65, 75
  attribution error, 44, 46 (*see also* Attribution error)
  from availability heuristic, 64–65, 75, 188, 196
  avoiding of 182–85, 198
    through consideration of alternatives, 66
    through open mind (Kundel), 198
    Orwig's systematic approach to, 182–85, 198
  from commission bias, 169
  as constraining, 263
  from deductive logic instead of empirical data, 148–49
  doctors' unawareness of, 147
  electronic technology as contributing to, 99
  from haste, 88
  learning from, 21, 55
  outcome bias, 47
    in case of cancer patient, 58
  in reading MRI scan (Kressel), 202
  representativeness, 44
  from satisfaction of search, 169–70, 185, 197–98, 263
  technical vs. misguided thinking, 24, 40
  in test administering, 68
  and variability in interpretation, 179–82
  from vertical line failure (thinking inside the box), 170–71
  "yin-yang out," 72, 76
  See also Misdiagnosis
Estrogen replacement (menopausal women)
  breast cancer risk in, 214
  Delgado on, 218
  and heart disease, 215, 216
  See also Hormone replacement therapy

Estrogen therapy for premenopausal
    women, 214
Ether Dome, 28
Ethical marketing of drugs, 221–22
Evaluation of patient, 11
Evidence-based medicine, 5–6
Expected utility theory, 150–51. *See also*
    Bayesian analysis
"Eyeball test," 22

Faith. *See* Religious faith
Falchuk, Myron, 3, 8, 10–18, 20–21, 39,
    47–48, 58, 263–64
FDA (U.S. Food and Drug Administra-
    tion)
    and doctors' freedom to prescribe, 211
    and testosterone replacement therapy,
    210, 211
Fear of failure, and oncologists, 258
Feedback, use of, 21
Feldstein, Vickie, 199–202
Feminine Forever (Wilson), 210
"Figure it out," as surgeon's strategy, 164,
    171
Financial disclosure, requirement of,
    231–32
5-azacytidine, 248
"Flamers," 127
"Flogging" of advanced cancer patients,
    252
Fox, Renée, 152
Foyer, Bert, 205, 207, 211, 212, 216, 227
Framing
    of clinical situations (Lock), 146
    of patient information, 22
Framingham Heart Study, 215
Franklin, George (patient), 240–42, 243–
    44, 257, 267–68
"Frequent flyers," 69
Freylich, Naomi (patient), 250–51
Fuchs, Richard M., 217
Fusion surgery. *See* Spinal fusion

Gardner, Constance (patient), 92–93
Gatekeepers, 9

primary care physicians as, 82, 100
    Bigby as, 88
    See also Primary care medicine
Gemcitabine, 211
Generic drugs, 222–23
Generic profiles, 238
"Gestalt," 178, 179, 186
Gift-giving, and doctors' thinking, 231
Gould, Stephen J., 256
Grady, Deborah, 217
Graft-versus-host disease, 118–19, 121

Halifax, Nova Scotia, 59
Hall, Judith, 17, 18–19, 24–25, 88, 94,
    181
Halstead, William, 224
Hamm, Robert, 34
Hand, human, 156
    author's problems with, 156–58
    doctors consulted on, 158–67, 170,
    172–73, 175–76
    explanations for, 174–75
    See also Surgery, hand
"Handbook of Religion and Health"
    (Koening, Larson, and
    McCullough), 130
Harvard Medical Alumni Bulletin,
    McEvoy article in, 81
Hayes, Frances, 209
Heart
    anatomy of, 138–39, *139*
    sounds of, 33
Heart disease
    in example of miscommunication, 93
    Framingham Heart Study on, 215
    Heart and Estrogen/Progestin Replace-
    ment Study (HERS) on, 215–16
    and hormone therapy, 217, 218
    myocardial infarction, 43, 182
    and Women's Health Initiative, 214
Heart disease, congenital, 132
    and Lock on errant reasoning, 140,
    147–49, 150
    of Baby O'Connell, 143–46
    See also Pediatric cardiology

Hematology and hematologists
acquaintance with cases in, 186
and "bad diseases," 239
and bone marrow transplants, 238
and case of Anne Dodge, 7, 12
and case of George Franklin, 241
and case of Naomi Freylich, 250
and case of Vincent Rivera, 248
and Nimer doing rounds, 236–38
repeated examinations in, 262
Tepler as, 249, 251
Herceptin, 253
Heuristics (shortcuts), 35–36
anchoring as, 65, 75
"availability," 64–65, 75, 188, 196
and conferences on misdiagnoses, 125
errors from, 36 (*see also* Errors, medical)
Hi-Fi (high-frequency ventilation), 109,
110, 112, 113, 116
HIV, and Shira Stein, 109, 115
HMOs, practice guidelines set by, 97
Holmes, Sherlock, 133, 134, 149
Holmes-Bernstein, Jane, 85
Hormone replacement therapy, 210,
214–16
conflicting judgments on, 217–19
Hospital administrators
and Bigby's schedule, 90
and cost control (Cassell), 97
economy demanded by, 262
McEvoy on surrender to, 82
Hydrocephaly, 200
Hyperreactive synovium, 160–61, 165,
175
Hypotheses, in diagnosis, 11–12, 35

ICE (ifosfamide, carboplatin, and
etoposide), 241, 243
ICU, Shira Stein in, 106–12, 113, 114, 119–
20, 128
Immune deficiency
of Brad Miller (and incomplete examination), 52–53
and nutritional inadequacies, 127–28
of Shira Stein, 105, 115–16, 117, 121, 122–
23, 126–27

Incomes of physicians
decreases in, 86
procedures more profitable than examinations, 226
"Incredibles, The" (McEvoy), 81
Informed choice, 233
Inner-city hospitals, alcohol-abuse
patients in, 65
Institute of Medicine, of National Academy of Sciences, 24
Insurance benefits, and surgery, 228
Insurance companies
and algorithmic diagnosis, 5
practice guidelines set by, 97
and primary care, 85–86
Bigby's schedule of, 90
as rewarding procedures more than
examinations, 86, 226
and surgery
spinal fusion over discectomy, 228
and spinal fusion panel, 229
International Prognostic Scoring System,
237
Internet, diagnostic ideas from, 261
Internship, 27, 28–30
Intuition, clinical, 9, 20
Irritable bowel syndrome
in case of Maxine Carlson, 69–70, 71,
76
in case of Anne Dodge, 2–3, 12, 14, 18
Ischemic bowel, 184

*Journal of the American Medical Association
(JAMA),* 215–16
paper on undue drug industry influence, 231–32
Journal of Clinical Oncology, 215
Journalists, and public understanding of
medications, 215, 216
Journal of Women's Health, hormone
replacement article in, 215

Kahneman, Daniel, 64, 65
Katz, Jay, 152–53
Kidney stone, in aortic aneurysm case,
75

Klebsiella (bacterium), 115, 118
Klinefelter syndrome, 207
Kressel, Herbert, 190–92, 202, 262
Krupinski, Elizabeth, 190
Kundel, Harold, 197

Language
    and clinical practice, 8
    and doctor-patient relationship, 10, 23
    and Falchuk, 11
    Latin and Greek terms, 175
    need for sensitivity to, 94
    of radiologists, 194–95, 202
    See also Communication
Lateral thinking, 170–71
Lawsuits. See Legal ramifications and law-
        suits
Lawyers, neurologists' group working
        with, 227–28
Leaf, Alexander, 28, 29
Legal ramifications and lawsuits
    and decision on communicating fetal
        abnormality, 201
    and mammograms, 187, 188
    and treatment choice, 254–55
"Less Than Ten" (Brown), 168
Leukemia, 239
    chronic lymphocytic, 250–51
    lymphoblastic, 63
    and Nimer, 236, 239
Leukemia, acute
    in case of Vincent Rivera, 248, 249
    from chemotherapy due to
        misdiagnosis, 250
    treatment choice for, 244
Lewis, Linda, 169, 174
Light, Terry, 156, 157, 159–60, 161, 165,
        167–69, 171–72, 173–74, 175,
        176
Listening, active, 18
Lock, James, 132–33, 136–38, 140–51, 179,
        246
Lumpectomy, 195, 224
Lymphoblastic leukemia, 63
Lymphoma, 239, 241
    and "bad disease," 239

and case of Max Bornstein, 236
and case of George Franklin, 241–42,
        243
and case of Naomi Freylich, 250
and case of Joe Stern, 48
patient's casual remark reveals, 88
repeated examinations for, 262

Magical thinking, 261
Malabsorption, and Falchuk diagnosis,
        20–21
"Male menopause" (andropause), 208,
        209, 211
Malpractice suits
    radiologist's aggressive assessment from,
        188
    See also Legal ramifications and lawsuits
Mammography, 187–88
    and computer-aided systems, 198
    example of missed cancer in, 265
    example of uncertainty in, 195–97
    variability in interpreting of, 181
Managed care, demands of, 69. See also
        Hospital administrators; Insur-
        ance companies
Mancini, Nick (patient), 204–5, 207, 210,
        212
Mannequin
    and McEvoy's group, 81
    in medical school exercises, 37–38
Manning, Gloria (patient), 90–92
Manual dexterity, for surgery, 141, 168
Marin General Hospital, 177
Marx, Karl, on religion, 130
Massachusetts General Hospital
    internship program at, 28–29
    author in, 27
    and therapy rationale, 163
Mastectomy, radical, 224
McEvoy, Victoria Rogers, 77–86, 88, 95,
        100, 114, 178
McKinley, Evan (patient), 41–44, 46–47,
        48, 58, 68
MDS (myelodysplastic syndrome), in
        examples of treatment choice,
        236–37, 248–49

Medical decision-making. *See* Decision-making, medical
Medical literature, and Tepler's practice, 252
Medical training
  and algorithmic decision-making, 4–5, 6
  dogmatic certainty in, 153
  emotional suppression in, 54
  in internal medicine (Bigby), 89
  internship, 27, 28–30, 38
    and case of William Morgan, 30–33
  medical school, 27–28
    mannequin used in, 37–38
    paper cases in, 33–34
    merit vs. social position in admission to, 95–96
  residency, 38
Medicare, and spinal fusion panel, 229
Medications
  incomplete instructions about, 86, 266–67
  patients' reports of, 67–68
  varying benefits from, 267
Memorial Hospital/Sloan-Kettering Institute, 234, 256, 258
Methicillin-resistant staphylococcus aureus (MRSA), 72–73
"Me too" drugs, 220
Miller, Brad, 48–54, 58
Minkin, Mary Jane, 216
Misdiagnosis, 24–25, 263
  of abscess for pharyngitis, 72–73
  of aortic aneurysm, 75–76
  of aortic dissection, 25
  of aspirin toxicity (Blanche Begaye), 63–64
  of cancer, 265
  of celiac disease (Anne Dodge), 15–16
    from diagnosis momentum, 128
  clinical conferences on, 125
  of ectopic pregnancy (Maxine Carlson), 71–72
  from familiar prototypes, 126
  leading to judgment of cancer, 92–93

  of lymphoma
    in Naomi Freylich, 250
    in Joe Stern, 47
  of myocardial infarction (Evan McKinley), 43
  of pheochromocytoma (Ellen Barnett), 57
  and second condition, 263–64
  on Shira Stein (apparent nutritional deficiency), 124–25, 128–29, 154
    from diagnosis momentum, 128, 154
  of Wegner's granulomatosis (Constance Gardner), 93
  of Wilson's disease (Charles Carver), 46
  from "zebra retreats," 126–27
Mistakes, medical. *See* Errors, medical
Money, and medicine, 9. *See also* Corporate influence; Cost control; Pharmaceutical industry marketing
Moral constraints to research, 140
Morgan, William (patient), 30–33, 34, 36, 38, 39–40
MRI scan, 177, 189, 191
  as constraining, 171
  doctor's challenging of, 176
  example of missed abnormality on, 202
  improved version of, 172
  increase in number of, 190
  overreading of, 161, 167, 172
  and surgery for chronic back pain, 224, 225, 226, 228
Myelodysplasia syndrome (MDS), in example of treatment choice, 236–27, 248–49
Myocardial infarction
  in case of Evan McKinley, 43
  erroneous EKG readings of, 182

Naftolin, Frederick, 217
National Academy of Sciences, Institute of Medicine of, 24
National Institutes of Health
  on andropause hypothesis, 211
  and Women's Health Initiative, 214, 218
National Marrow Donor Program Registry, 120–21

New England Journal of Medicine, 215
   Women's Health Initiative study in,
     216
   on stethoscope as obsolete, 192
New Yorker, The, "Superaspirin" article in,
   212
New York Times, hormone replacement
   article in, 215
Nimer, Stephen, 236–39, 240, 241–49, 259,
   267–68
Noncompliant patients, 91
   inability to read as cause of, 91–92
Nonverbal behavior (body language), 17,
   19
   in case of Anne Dodge, 11
Normality, psychological, 84–85
Norman, Geoffrey, 142
North American Spine Society, 229
"Nothing is wrong with you," as misguided and dangerous response,
   264, 265
Nurses' Health Study, 214, 216
Nutritional deficiency
   and immune deficiency, 127–28
   and Shira Stein, 117–18, 120, 121, 124–
   25, 126–27

Observational studies, 214
Obsessive-compulsive disorder, as diagnosis, 210
Ockham's razor, 171–72, 263
O'Connell, Baby, 142–47
O'Connell, Tom and Helen, 142, 146
Oncology
   and "bad diseases," 239
   and bone marrow transplant, 238
   perfection often not proper goal in,
   256
   schism in (data-driven vs. innovative),
   259
   and Tepler, 249, 250, 251
   and treatment choice, 10
   wider applications for drugs in, 211
   See also Cancer
"Opinion leaders," drug companies'
   enlisting of, 206, 211

Delgado as, 206
Oriol, Nancy, 37–38
Orwig, Dennis, 177–79, 182–87, 188, 192–
   93, 195–97, 198
   as husband of Feldstein, 199–200
Osler, William, 16
Osteoporosis, example of (side effects),
   245–46
Ovarian cancer
   drugs for, 211
   metastasis of in colon (Rachel
   Swanson), 254–56

PADAM (partial androgen deficiency in
   aging men), 208. *See also*
   Andropause
Pancreatic cancer, 192, 211
Paper cases, 33, 36
Parainfluenzae, 115, 118
Pathologists, variability among, 182
Patient(s)
   attractive and unattractive, 19, 45, 46–
   48, 57–58
   confidence of, 155, 172
   empowerment of (Delgado), 247
   individuality of, 6, 56, 173–74, 218, 238,
   257
   and medications, 67–68, 86, 266–67
   noncompliant, 91–92
   prototype of, 126
   questioning by, 23, 76, 163, 175, 263–64
   and side effects, 245–46
   values of (and treatment), 247–48, 256–
   57, 259
   See also Doctor-patient relationship
"Patient activation and engagement,"
   17
"Patient Site" Web site, 194
Patient templates, 98–99
Pattern recognition, 34–35, 38, 39
   distorted, 65
   in pediatrics, 78
   without preconceptions (Lock), 146
   stereotypes in, 56
   for surgery (Light), 167
Peabody, Francis Weld, 54

Pediatric cardiology
 and cardiac tamponade case, 136–37
 and case of Baby O'Connell, 142–47
 and congenital heart disease, 132
 Lock on reasoning in, 135, 147–49, 150
 See also Heart disease, congenital
Pediatrics
 doctor-patient relationship in, 121
  as partnering, 114
  and Rachel Stein's interventions, 119,
   121–22, 128, 129, 263
 emotional burden of, 114
 excessive haste in, 86–87
 McEvoy on, 77–81, 82–85
 and normal development, 84–85
 and parents' fears, 88
Pharmaceutical industry marketing, 9–10
 and access to doctors' prescription patterns, 207
 as creating demand beyond medical
  need, 206, 220, 222–23
  labeling of personality traits as illnesses, 210
  and testosterone replacement, 209,
   211–12
 and Duggan as representative, 203–4,
  206–7
 and estrogen replacement, 210, 215–16
 ethical/educational forms of, 221–22
 and FDA-approved uses, 211
 industry executive's views on, 219–23
 and *JAMA* article on undue influence,
  231
 need to be wary of, 268
 and need for extensive assessment, 214
 for testosterone replacement therapy,
  203, 208–12
  cultural shift as instrumental in,
   220–21
Pheochromocytoma, 57
Phillips House, Massachusetts General
 Hospital, 29, 95
Physician-patient relationship. *See*
 Doctor-patient relationship
Pituitary gland, 204–5
"Plate-spinning on sticks," 66–67

Pneumonia, 108
 and false x-ray, 68
 misdiagnosis as, 63–64
 of Shira Stein, 106–7, 115, 126–27
Potchen, E. James, 179–81, 186–87, 193
Pregnancy, ectopic, misdiagnosis of, 71–72
Prejudice, against minority doctors, 96–97
Primary care medicine, 9, 99–100
 and Bigby, 88–95
 Cassell on demands of, 97–98
 communication important in, 94
 and competence of physicians, 95
 and McEvoy, 77, 81–82
 passing-train metaphor for (McEvoy),
  77, 79, 100
 pressures of, 77, 81–82, 90, 100, 185
 "quality" in, 100
 and uncertainty, 153
 See also Pediatrics
Probability
 in Bayesian decision-making, 11, 62,
  151
 Bigby on, 89
 difficulty in assessing, 151–52
 in experimental outcome, 155
 failure to estimate (case of Nathan
  Talumpqewa), 66
 patients' questions about, 175
 See also Uncertainty
Productive anxiety, 37
*Professional Judgment: A Reader in Clinical
 Decision Making* (Dowie and
 Elstein), 150
Prostate cancer, 154, 240
Pseudogout, as hand-problem diagnosis,
 164
Psychiatric labels, on children, 85
Psychiatrists, in case of Anne Dodge, 2, 3
Psychological disorder, doctors' negative
 feelings toward, 39, 264–65
Psychologists, in case of Anne Dodge, 2
Psychosomatic symptoms, 264–65
 of author, 265–66
 Maxine Carlson's complaints taken for,
  70
Psychotropic drugs, 210

Pulmonary edema, 143
Pulmonary embolus, 190, 194, 261, 262

"Quality," in primary care, 100
Questioning
    close-ended, 18
    as guide in diagnosis, 17–18, 67, 261–62
    open-ended, 18, 20, 88, 99
    by patient or companion, 23, 76, 175,
        263
        about arthroscopy for author's hand,
            163
        about possible second problem,
            263–64
    and Socratic method, 4

Radiology, 177–79, 188–91
    "cine" model vs. "tile display" of, 189
    and clinician, 192–94
    and eye movement study, 197–98
    language of, 194–95, 202
    mammography, 181, 187–88, 195–97,
        198
    and Orwig, 182–86, 187, 188
    quality assurance program of, 185
    and search satisfaction, 185
    tracker ball in, 191–92
    uncertainty in, 195–97
    variability and error in, 179–81, 262
        and example of MRI error, 202
    See also CT scan; MRI scan
Rainville, James, 227
Redelmeier, Donald, 21, 44–46, 91, 188
Religious faith, 129–30
    and nonreligious strategies, 130–31
    of Rachel Stein, 116–17, 120, 123, 124,
        129, 130, 131
Remicade, 91
Representativeness (prototypical) error, 44
    and case of coronary artery disease, 44
Research
    and evidence-based medicine, 5–6
    moral constraints to, 140
    and "optimal" medical decision-
        making, 7
    as valued over practice, 97

Risk aversion, and radiologists' false nega-
    tives, 180
Ritalin, 133
Rituxan, 259
Rivera, Vincent (patient), 248–49
Rockefeller, John D., Jr., 236
Roter, Debra, 17, 18, 24–25, 88, 94, 181
Rounds, conducting of, 3–4
    by Nimer, 236–38

Salem, Deeb, 95, 96
Samei, Ehsan, 181
Sarcoma, in case of Elizabeth Dashiell, 235
Satisfaction of search, 169–70, 185, 197–
    98, 263
Scans
    overreliance on, 166
    repeating of, 262
    See also CT scan; MRI scan
Schemas, 239
Schön, Donald A., 35, 151
Sciatica, discectomy for, 226
SCID (severe combined immunode-
    ficiency disorder), and Shira Stein,
        115–16, 118, 119, 120, 121, 123, 124,
        126, 128
Scoring schemes, 236–38
Search satisficing, 169–70, 185, 197–98,
    263
"See one, do one, teach one," 38
Self-diagnosis, 261
Selzer, Richard, 169, 173
Septic shock, in case of Brad Miller, 52–53
Serologies, 226
Sherman, Max, 213
Shortcuts. See Heuristics
Shunt, 140
Side effects, patients' fear of, 245–46
Sloan-Kettering Institute, 234, 256, 258
Social affective disorder, as diagnosis, 210
Social context, need to consider, 90, 92
Socratic method, in training of medical
    students, 4
Sosman, Merrill, 187, 198
Spatial sense, as needed in cardiac surgery
    (Lock), 141

Specialists
  and Cassell on primary care, 98
  clinical certainty of, 150
  as technicians vs. diagnosticians
      (Falchuk), 16–17
  and uncertainty, 153–54
  and "We see this sometimes," 62, 63
Spinal fusion, 223, 224, 227–29
  and Agency for Health Care Policy and
      Research, 229–30
  for author, 164–65, 174
  proliferation of, 230
  and surgeon's company-financed trip,
      230
  surgeons' refusal to participate in trials
      on, 232
Stein, Rachel, 101–24, 126, 128, 263
  religious faith of, 116–17, 120, 123, 124,
      129, 130, 131
Stein, Shira (daughter), 101–10, 111–24,
      142, 154, 263
Stereotypes, 56
  attribution error from, 44
  in case of Ellen Barnett, 57
  See also Prototype patient
Stern, Joe (patient), 47–48, 58
Stossell, Thomas, 232
"Study in Scarlet, A" (Doyle), 134
"Superaspirin" (Groopman article),
      212
Surgery
  for chronic back pain, 223, 224–29
    spinal fusion, 223, 224, 227–29 (see
        also Spinal fusion)
  disappointing procedures, 223–24
  education in, 168
  primary care complexities contrasted
      with, 100
  for prostate cancer, 240
  requirements for success in, 141–42,
      168–69
  See also Pediatric cardiology
Surgery, hand
  and individual patients (Light), 173–74
  recommended for author, 160, 161, 162–
      63, 164, 165, 166–67

Sutton's law, 138
Swanson, Rachel (patient), 254–56

Talumpqewa, Nathan, 60–63, 66, 74
T-cell lymphoma, example of, 241–42,
      243–44
Tepler, Jeffrey, 249–56, 259
Testosterone
  and aging, 209
  clear uses for, 210
Testosterone replacement therapy, 207–8
  FDA approval of, 210
  marketing of by drug companies,
      208–12
    cultural shift as instrumental to,
        220–21
  studies on benefits of, 211
Thinking inside the box, 170–71
Thyroid cancer, 58
Time management, 88, 268
Training, medical. See Medical training
Transplantation of bone marrow, 118–19,
      242
  and case of Max Bornstein, 238
  and case of George Franklin, 242,
      243–44
  and case of Shira Stein, 120, 124, 125
Treatment choice, 247, 259
  in case of George Franklin, 242, 243,
      267–68
  and corporate influence, 231, 268
  doctor-patient discussion of,
      266–67
  doctors' unwillingness to risk change
      in, 239–40
  and lawsuit threat, 254
  and oncology, 10
  and patient's values
    in case of artist, 256–57
    in case of Rachel Swanson, 256
    in contrasting cancer examples,
        247–48
  and side effects, 245–46
  and unjustified treatment (Tepler),
      252–53
  See also Spinal fusion

Triage system
    of Children's Hospital ER, 105
    and McEvoy on primary care, 82
Tuba City, Arizona, 59, 60, 68
Tversky, Amos, 64, 65

Ultrasonography, 199–200
    in cardiac tamponade procedure, 138
    questions arising from uncertainty in,
        200–202
Uncertainty, 151–52
    acknowledgment of, 155
        as advantageous, 172
        in predicting outcomes (Tepler),
            255–56
        as reassuring, 159
    basic types of, 152
    Bayesian analysis for, 61–62 (*see also*
        Bayesian analysis)
    in case of Shira Stein, 113
    of chemotherapy, 246
    deductive reasoning blocked by, 149
    denial of, 152–53
    doctors' responses to, 149–50, 151,
        152–53
    and specialization, 153–54
    experiment inadequate to dispel, 154–55
    managing of (radiologists), 180
    of pediatric cardiologists, 132
    in radiologist's report, 195
    as surfacing through patient's questions,
        263–64
    in ultrasound example, 201–2
    See also Probability

Vena cava, 144
Ventricle 138, *139,* 143
    cerebral, 200

Vertical line failure, 170–71
Viagra, 220–21. *See also* Testosterone
    replacement therapy
Vioxx, 212, 213, 220
Visual-spatial ability, in surgical proce-
    dures (Lock), 141–42

Wall Street Journal, hormone replacement
    article in, 215
Waters, Diane (patient), 253–54
Watson, Douglas, 219–23
Wegner's granulomatosis, 93
Weinstein, James, 232–33
West, Harriet, 93–94
"Who You See Is What You Get" (study),
    225
Wilson, Robert A., 210
Wilson's disease, 46
Women's Health Initiative, 214, 215–16,
    217, 218, 219
Woo, Alex (patient), 253, 254

X-rays
    chest, 189
        Orwig's reading of, 183
        in trial of computer-aided systems,
            198–99
        variable interpretation of, 181
    See also Radiology

Yazdans (family with autistic child), 83
Yerkes-Dodson law on task performance,
    36–37, 38
"Yin-yang out" mistake, 72, 76

"Zebra retreat," 126–27